Women in Transition

Between Socialism and Capitalism

Ingrid Sandole-Staroste

Foreword by Anita M. Taylor

Westport, Connecticut
London

Library of Congress Cataloging-in-Publication Data

Sandole-Staroste, Ingrid, 1948–
    Women in transition : between socialism and capitalism / Ingrid Sandole-
Staroste ; foreword by Anita M. Taylor.
        p. cm.
    Includes bibliographical references and index.
    ISBN 0–275–97370–0 (alk. paper)
    1. Women—Germany (East)—Social conditions.   2. Women—Germany
(East)—Interviews.   I. Title.
HQ1630.5.S26   2002
305.42′09431—dc21   2001058945

British Library Cataloguing in Publication Data is available.

Library of Congress Catalog Card Number: 2001058945
ISBN: 0–275–97370–0

First published in 2002

Praeger Publishers, 88 Post Road West, Westport, CT 06881
An imprint of Greenwood Publishing Group, Inc.
www.praeger.com

Printed in the United States of America

The paper used in this book complies with the
Permanent Paper Standard issued by the National
Information Standards Organization (Z39.48–1984).

10 9 8 7 6 5 4 3 2 1

This book is dedicated to the women of Güstrow, (East) Germany, who gave generously of their time and entrusted their life stories to me.

Contents

Contents

Foreword

In this moving and insightful analysis, Ingrid Sandole-Staroste lets us hear the voices of women affected by the transition from state socialism in the German Democratic Republic (GDR) to a radically different set of systems when the reunification of Germany took place beginning in 1989.

Hearing these voices is crucial to understanding fully the scope and impact of the changes that occurred. The perspective provided by paying attention to the women of the GDR is unique and important. Similar to women throughout the former Soviet states, the women of East Germany had attained a high level of education and played important roles in the social, economic, and political fabric of the system, even as they demonstrated (and knew) that the rhetoric of equality (of both gender and class) propounded by the state and its apologists remained elusive. Their lives also demonstrated (and they also knew) that the socialist system had not and was not producing the economic benefits that should accrue to all members of a productive "classless" society. Unlike women in many of the other Soviet states, they were relatively well off. Even though they encountered many shortages of essentials (food, clothing, adequate housing) and did not have access to the myriad consumer goods that characterize the "good life" as lived and believed in Western, non-Soviet states, they were able to find (and often produce) adequate food and clothing. Moreover, as Sandole-Staroste lets us hear, they developed a social fabric that built a strong sense of community and sharing that accompanied their strong sense of an autonomous nondomestic self, which enabled them to enjoy a kind of security, they later came to realize, that was not available to their "sisters" in West Germany even as those Western women had many more material goods and a higher standard of living when measured in economic terms.

One of the strengths of this book is Sandole-Staroste's combination of critical analysis and judicious listening to what the women said. The women demonstrated a reflective perspective on their pre- and postunification lives, valorizing neither the state socialist system nor the unified Germany that followed it. Much of the power of this book is in the voices we hear, which demonstrate recognition of imperfections in both systems and a strong sense of what was good about the Soviet system as applied in Germany even as it was deeply flawed. We can hear through their words their disappointment as the best of the prior system was destroyed even as it often seemed they encountered the worst of the new economy. They learned that finding one's way into the "prosperity" of the new system was far from guaranteed. Sandole-Staroste brings another strength: her knowledge of feminist theory and scholarship, which permit her to go beyond the words and the facts she artfully marshals to explore the fabric of life in the GDR and the reunified, now market-based, "new" Germany. Using her feminist lens, Sandole-Staroste can explain why the Soviet system never really delivered gender equality and what was lost and why as the women of the GDR moved into a system where they became economically dependent on men. She is able to note how the well-being of that system is implicated in the high unemployment rates in the former GDR and place into context upon what these women saw as excessive consumer spending on relatively unimportant consumer goods. She can explain why the new system made it extremely difficult to manage a life that included both family and work. Among the most delightful parts of the book is hearing the women protest that they did not see why there is a conflict between paid employment and the work of family. The book, through the eyes of these women subject to wrenching changes in their lives, demonstrates yet one more time and quite vividly, how much the "free" market system of which we in the West are so proud requires vast quantities of unpaid labor, almost all of it to be done by women.

Anita M. Taylor

Preface

To see a book through to completion involves many people who take it upon themselves to nurture and sustain the author over a long period of time. There are several people without whom this work would never have been completed.

Many thanks and acknowledgment go to Dr. Sharon Hays for invaluable advice and continuous encouragement over several years. Drs. Rae Blumberg and Bethany Bryson provided thoughtful feedback. Dr. Seymour Martin Lipset taught me the craft of research and writing when I worked as his research assistant for several years.

My heartfelt thanks goes to Angelika Schmiegelow-Powell, Uschi and Willi Reichel, Sheila Smith, and Dr. Daniel Stuhlsatz for their intellectual and practical generosity and support. Without them this book would not have come about. Angelika Schmiegelow-Powell (who was, until her retirement in 1997, bibliographer for Slavic/German Social Sciences at the Alderman Library at the University of Virginia) took me under her wing and not only searched herself and supplied me with important research materials, but she also built a bridge to the women in East Germany, who made up my sample. She introduced me to Uschi and Willi Reichel, who provided me with an apartment in Güstrow so I had a home away from home while conducting my interviews. Sheila Smith and Dan Stuhlsatz opened their home to me in Charlottesville, Virginia, and looked after my physical and emotional well-being during my visits to the University of Virginia. They were generous with their time, ideas, good humor, many cups of tea, and home-made meals.

Dr. Marcella Ridlen Ray was my steady fellow traveler on my book-writing journey. We met regularly, talked through the "sticky" points, endured frustration, and appreciated the moments when everything just flowed along. I am immensely grateful to her for her friendship, diligent work, thoughtful comments, moral support, and good laughs. What would have become of us had we not learned to laugh at ourselves in the process?

My long-term teacher, mentor, colleague and friend Dr. Anita M. Taylor, who has guided me directly with her leadership by example, graciously consented to take valuable time away from her busy schedule to write the foreword.

And last, but not least, I am deeply indebted to my life-partner Dennis Sandole, who nurtured and sustained me with his love, patience, practical support, and professional expertise, and who graciously tolerated and alleviated the inevitable ups and downs in the life of an author. Our son Tim chose to be more to the point and asked direct questions, such as, "why does it take you so long to finish?" and "why don't you get a real job?" Only the future will show whether I provided him with a model to emulate or one to avoid.

I also wish to thank Suzanne I. Staszak-Silva, editor of sociology and religious studies for taking on this project; Marcia Goldstein for ensuring that all information was complete and submitted in a timely fashion; and K. McBride for doing a fine job of copy-editing. I am also indebted to Arlene Belzer, production editor, for seeing the book through to completion.

Beyond these particular acknowledgments, I have never lost sight of the broader social and intellectual debt that I owe to many feminist teachers and mentors, who for years have been the only ones insisting that it is important to ask questions about the state of women, and in that sense, I am deeply indebted to the women of Güstrow, (East) Germany—my "sample"—for clearly without them this book would not have been possible.

1

A Survey-Based Study of East German Women in Transition

INTRODUCTION

Because of my particular history of growing up in a divided Germany, I had no sentimental attachment, no connection with, nor any particular interest in East Germany. I had learned to fully accept that Germany was a divided country. Unlike so many members of the older German generation, I did not entertain the idea that, one day, Germany might be united again.

After the collapse of the Berlin Wall in 1989, I realized that I knew little about East Germany, and as a feminist, less still about the lives of East German women. As events unfolded, I was fascinated by the high visibility of East German women. They were actively involved in decision making, public speaking, protests, and publishing their ideas (Rosenberg, 1991, p. 139). Until the fall of 1989, there was no independent women's movement, no mass solidarity. Yet, they came together and established the *Unabhängiger Frauenverband* (UFV) (Independent Women's Union) (Dahn, 1990).[1]

I was equally fascinated when, by 1990, the majority of women had disappeared from public life. They had taken over the *invisible* labor of integrating, in their daily work and family lives, the enormous political, economic, social, and cultural changes that had occurred as a result of German reunification.[2] These and other events encouraged me to undertake the study reported in this volume.

THE PURPOSE OF THE STUDY

The purpose of the research, therefore, was to examine how East German women experienced 40 years of socialist institutions, ideology, values, and norms; how they dealt with the elimination of them; and how they cope with the new social order in reunited Germany.[3]

I interviewed 52 East German women in the city of Güstrow and asked them to describe their daily lives under state socialism and how these had changed in reunified Germany. I explored how they defined themselves and the visible and invisible work they performed before and after reunification. I analyzed their experiences, perceptions, and actions to determine to what extent, if at all, they embraced the new social order. That is, to what extent they responded to the efforts of the new German elites—political, economic, social, and cultural—to redefine East German women's social space and status to make them "fit" into the newly established capitalist society.

Accordingly, this study had four central goals: *First*, to listen to the voices and to recognize as valid the experiences of 52 East German women who lived from 1949–1989 under state socialism and since 1990 in reunified Germany. *Second*, to create a record of East German women's knowledge and actions, and thereby direct the focus of German reunification away from *macro*-level changes to changes at the *micro* level experienced by these women in their daily lives. *Third*, to focus on the crucial importance of the daily visible *and* invisible work women performed to mend the social fabric so that social stability can be maintained; and *Finally*, to explore why East German women resisted shifting their identities to fit the new social structures of reunified Germany. In this regard, I examined how the changes of the larger institutional structures were linked to individual lives.

BACKGROUND TO THE STUDY

The Sociopolitical Context in East Germany in 1989

In the autumn of 1989, East German opposition groups rallied in protest and helped to end the Cold War.[4] They dismantled the Berlin Wall, rejected 40 years of *Real Sozialismus* (real socialism) and, in general, East Germans chose to reunite Germany.[5]

Several (mostly women's) groups voiced early suspicions that the German reunification process was, in many ways, a *gendered* process. They saw mostly male actors vying for dominant positions and power in order to define what is just for everyone in a reunified Germany. Initial attempts by East German women at the *roundtables* to rethink what the West German

system would entail, especially for East German women, were quickly sti-
fled.[6]

Calls for addressing gender relations, family structures and their influence on individuality and the economy, abortion, quotas for political leadership positions, full employment, and child care were dismissed by West
Germany's political parties. East German men and some women in opposition groups maintained that "we have more important items on the agenda
than equality for women" (Helwerth, 1991, p. 137; also see *Unabhängiger
Frauenverband*, 1990). This substantiates Chafetz's theory that:

[G]ender equality does not constitute the first or primary priority of real and
would-be elite members. Their commitment to ameliorating women's disadvantages is [mostly] strategic. It constitutes a means that they perceive as enhancing the
probability of achieving or maintaining power and perquisites or other goals they
seek. (1990, p. 152)

Accordingly, the treaty between East and West Germany to establish
monetary, economic, and social union was negotiated and signed *exclusively* by men on May 8, 1990. Addressing the subject of "unemployment
insurance and employment promotion," Article 19 referred to the status of
women *and* disabled persons only once and in the same sentence: "Consideration shall be given to the interests of women and disabled persons"
(Press and Information Office of the Federal Government, 1991, p. 20). East
German women's emancipatory demands in the autumn of 1989 did not
"carry very much weight in the developing struggle for the consolidation of
political power [because] the distribution of positions is primarily a matter
for men" (Dölling, 1992, p. 128). In Germany, like all patriarchal societies,
positions are distributed in such a way that women end up in those that are
valued less by society (Costas, 1994, p. 58). Indeed, "there is something
very 'old' about [this newly established] democracy" in the eastern part of
Germany. It is based on the age-old concept that assumes its citizenry to be
male and politics to be "the relations of power within the economy and the
market" (Eisenstein, 1993, p. 304). A historical phenomenon repeated itself in Germany: "as soon as a political revolution [was] successfully
brought about with the considerable support of women, and new social
structures [were] instituted, the majority of female activists disappear[ed]
quietly from the political stage" (Baureithel, 1994, p. 155).

Rita Süssmuth, a member of Germany's conservative Christian Democratic Party (CDU) and former president of the Lower House of Parliament,
concluded that:

No one can deny that the reunification [process] of 1990 will be associated with men and not women. . . . The "masculine" gains expression not because there is a conscious exclusion of the specific interests of women and children, but in the non-consideration of the different life situations of men and women. It is being ignored that inequalities [between women and men] demand unequal remedies. Men dominate the political sphere and they cannot see how different the life situations of women and men are. Many men have no sensitivities for the economic dependence of women, the devaluation of women's unpaid work within families, and the insufficient social security of women in old age. (Quoted in Haller, 1992, pp. 44–45)

Many East German women activists were torn during the reunification process. They were aware of the importance of assuming positions of political power, yet, at the same time, they were repelled by its practice and wanted to withdraw entirely from a process that worked hard to marginalize them. East German men, meanwhile, consolidated their power positions by committing themselves to the new political, economic, and social institutions, recruiting their own and taking up well-paid positions.

The Sociopolitical Context in Reunified Germany

German reunification had come faster and in a way that no one was prepared for or had expected.[7] No one had "categories, . . . concepts, and . . . prognoses at hand" (Hagemann-White, 1997, p. 558). The new hopes, ideas, and opportunities that had presented themselves in 1989–1990 to build an East German society based on *actual* equality between women and men disappeared with the Berlin Wall. West Germany had moved quickly to fill the vacuum and, with the approval of most East German women and men, had installed its own institutions in East Germany. These fast-paced changes eliminated opportunities for reflection on, and critical evaluation of (not to mention actual changes in), the East and West German gendered structures, institutions, and relations.

Even though profound changes in the prevailing political and economic systems occurred, the superior power of men remained basically unaltered, because the existing power disparity was not redressed and guarantees were not given to women for equal "access to scarce and valued societal resources—material and nonmaterial," that is, income-generating roles, incumbency in elite roles, and time for leisure and personal growth (Chafetz, 1990, pp. 83, 188–192). Quite to the contrary, according to a high-ranking politician of the German Democratic Republic (GDR)[8] and a member of the delegation that had negotiated with West Germany's delegation the terms of reunification, "the time of giving women privileges is . . . over" (Dölling, 1992, p. 132). The "privileges" were women's social rights, which enabled them to combine, albeit imperfectly, family and paid work responsibilities and guaranteed them access to education and promotion.[9] Although these were important *formal* rights, in practice, they also served the predominantly male elites of the GDR as important instruments to encourage East German women to "work . . . like a man," but still "perform by far the greatest part of unpaid household labour" (p. 132).[10]

By granting women social rights, the GDR state promoted women's economic independence from individual men, but dependency on "Father State." These were paternalistic policies of equality, granted to women because the GDR decision-makers needed women's domestic and nondomestic labor to secure their own power positions (Dölling, 1992, p. 131).

Social rights became a problematic issue for the East German elites during the process of reunification because they were regarded as too costly by the transition team (Costas, 1994, p. 64). Officials did not hesitate to discard them without negotiating transitional conditions or time. The relationship between East German women and the state was swiftly reversed: Women's dependency on the state was shifted to dependency on the husband and/or father of their children (Ostner, 1995, p. 10).

After German reunification, the less extensive West German family and labor laws replaced the East German laws. The right to gainful employment was eliminated for everyone under the new market conditions, and state-sponsored child care was all but abolished. Reconciling work and motherhood became next to impossible. According to a former school principal from the state of Saxony in East Germany:

In our town [where most women were employed in textile mills] it is very problematic for mothers to find work or to get into a retraining program. Often grandmothers or great-grandmothers help out with the children, because mothers have to tell how many children they have, and have to prove that their children are looked after before anyone considers employing them or enrolling them in a retraining program.[11]

The women who remained employed found that their wages did not keep pace with the increasing costs of living, especially for food, housing, child care, and transportation (see Einhorn, 1993; Rueschemeyer, 1994; Scholz, 1994).

The newly imposed institutional structures—political, economic, social, cultural—have been implemented by a predominantly male elite in whose interest it is also to redefine East German women's social roles and space. Thus, they set the boundaries for women's choices, opportunities, and spaces in reunified Germany. These boundaries clash with East German women's expectations because they violate how East German women define themselves. This has created tensions that, to this day, remain unresolved. According to Bütow and Stecker (1994, p. 8):

There is obviously a vital interest in . . . preventing East [German] women from entertaining the idea that they should think about their own *identity*. . . . West German patterns are imposed and those who do not fit these patterns have never existed. The [West German] models that are being offered miss our most fundamental needs. We East [German] women are independent, we do not conform. We do not fit into Western patterns of interpretation. We did not conform the way many Western authors try to make us believe. We are diverse in our thinking, feeling and actions—and defiant too (emphasis added).

THE CENTRAL ARGUMENT AND IMPORTANCE OF THE STUDY

Before proceeding, I offer a glimpse of the central argument to which I will return throughout the book. Both systems—West Germany's capitalism *and* East Germany's state socialism—rest/ed on deeply rooted *patriarchal* structures that are/were sustained by male elites. It is striking that, despite profound political, economic, social, and cultural change, these structures have not only remained untouched, but have often been reinforced.

Patriarchal structures can be likened to "soil" and male elites—or more precisely *Männerbünde* (male associations)—to cultivators who produce and sustain *traditional* gender relations on all levels of society irrespective of what type of political and economic system they "cultivate."[12] Patriarchal structures, like soil, are flexible. They are also "progressive" if they serve the interests of male elites. In that sense, the socialist elites responded in a more "progressive" and comprehensive way than the capitalist elites to the needs of women, particularly with regard to combining the responsibilities of family and paid work.

This was rooted in socialist ideology, and in the socialist system, which depended for its very existence on women's labor in the public *and* private spheres. Achieving any goal in the socialist system was possible only with—never against—one another and, therefore, cooperation and not competition (both between women and men) was emphasized. This explains, in part, why women in East Germany look for ways to work and solve problems together with men: Socialist ideology shaped, in profound ways, the relations between women and men.

Although notable gains were made, gender equality was not achieved under state socialism, in part, because a complex and contrary belief system, rooted in the patriarchal organization of socialism, prevailed. Given equal rights and opportunities, women and men were *not* different, but given their biological distinctions, women and men were *essentially* different. Whereas the former view was officially articulated and dominant, the latter remained unspoken and unchallenged and continued to exist beneath the surface, reproducing and reinforcing patriarchal relations and social inequality, which women resisted only on an individual level.

The *central argument* here also alludes to the East-West divide. Thus, in the eyes of Westerners, the German Democratic Republic (GDR) had always seemed an archetype of the Leninist, totalitarian state in which life was strictly regimented and controlled by the state. The reality turned out to be far more complex, however. Everyday life may have been routinized for most East German women, but it was not as rigid, subordinate, or linear as it is often portrayed from a Western point of view. Instead, everyday life was full of improvisations and contradictions. Particularly during the last decade of the GDR's existence, many East German women astutely bent the Communist Party's rules, or evaded them altogether, if those rules complicated their lives. East German women did not just survive, as many Westerners tend to assume. They perceived opportunities and took advantage of them and asserted themselves in the work place and at home. They continued their education and took on public responsibilities. They identified strongly with their immediate communities though not necessarily with the state (Rocksloh-Papendieck, 1995, pp. 189–190). East German women's emancipation took a different, unnamed, and quiet path. It was more personal and inconspicuous than that which characterized West German women (Szepansky, 1995).

During the process of German reunification, when power—political, economic, social, cultural—was consolidated on all levels of society, the age-old patriarchal structures began to assert forcefully their most fundamental value: control over East German women's lives and bodies (Funk, 1993). One essential task of the predominantly male elites was to draw a clearer and more hierarchical division of public and private labor. East German women's roles were confined, once again, to being primarily responsible for home and family. Another task was to implement throughout reunited Germany West Germany's abortion law, which was one of Europe's most restrictive. This met with such resistance that the process of reunification was put at serious risk. To proceed and not jeopardize this historical opportunity, political decision-makers decided that East and West

7

Germany would retain their original abortion laws until 1992 when a new law was to take their place.[13]

These experiences created the perception in East Germany that West German democracy was not as egalitarian and liberating as many Westerners assumed. Instead, many of the East German women I interviewed said that reunified Germany limited their individual opportunities, choices, and actions in everyday life to a larger extent than socialist East Germany had done.[14] In their view, the capitalist system had not turned out to be more socially and economically just. It had not given more women better opportunities as many had expected, but pitted them against each other in competing for scarce resources. It had prevented many women from asserting greater influence in the creation of a better society.

Whereas the socialist, predominantly male elites had defined East German women's social roles first and foremost as being members of the paid labor force, the capitalist, predominantly male elites define women's social roles as primarily taking care of home and family. This has created a field of tension. Institutional expectations relentlessly collide with individual expectations and needs. West Germany's definition of women's primary social roles and identities clashes with the ones East German women have internalized. Identities have proven to be resilient and to conflict with systemic changes. Yet, these tensions have largely been left unexplored. Women have remained *invisible* as actors in the process of societal transformation, and their contributions and resistance have gone unrecognized because everyday life is deemed too "normal" to command special attention. Thus, Sauer (1996, p. 134) observes that "the marginalization of women in the transformation process . . . corresponds to women's marginalization in the accompanying social sciences."[15]

My analysis of the data generated by the interviews shows that East German women were important actors in the transformation process. Daily life demanded their full participation and actions. They often, though not exclusively, endured substantial setbacks as revealed by their stories of three closely intertwined areas of everyday life—occupational, family, material—before *and* after German reunification. The focus on the "ordinary" reveals the inseparable link and tensions between the newly imposed social institutions and individual perceptions and actions. The women I interviewed resisted (though not always successfully) "falling into line" with institutional changes in reunified Germany, especially if it required them to relinquish a crucial part of their *identity*.

It will be the voices of these and other women that contribute, in an important way, to how the transition from state socialism to capitalism is conceptualized, implemented, and recorded. Their voices will add depth, clarify interpretations, and contribute another piece to the already complex picture of societies in transition. I hope the findings of this study will advance our understanding of the paramount importance of women's social roles during times of social upheaval, when decision-makers expect women to make crucial contributions to political and economic stability. As a result, women's *private* lives and emotional capacities take on vital *public* significance (Coole, 1988). This is neither obvious nor publicly acknowledged, yet (mostly male) decision-makers expect women "to keep things running smoothly" in the day-to-day routines of their families and, by implication, in the day-to-day life of the larger society. To this end, the ruling elites shape women's social status and space through policies that supply (or withhold) resources in such a way that the power positions of elites on all societal levels—social, economic, political, and cultural—are not threatened. Thus, the underlying patriarchal structures and male privilege remain intact.

THEORETICAL SETTING AND METHODOLOGY

... the facts of experience do not present themselves immediately to us; rather, they are known only in terms of a conceptual framework which acts like a filter, in that it emphasizes some features of our experience while ignoring other aspects or even rendering them invisible. (Jaggar and Rothenberg Struhl, 1984, p. xi)

The conceptual framework that has guided my work derives from feminist thought and scholarship.[16] It has informed the conception and design of my study, including the methods of data collection, analysis, and interpretation (see Appendices 1 and 2).

The feminist framework appears to be the most complete and suitable for understanding the present situation of East German women. It is both *descriptive* (empirical), in that it examines the lived experiences of East German women, and *prescriptive* (normative), in that it identifies sources of those experiences that should be changed—bias, discrimination, and injustice (p. xi).

Almost all East German women I interviewed shared a sense of feeling devalued in reunified Germany. Arguably, this reflects a climate that Watson (1997, p. 145) has termed the *creation* of antifeminism. It is part of the process of democratization and "encompasses the rise of both a masculinist and feminist political identity" (p. 145).[17] The creation of general hostility toward women is facilitated by conditions that existed under state socialism such as the unchallenged, but persisting notion that given the biological distinction, women and men were essentially different, and that the family (society) existed in opposition to the state. The process of democratization politicizes these differences with the institutionalization of "universal rights of citizenship and the creation of liberal civil society" (Watson, 1997, p. 145). Democratic citizenship rights assign new political meaning to social differences such as gender, ethnicity, and nationality, making "abstract rights concrete" (p. 145). Gender is constructed as "a politically exclusionary/inclusionary social category" resulting in a "politically polarizing effect." This reality is obscured by the flawed (Western) assumption that democratization is an "evolutionary process," placing the "legacy of state socialism" on one side and "feminism/civil society/democracy" on the other. In reality:

Democracy creates a division because it replaces a communist system where political citizenship was universal both in a positive (abstract) and negative (concrete) sense with a system of democratic political citizenship which is universal in abstract terms but within which the concrete rights of some are formed at the expense of the rights of others. (Watson, 1997, p. 146)

The process of constructing women as a "minority grouping" as different from men, in effect, politically, economically, and socially excluding them, is constitutive of democratization in most former communist countries. A Polish representative to the Council of Europe illustrates the point: "it is impossible to speak of discrimination against women. Nature gave them a different role to that of men. The ideal must still be the woman—mother for whom pregnancy is a blessing" (Bielicki, 1993, cited in Watson, 1997, p. 149).

In the reorganization of social and political power, "gender" has emerged as a prime category and as a useful conceptual tool that helps reveal how social spaces, status, and identities are being redefined and reorganized in the transition from state socialism to capitalism (Watson, 1997, pp. 151–152). One East German health care worker illustrates this when she says:[18]

I really believe that most women considered themselves equal in the GDR, because their opinions counted as much as those of men. The result has been a certain self-respect, a certain self-assurance. Women simply said, "ok, I am independent. I make my own decisions. I can stand on my own two feet [economically and otherwise]."Since reunification, women are seriously slipping [in all respects]. Look around and see who is unemployed. Mostly women! When a woman with three children applies for a job now, she might as well forget it. There is no chance that she will be offered a job. [In the GDR] we used to think, "let's see how we can help this woman." That is how it used to be. Now women are hit very hard, indeed.

Many East German women I interviewed concluded that under state socialism there was a general recognition that women's knowledge, skills, and talents benefited society. In reunified Germany, that is not the case anymore. These women also considered women's opportunities for education and professional advancement an important socialist achievement, even though it did not lead to real gender equality. Many considered socialist society far from perfect, but perceived it as more fair and equal than capitalist society.

As a consequence, many East German women are reluctant to embrace the West German system as truly theirs. They perceive it as having been imposed on them by West Germans. They also voice skepticism of Western approaches to solving problems—including Western feminist approaches—because they perceive themselves to be in a hierarchical relationship in which everything Eastern is relegated to a lower status and everything Western is elevated to the higher ranks of the social ladder.

Most of the women I spoke with resented that definitions of their status and place in society were imposed on them by West Germans. They insisted that they themselves must define the issues that concern them, their interests, and possible solutions to problems, and that this must be recognized as legitimate.[19] Most wanted to include their past—the good and the bad—to better understand the present and plan the future. They wanted to determine for themselves which aspects of their former society to keep and which to discard. As one educator said, "We did not only suffer [in the GDR]. We laughed and lived."[20] It was clear to most women that the unexpected and rapid process of German reunification had foreclosed more options than it had opened.

Although the women I interviewed would not define themselves as acting in the feminist spirit, their struggle nevertheless exemplifies it: They were trying to overcome a newly imposed subordination and to achieve justice and equality, not just for themselves, but for all members of society.

PERSISTENT THEMES ACROSS INTERVIEWS

Three closely interrelated aspects of daily life—*occupational life, family life,* and *material life*—constituted the focal points of the interviews.[21] It became clear that in the GDR, unlike in reunified Germany, these aspects of women's everyday lives were not necessarily hierarchically ordered. Under state socialism, for example, most women did not perceive important differences in material status between themselves and those with whom they lived and worked. Most did not consider family work more important than paid work. When I asked what they considered more significant, the women could not quite see the point of my question—"you don't just have one or the other!," many told me. And they did *not* choose one over the other! In the

GDR, the norm was to have both. To maintain or improve one's material well-being depended less on money and more on the cooperation among family members and on their embeddedness in the larger community. It did not necessarily reflect a gendered hierarchy.

In reunified Germany, by contrast, material well-being depends on money and private property. Yet, work places have been reduced drastically and men receive priority in the labor market. More women are unemployed and depend economically on their husbands or partners. The division of labor and access to resources is again more gendered. Women have assumed the responsibility of helping their families adjust to the new social order, often with no choice in the matter.

THE ORGANIZATION OF THE STUDY

In chapters 2 and 3, I discuss the demographic profiles of the 52 women I interviewed, and analyze their *occupational* experiences under state socialism and under capitalism to provide a deeper understanding of why the impact of rapid social change has not only affected their social roles and economic independence but also shaken their confidence in capitalism. Many, including those who prospered, were critical of the new order. In chapters 4 and 5, I focus on East German women's *family* situation to emphasize the multitude of hidden tasks they performed *before* and *after* German reunification to keep their families and, by implication, their country together and the economies functioning. In chapters 6 and 7, I explore East German women's *material* well-being. The deficiency of the socialist state, particularly toward the end of its existence, created shortcomings of consumer goods but also opportunities to act independently, revealing entrepreneurial skills and spirit. Reunification reversed the situation. A host of consumer goods became instantly available but women's economic independence was diminished. Finally, in Chapter 8, I summarize the study's main findings and discuss their implications for further research in reunified Germany and their relevance for Eastern Europe and the newly independent states in the former Soviet Union.

NOTES

1. On the subject of women as revolutionaries, see Giffin (1973).

2. For further details on the political, sociological, and economic aspects of the transformation process, see Icks (1995).

3. For an indepth analysis of the process East Germans go through to accept West German values and norms, see Heins (1994).

4. The opposition included the newly formed *New Forum*, the *Greens*, *Free Democrats*, *Democratic Awakening* and the *Social Democrats* (Derbyshire, 1991, p. 142).

For an indepth analysis of the transformation of East Germany, see Fisher (1995), Grosser (1998), Jarausch (1995), and Pond (1993). For further analysis of the collapse of communism and transformation of Eastern Europe and Gorbachev's role in the process, see Kumar (1992, pp. 309–356).

5. East Germans distinguished between *Ideal Sozialismus* (ideal socialism), with its emphasis on equality and justice, which they regarded as compatible with democratic practices, and *Real Sozialismus* (real socialism), with its repressive and dictatorial practice throughout East Germany's 40-year history (see Simon, 1995).

6. The *roundtables* were a notable achievement of the fall 1989 revolution. Women asserted considerable influence in instituting them as a way to practice democratic participation and tolerance. Thus, the *roundtables* came to be recognized as the most important achievement Europe's male democracies had accomplished over the last 200 years. But neither the separated Germanies, nor the unified Germany, were prepared for the roundtables or the influential positions women assumed at them. Instead, the tables were viewed with great suspicion (see Keller, 1990, p. 135, cited in Häder and Häder, 1995, pp. 30–31; Baureithel, 1994, p. 155; Böhm, 1992, p. 32).

7. Early in 1990, all political parties concerned themselves with the question of reunification. They viewed this as a process involving several steps, beginning with a monetary and economic union, the completion of which was believed to be possible by the end of 1992. Once established, it was assumed that a full political union would follow after a number of years. However, with a rapidly deteriorating economic situation in East Germany, rising expectations among East Germans, an increasing number of East Germans leaving for West Germany, and growing concerns among West Germans about the impact of the exodus on their lives, the monetary and economic union proceeded rapidly. After short and tense negotiations, it came into effect on July 1, 1990, and was followed, only three month later, on October 3, 1990, by formal reunification (Derbyshire, 1991, pp. 158–169).

8. I use the terms *German Democratic Republic*, *GDR*, and *East Germany*, to refer to the Eastern part of Germany that was under Soviet control from 1949 to 1989.

9. East German women managed to combine work and family responsibilities largely because *formal* gender equality simplified their efforts in this regard by providing legal guarantees, such as a comprehensive child-care system; special protection during times of pregnancy and maternity; maternity leave at full pay; financial subsidies for childbirth; time off to take care of a sick child without loss of pay; monthly child subsidies; measures for further education and professional advancement; a day off per month for housework at full pay; free medical care; free contraceptives; free medicine; the right to abortion; and affordable

housing (see Berghahn and Fritzsche, 1991, pp. 39–42, 63–108; Dölling, 1990, pp. 128–133).

10. In this regard, see Berghahn (1992) and Böhmer (1994).

11. The interview was conducted in Washington, DC, October 19, 1995.

12. According to Kreisky (1996, p. 19), *patriarchal* refers to those aspects of societal organization that are based on male-dominated gender relations: Mechanisms that institutionalize male power within different social relations.

The concept of *Männerbünde* was initially associated with formal male associations. There is, however, a growing consensus that the essential characteristic of *Männerbünde*, as deliberate and voluntary associations of men, is not the unique decision to join an association, but instead the permanent exclusion of unwanted persons, that is, women. It is not the self-declaration of groups and organizations that is important, but the existence of mechanisms to exclude women.

Hence, *patriarchy* and *Männerbund* (male association) refer to the same social fact: Most social and institutional relationships are dominated by men in terms of numbers and values. Male domains are increasingly characterized as *Männerbünde*.

13. Abortion was the single issue that remained unsettled in reunified Germany. East and West Germany were unable to reach agreement during the unification process in 1990. In June of 1992, the parliament of the reunified Germany cast 357 to 284 votes for rejecting the restrictive West German law. However, the Federal Constitutional Court voted unanimously to block the change from taking effect, siding with then Chancellor Helmut Kohl, 247 conservative parliament members, and the predominantly Catholic state of Bavaria, which had requested the injunction (Fisher, 1992, p. A25).

In July 1995, the parliament passed a law that reflected a compromise. It was less liberal than the East German law, but more liberal than the West German law. The new law "allows abortion only when a pregnancy results from rape or threatens the mother's life." In all other instances, counseling from a doctor is mandatory. The doctor must emphasize the "protection of the unborn life." Doctors and women who disregard counseling and carry out the abortion are not subject to punishment, however; and health insurance has to pay for abortion if women are poor (Associated Press, 1995, p. A18).

14. For instance, in the spring of 1996, a representative survey (Allbus) found that 67 percent of East German men and 67 percent of East German women said that it should be possible to have an abortion "if the woman wants it." By contrast, only 36 percent of West German men and 37 percent of West German women expressed that opinion (Kaufmann, Schröter, and Ullrich, 1997, p. 24).

15. All translations in this volume from German into English have been made by the author.

16. Feminist frameworks cut across academic disciplines, adding to the richness of the debate from which springs a variety of feminist theories—for example, *liberal, Marxist, radical, socialist, postmodern, gender, African American*, to name a few. (See, for example, Blum, 1997; de Beauvoir, 1952; Eisenstein, 1979;

Eisler, 1988; Flax, 1990; Fox Keller, 1985; French, 1985; Friedan, 1976; Harding and Hintikka, 1983; Hartmann, 1981; Hartsock, 1983; Hill Collins, 1991; Jaggar, 1983; Johnson, 1997; Kurz-Adam, 1994; Lengermann and Niebrugge-Brantley, 1992; MacKinnon, 1989; Marks and de Courtivron, 1981; Ortner and Whitehead, 1981; Tong, 1989; Trebilcot, 1984.)

17. Watson argues that feminism developed as a response to Western (male) democracies. Therefore, the emergence of feminism in former communist countries is part of the democratization process. Feminism emerges in the former communist countries because the gendered organization of Western democracies has been instituted without examining its gendered aspects. Antifeminism is a response to a new feminist consciousness and actions that unsettle traditional gender relations.

18. To preserve confidentiality for the women I interviewed, I identify them in the text by the occupational status they held before reunification, as many had lost their positions after reunification.

19. In this regard, see Gerhard (1990).

20. Begenau (1995) observed that social scientists describe a "very incomplete view of life in the GDR." She is quick to admit that the GDR was an authoritarian society but that, at the same time, social conditions were such that space was created in which women were able to seize opportunities to act and make decisions that increased their individualization and self-worth. She has urged Eastern and Western social scientists to be conscious of the fact that their research about the GDR reflects the deeply internalized standards of their respective societies, coupled with the emotional ethnocentric dimension that lets their own society appear "eternal" and the perceived "bad" society appear even worse (Begenau, p. 41). She demonstrates show a picture is constructed of East German women's life that appears standardized and grey: A picture that portrays life as having less of everything that is "good" and much more of everything that is "bad" (Begenau, p. 35). She questions the methodologies of the studies under review and encourages a "dialogue of reciprocal reflexivity." She suggests that only by reconstructing, *in context*, the "reality" that was, and the "reality" that is today, can East and West German social scientists begin to meaningfully compare the two worlds.

21. When I designed this study, my focus was on the occupational and family life of East German women before and after German reunification. While conducting the interviews, and later while analyzing the interview texts, it became clear to me that the material life warranted being looked at more closely. The transformation of state socialism or communism into capitalism introduced capitalism's essential pillars—consumption and private property—into the everyday lives of East German women, which contributed to more clearly defined gender roles and class distinctions. This impacted widely on women's material status and often, though not always, limited their opportunities.

2

Work Life under State Socialism

DEMOGRAPHIC PROFILES OF 52 EAST GERMAN WOMEN

Before Germany was reunified in October 1990, all but one of the women I interviewed (98 percent) had enjoyed the security of full-time, long-term employment; the one who was not employed finished school in 1989.[1] About 25 percent of the women were employed in agricultural production cooperatives.[2] The other 75 percent held various positions in different sectors (see Appendix 3 for a description of the jobs before and after German reunification).[3] They had each worked, on average, for 19 years. The incomes of nine women (18 percent) were concentrated at the higher end of the income scale (between 1,300 and 2,999 East German Marks a month), whereas the incomes of 42 women (82 percent) were at the lower end of the scale (between less than 400 and up to 1,300 East German Marks a month).[4] Thirty-seven women (72 percent) had between 11 and 18 years of education, while 15 (28 percent) had between 7–10 years.[5]

The ages of the women I interviewed ranged from 18–74 years, with the majority (84 percent) between 25 and 54 years of age. Forty-five (87 percent) were born, educated, and trained in the former GDR. Seven women (13 percent) were born before and during the Third Reich. Thirty-two of them (61 percent) were married; 17 (33 percent) were either single, divorced, or separated; and three (6 percent) were widowed. Except for three women (6 percent), all (94 percent) had between one and five children, with an average of 2.5 children.

THE PROMISE OF GENDER EQUALITY

Most of the women I interviewed took the 1968 amendment to the constitution for granted, which not only guaranteed equal rights for women and men but provided preferential treatment for women.[6] Seven years later, Erich Honeker, first secretary of the Central Committee of the *Sozialistische Einheitspartei Deutschland* (SED) (Socialist Unity Party), told East Germans that "women's equality is indeed one of the greatest achievements of socialism, which our state has realized not only in the legal sense but to a large degree in everyday life. No capitalist country can claim anything similar" (*Staatliche Zentralverwaltung für Statistik* [State Central Office for Statistics], 1975, p. 1).[7]

Inge Lange, responsible for the "women's question" within the ruling party (SED), asserted in the same year (1975) that the SED had succeeded in developing a socialist society and had, therefore, succeeded in achieving the emancipation of women (Horn, 1992, pp. 99–108; *Staatliche Zentralverwaltung für Statistik*, 1975).[8] In the GDR, the definition of equality for men and women rested on an ideological premise that did not recognize the existence of gender difference. Women and men were subsumed under the notion of "citizen," not unlike the middle-class definition in Western countries (Horn, 1992, p. 101).

In theory, the problem of gender inequality was solved; in practice, however, gender inequality remained a structural feature throughout the 40 years of state socialism. Because the problem of gender inequality was declared solved, gender roles were not questioned and a gender consciousness did not come into existence. Gender equality was confined to the level of state ideology and became a tool for denying the existence of any discrimination against women (Rai, Pilkington, and Phizacklea, 1992, p. 6).[9]

THE REALITY OF GENDER (IN)EQUALITY

In the legal sense much was accomplished with regard to gender equality in the GDR. Legal equality was a necessary condition for achieving gender equality, but it was insufficient. The gap between *Real Sozialismus* (real socialism) and *Ideal Sozialismus* (ideal socialism) was never closed.

In accordance with Marxist-Leninist ideology, the means of production became the property of the socialist state, but Marxism, as practiced, neither abolished social classes nor made women truly equal to men. A nurse I interviewed described how unprepared she was to deal with class differences and gendered expectations when she went for an interview arranged by a government minister in a well-recognized hospital in East Berlin:

I finally . . . went to the government hospital in Berlin. Well, I thought, hospital is hospital. I had this socialist image of the world that everyone is equal . . . I was taken up in an elevator [to see the minister]. The elevator was carpeted and had armchairs in it. I thought I was in some kind of luxury hotel. I had only seen something like that on television, but never in reality. No one could afford anything like that [in the GDR]. Well, and then I was brought to the minister. He had a real suite with everything: television, telephone, a menu with five different choices. Five minutes before the meal was served, he could ask for specials.

Then a nurse entered [the room], and I realized she was [the minister's] servant and waitress. I told the minister, "This is unacceptable to me. This is such a difference, such an injustice. I thought it does not exist under socialism. I don't want to work here even if you do pay me more than 1,000 Marks. . . ." He was surprised but also understanding. He said, "Differences exist in all countries."

This nurse was not alone. Other East German women found themselves in similar situations. Unless they were confronted with a starkly contrary reality, class and gender structures had almost become invisible. Generally, East German women (and men) had accepted the state's declaration that gender equality had been achieved, and the class system abolished. There were no alternative conceptual lenses through which to "see" the extent to which work—within the family, the labor sectors, and society—was divided, not equally between women and men, but in such a way that women were generally placed in subordinate, and men in superior positions (Böhm, 1992, p. 33; Horn, 1992, pp. 99–108). This may explain, in part, why half of the women in my sample believed that the affirmative action policies of the GDR had brought about gender equality.[10] This was true particularly for those who occupied high-ranking positions and who were, therefore, also more committed to the Party ideology. They perceived themselves to be equal to their male colleagues. In the words of one educator:

In our time, there was no need to discuss [gender] discrimination. I have never felt discriminated against, or that I was less important because I was a woman. I was elected to our local administration, I was a member of the government council, I was active in the parent advisory board in our school. I have to say, I have never felt like a second-class citizen in the GDR.

Another educator, who regarded herself as equal to her male colleagues in every respect, reflected on how her pregnancy affected her work. She did not critique the standards, norms, and values predominant at her work place, but "nature," which "disadvantages women with pregnancy." She reflected the dominant (male) values when she assessed her circumstances:

19

[Women cannot be as effective in the work place as men] because often nature does not play along. I was unavailable for an entire year. I had a very problematic pregnancy. I was afraid that I would really fall behind with my research. It would have impacted negatively on how I was perceived by my colleagues.

East German women had internalized the socialist ideology. Their identities and expectations were shaped by full employment, which they considered not only their right, but also their duty. However, their employment opportunities and job promotions were limited by gender prejudice and gender-segregated employment sectors. Because gender prejudice was not supposed to exist under state socialism, it could not be publicly articulated and questioned.

EAST GERMAN WOMEN'S SELF-CONCEPT AND EXPECTATIONS

Although gender equality was not achieved under state socialism, for those who were born and grew up in the GDR, opportunities were, nevertheless, significantly better than they had been for their mothers' and grandmothers' generations before the GDR was established in 1949.

Most of the East German women I interviewed were born, socialized, and educated in the GDR and had internalized, to different degrees, the teachings of their ideological fathers and mothers—Karl Marx, Vladimir Illich Lenin, August Bebel, and Clara Zetkin.[11] They were educated "to choose a work place that was in accordance with social demands and personal qualifications" (Article 24 of the GDR Constitution, cited in Häder and Häder, 1995, p. 48; Horn, 1992, pp. 101–102). According to a bookkeeper, "We all had work because every enterprise was a state enterprise and those in charge had to employ people. They were ordered to do so [by the state]."

Women's full integration into the work force was the result of government policies that were introduced during the 1960s and 1970s. These policies had three objectives: (1) to regard women and men as equal before the law; (2) to improve women's employment and educational situations; and (3) to grant special protection to mother and child (Penrose, 1990, p. 64).[12]

Factories, institutions, and administrations were mandated by law to employ women. Laws were enacted that aimed at equality between male and female professional qualifications and preparing women for leadership roles. Institutions such as communal kitchens, child care, and laundry facilities were established to assist women in entering the labor force (Penrose, 1990, p. 65).

In accordance with the dominant ideology, it was assumed that women would be emancipated as soon as they were fully integrated into the production process and individual households were transformed into community households. However, the question of who was to rear and educate the children in community-run centers and schools, and who was to be responsible for the chores in community households, was not publicly discussed (Penrose, 1990, p. 64).[13]

Nevertheless, as a result of those policies, their high level of integration in the world of paid work, and the perception that their work was of value, women's self-concept underwent a change.[14] Dr. Regine Hildebrandt, social democratic Minister for Women, Labor and Health in the East German state of Brandenburg, [said in this regard], "We did not have equality in the way [the government] made us believe, but self-awareness was forged by participation in the work process" (cited in Einhorn, 1993, p. 141).

Because of their uninterrupted work experience outside the home (which also defined their status within the family [see chapter 4]), most women in my sample generally regarded themselves as emancipated.[15] One interviewee, who managed a division in a large state enterprise, said: "I think we have been formed by a certain [work] discipline. My generation has worked the longest without interruption [in the paid work force] and it has given us a sense of strength and independence."[16]

In 1989, the income of East German women made up 37 percent of the household income, in contrast to West Germany, where the income of women made up 18 percent of the household income (Szepansky, 1995, p. 121).[17] East German women were also more independent economically, and educationally and professionally better qualified than West German women (p. 121).[18] Further, they experienced less discrimination in the labor market under state socialism than they have in reunified Germany. For all 52 women I interviewed, the security of full-time, long-term employment was a given. It never occurred to them that their situation could be otherwise.

OCCUPATIONAL CHOICE AND CONFORMITY

In the GDR, reality was such that women had little choice between nondomestic and domestic work. The women's policies had been introduced not only to emancipate women, but to ensure that women would play their part in promoting the centrally planned goals of the socialist state.[19] Integrating them into the work force allowed the state to have greater control over their lives. Wages were structured in such a way that men were generally unable to support their families alone. Therefore, according to one agricultural worker, "[working outside the home] was a question of money, because our salaries were very low."

In addition to financial needs, 20 women (38.5 percent) felt political pressure from the Party. Participation in the work force was mandatory, and violating that norm entailed sanctions. Sooner or later, everyone was faced with the demands to join the ever-present Socialist Unity Party (SED) and to become politically active in their collectives. One nurse recalled how ignoring those demands almost always incurred retribution of one sort or another:

Everywhere one was asked to become a member of the Party. As head nurse, I was still able to get away without joining, but I was asked. [If I had wanted to get ahead professionally] my political perspective would have counted. My professional expertise was not very important. . . . You have no idea how careful we used to be. We knew very well that if we said anything against the state, the party functionary would have recorded it and would have passed it on, guaranteed. . . . [Anything against the state] would have had an impact on my job situation. Most likely I would have lost my job.

A child-care worker who was taught at home not to trust any mass organizations paid a price for her persistence: "If you did not belong to the Party, there was no way that you could advance in your career. That was just not possible. I never let myself be influenced [by the Party]. I had to leave university because I was not a member. . . . Those who joined had it easier."

And a gardener naively told her supervisor, "I don't want those advantages [that came with party membership]; if I succeed, I want to do it on my own account, and not because I am active in the Party." As a consequence, she had to endure years of constant ridicule, and, despite her hard work, was given small salary increases. A teacher was a member of the Catholic Church, whose teachings conflicted with the Party. She had to decide between her profession as a teacher and her faith. She decided for her faith, and lived with the professional consequences. And one cook had to leave school and her father lost his job, when she steadfastly refused to report on who in her family, and who among her neighbors and friends, watched Western television, which was strictly forbidden but could be received in certain areas of the former GDR.

However, five women in my sample (10 percent) joined the Party and actively worked on its behalf. A teacher, who was also a Party functionary, explains:

I worked in the [government ministry] for *Volksbildung* (people's education). I was a small overseer, so to speak. . . . We had a certain educational concept that schools were supposed to realize. Of course, there was a political ideological emphasis. There is no question about that. Ideology did play a role. It simply was part of it. That was the way I grew up. As a teacher, I taught German from texts that led students in a certain direction. That's how I was evaluated. There was no doubt about it. In mathematics it was the same. When we taught numbers, we did not exactly say "three red flags and three red flags [equal six red flags]," but the political emphasis was always there.

And another teacher, who became an influential Party member in her community, added: "I was a member of the SED. I became Party secretary. I actually believed in the good of socialism. I was very much involved at the time. I really believed I was doing something good."

The women (or their parents) who supported the goals of the SED Party had done so because of the horrors of the Third Reich and sincerely believed that a socialist society was the better and only alternative for their children. Later, they reaped social and economic benefits from supporting the system. One Party functionary loyal to, and active in, the Party experienced harsh personal and professional consequences when her loyalty to the Party was tested and she refused to live up to the Party's expectations. She and her husband lost their jobs and were demoted. Yet, she was pained by the collapse of the socialist system that she had once believed in and that had not fulfilled its promise.[20]

Most women I interviewed were neither supportive of the old system nor rejected it completely. One white-collar employee spoke for the majority when she said that she had learned to live with it and had carved out a *niche* for herself in which she was able to work and live: "I cannot say that I was unhappy. I always said my family life and my immediate surroundings are my island on to which I could withdraw and which gave me what I needed to be happy."

Despite the harsh retribution that some women experienced, most believed that socialism, with all its imperfections, was more equitable than capitalism and that it had achieved some of its promises, that is, integrating women into the work force and promoting women's educational and professional advancement, and their economic self-sufficiency. One interviewee who succeeded in starting an independent business under state socialism, remarked, "Until we had socialism, women were of no importance in society. That is what I liked about socialism. Until we had it, women were subordinate. Socialism gave women status in society. That is the positive side, I think. . . . Socialism took women out of their shadow existence."

And a teacher who lost her job after Germany was reunified noted, "I really don't understand why socialism has not worked out. I really believed that, by and large, it was a good system. . . . I am actually still convinced about [the ideal] of socialism [with its emphasis on equality]."

An independent book dealer reflected that: "Those who formed the first government after the collapse of the Third Reich, . . . they were honest [socialists]. They sincerely believed that they were able to build a state where there was no more human suffering and where the disadvantaged, including women, were given a chance as well."

The *Institut für Demoskopie Allensbach* (1993) survey found similar opinions. More than two-thirds of East Germans said that they believed that socialism was superior to capitalism. This did not, however, exclude harsh criticism. Most of the women I interviewed disapproved strongly of the way the economy was run and how people were prevented from doing a good job. They held the entire chain of command responsible, from the local Party functionary to the Party leadership, for ignoring everyday reality. And yet, most women held on to *Ideal Sozialismus* as a social alternative to capitalism. They did not want to dismiss it as obsolete.

COMBINING WORK AND FAMILY OBLIGATIONS

Social policies were *for* and not *by* women. More precisely, they were for mothers in the work force. They did not include women who chose to work at home, or older women who had left the work force. One interviewee, who was active in her congregation as a volunteer for 26 years, said: "The ideal [woman] of the socialist state was the woman who worked outside the home and who successfully juggled family and shift work. [I] belonged to the nonworking part of the population (laughs). As if the work I do at home [as a mother of four children] is no work."

Nor did the policies apply to men. No new socialization methods or policies were introduced that aimed at integrating men in child-rearing and household duties to the same degree as women were integrated into the work force. Forty years of socialism did not change the idea that male experience is the norm and female experience a deviation from that norm. The thrust of women's policies was to bring women "up" to the male standard. This strategy partly explains why, despite an array of social supports, women still carried a triple burden—worker, mother, homemaker—a condition that theoretically did not exist under socialism and was, therefore, denied in reality (Penrose, 1990, p. 65).

Nevertheless, social policies translated into real, albeit insufficient, support for working mothers. As a result, the majority of women in my sample were not only fully employed, but perceived their occupational opportunities and conditions as equal to those of men, as exemplified by a division manager of a state-owned enterprise: "All avenues were open to us in the GDR. We were given special opportunities for further education; our children were cared for. Women received equal pay. We had this concept, equality for women. That was not only written on paper, that was reality."

And an agricultural worker concurred when she said:

Equal pay for equal work definitely existed in the GDR. No differences existed.[21] Today you hear that when women and men do the same work, they do not get the same pay. It may have been true in some cases in the GDR. But I think that, by and large, it was true, at least in my experience. A certain equality did exist.

Some women, however, felt that it was difficult to pursue professional advancements. They simply could not muster the energy to seek promotions to higher positions that demanded more of their time, energy, and additional duties. Yet, others were undeterred. They wanted to overcome the limitations of the positions they had been assigned to and pursued their personal agendas with the clear intention of increasing their status and income. In this regard, one interviewee, who became a director of a division in a state enterprise, described how she relied on her mother to realize her career goals and cope with family demands:

I changed workplaces. Even [in the GDR], there was material motivation. I simply was able to earn more at the new workplace. . . . I was in charge of a division. . . . [In that position] I had to make sure that I was not absent. My children had to be in child care. I would have had professional disadvantages, had I been absent a lot. I had my mom who would look after my children when they got sick.

A deputy school director noted that political conformity was necessary for advancing one's career. Education, professional experience, and ambition did not suffice under state socialism:

I think I can say that women in the GDR were equal to men. Women were appointed to leading positions if they were capable. Of course, it did play a role whether or not they were members of the Party. I do not want to diminish that. It meant they were socially active. That way they found it easier to get promoted. I do not want to say I was an exception in this regard. But women were as capable as men. . . . Women participated in decision making. And I knew I did good work, and my work was recognized.

And a book dealer commented: "Some women were . . . ambitious . . . [and wanted] to get into leading positions. Of course, women had a double, if not triple burden. But each had to come to terms with herself if she wanted to accept a position like that."

A vast majority (38 or 84.4 percent) of the women I spoke with said that, in general, employers were considerate of the obligations women had to their families and children. Both women and men assumed that it was the responsibility of women to respond to the needs of children and family. Thus, it seemed "natural" when most women refused to assume leadership roles and occupied the lower ranks of the occupational ladders; when they limited their choices to those jobs, work hours, and work places that allowed them to cope with both nondomestic and domestic work demands; when they assumed, generally, less responsibility at the work place than men, and as a result, received less pay. Close proximity between home and work made it easier to combine work and family responsibilities.

The remarks of an agricultural worker were typical in this regard, "my place of work was perhaps two and a half miles from my home. I used to go by bicycle and later by motorbike. There also was a bus." Those who relied on public transport considered it adequate in the absence of a driver's license and a car. But relying on public transport was not without difficulties, especially during the dark and cold winter months as described by a textile worker:

It was not easy. I had to take the children with me on the bus to Güstrow [to bring them to their child-care center]. We took the worker's bus early in the morning. The ride was not the worst, that was about 15 minutes, but all in all it took two hours [to commute] every day. That was stress, but sometimes it was fun, too.

The work days were long. East German women (and men) had the longest work day, week, and year in Europe. They worked 43 and three-quarter hours a week. The work day for mothers (but not for fathers) with two or more children was reduced to 40 hours a week (Winkler, 1990, p. 81). For most women, work began at home, hours before they arrived at their paid work sites. A nurse and mother of two children recalled:

My day started like this: Every morning I got up at five. I had the breakfast prepared the evening before so it would not be too hectic. Then I woke my children, got them dressed and each got their bottle. We had a goat and I had to go and milk it first. . . . When I think back, the things we did! After that, I put their jackets on. I put one child in the front of my bike and another one in the back and took them three kilometers (about a mile and a half) to the village nursery school. Then I rode another five kilometers (about three miles) to my work.

Shift work often complicated the daily work routine, and school schedules added additional pressure. An agricultural worker coped as follows: "I

went to work at five o'clock in the morning. I went back home at six thirty to
wake up my children and get them ready [for school]. Then I went back to
work again. We also worked on weekends."

And a cook who worked in a boarding school relied on her husband for
getting the children to school: "When I had the early shift [in a state-run
boarding school for the deaf] I started work at five. My husband had to get
the children ready. It had to work somehow. And somehow we managed it
all."

For some, meeting the needs of their families and the demands at work
proved arduous. A gardener said:

I liked my work a lot. But sometimes it was really hard because it was just too much
with family [responsibilities] and three children. I had to get up very early, 4:30, because I left at 6:00 A.M. and I came home at 4:30 P.M. There was many a time I wished
I was able to work fewer hours to have some time for myself.

The GDR's rigid system of work hours was based on a male model of
work; therefore, combining work and family in accordance with that model
proved problematic. Also, the state's static view of family life obscured the
daily demands women had to meet. As a consequence, women took matters
in their own hands and broke the rigid state rules. They devised schedules
that suited their needs, insisted on working shorter hours, dropped out of the
work force altogether for a while, and relied on family and friends to help
out. The government, unable and/or unwilling to ease women's daily burdens, could not do without women's labor, and tacitly condoned their independent actions. Some women who worked in the agricultural sector chose
to quit state employment altogether, deciding to raise and sell cattle on their
own terms. That way they were better able to combine family and work responsibilities, and they earned more money. One agricultural worker explained that:

Women in our village did not work outside their homes. Well, most didn't. They
made so much more money with the livestock they raised. . . . They would sell two
bulls they had raised and earn 10,000 Marks. And how many months did I have to
work in my job to make that kind of money?   And then they raised pigs as well.
[These] women liked their lives.

Women's independent actions to better combine their work schedules
and family responsibilities are also revealed in official GDR statistics. In
1989, 27 percent of all employed East German women decided to work
part-time (Winkler, 1990, pp. 83–86).[22] Among the 52 women I interviewed, 13 (25 percent) had decided to work shorter hours at one time or an-

other during their working lives, usually when their children were small. This was true for women who had their children during the 1950s and early 1960s when there was little support from the state for child care and other services, as experienced by this bookkeeper:

In 1961, I tried to work outside the home but my children were small. I stopped because at that time we did not have child care as we had later on. I was a housewife. Later I got an offer as a bookkeeper . . . but I worked only for four hours. . . . But then both children got sick with all those childhood illnesses and I had to quit my job again. I felt very sorry. I liked to work. I worked again when they were older.

This pattern was also true for later generations when child care was not a problem. Younger women who wanted to work shorter and more flexible hours when their children were small arranged to do so. Thus, one office worker negotiated a work contract that accommodated her needs: "My work contract included shorter working hours. If someone got sick or went on maternity leave, I would work full-time . . . [but usually I worked part-time]."

A midwife arranged her work schedule in such a way that: "I worked part-time, [that is] I worked full-time for two weeks, and was off for two weeks. I wanted time for my family and children. . . . It was not because we could afford it. My husband did not earn very much. I just wanted to have time for my children."

And within the agricultural sector women found a way to share a full-time position: "For a time, I worked half a day. I took turns with another woman. [We shared a full-time position]. That way, I always had enough time for my children. On weekends, we did it the same way. And we watched each other's children. Well, we actually liked doing it that way."

Those who worked part-time enjoyed full material and social protection, such as a salary proportional to their working hours, premiums, additional compensation for shift work, paid maternity leave, sick leave, paid vacations, pension plans, free health care, and the right to switch back to full-time work at any time (Winkler, 1990, p. 86).

The majority of East German women, including those I interviewed, worked full-time throughout their working lives. This was possible because a comprehensive child-care system was in place. According to Haller (1992, p. 16), nowhere in the world was child care as available and as thoroughly implemented as in the former GDR. Child care was available to 80 percent of the children in more rural areas and to almost 100 percent in cities. There were nursery school places for 94 percent, and after-school care for 82 percent of the children. Even other socialist systems, such as the

USSR, remained far behind the former GDR. One teacher said: "I was able to combine work and family without any problems. When I talk to my children—my daughter is 28 and my son 24 years old—they never felt oppressed or terrible because I worked full-time and they were in a child care center."

This view was typical and is supported by the findings of the *Institut für Angewandte Sozialwissenschaft* (Institute for Applied Social Science) (1990). Forty-eight percent of those surveyed believed that their work had a positive effect on their family, especially on their children, and 58 percent said that an employed mother is as good a mother as is a full-time homemaker. East German women considered employment, followed by partnership, family, children, and housing, the most important part of their lives. Sixty-five percent of the women said that they would work even if it was not economically necessary.[23]

Combining work and family life was not a *linear* process for most women. It was full of contradictions and required improvisation. As a consequence, the state was not able to strictly control women's lives to the extent it had intended. Although the majority of East German women combined an uninterrupted work life with family responsibilities, a sizeable number bent the rules to respond to a myriad of personal and family needs that could not be simply routinized and subordinated to rigid state demands.

CHANGED IDENTITIES AND PRIORITIES

Socializing and integrating several generations of almost all women of working age into the work force led to a change in women's *identities* and priorities. During the 1950s, East German women considered themselves secondary earners. By contrast, three decades later with employment possessing an independent value for most women, paid work became a primary *identity*. With better education and training, women wanted to be part of the work force, and for the majority, paid work went beyond financial needs. Equally important, if not more, was building self-esteem, recognition, developing skills and talents, creating and nurturing social relationships, communicating, contributing to the general good, and sharing in responsibility (Winkler, 1990, p. 70).

Although a gender division of labor persisted at all levels of employment, it can be argued that by socializing, integrating, and publicly valuing women as important members of the paid work force, the GDR government succeeded in shifting women's social *identity*. East German women's *identity* of a working self was not secondary to the mother/spouse self. The women in my sample had a strong sense that their nondomestic work was valuable and publicly recognized and that it enabled them to be economically independent of their spouses.

THE PERSISTENCE OF GENDER SEGREGATION IN THE PLANNED ECONOMY

In spite of the high integration of women into the labor force, equitable gender distribution across occupations did not exist in the GDR. Indeed, the gender distribution was similar to that of Western market economies. The higher the position, the less likely it was occupied by a woman. In industry, for example, only 20 percent of leading positions were occupied by women. In institutions such as science, education, health and social services, women worked predominantly (63.9 percent) in clerical positions (Rudolph, 1990, p. 3; *Unabhängiger Frauenverband*, 1990, p. 7; Winkler, 1990, pp. 55–73).

Of the women I interviewed, nine (17 percent) had supervisory positions, predominantly in food and material distribution, and in the health and educational fields. Two women had their own businesses—one managed her own drugstore and the other was an independent cosmetician. Although many women said that they were able to choose any occupation they wanted—"I liked it that a woman in the GDR could choose any profession she liked"—the majority "chose" traditionally *female* occupations. For example, they cared for handicapped children and adults, took care of the sick, worked in the communal kitchens and laundry rooms, taught the children and cared for them after school, took care of livestock and tended the fields, and filled supporting roles for male bosses. One child-care worker described how the work was divided up at the boarding school where she worked: "We had a brigade, which was divided into a laundry room, a drying area and ironing area. There were about 20 workers, all women. Well, we did have truck drivers and they were men."

A textile worker depicted her workplace as follows: "[In the garment factory] we were almost all women. There weren't many men. In the cutting room were some. Truck drivers and foremen were men. But mostly, we were women. The management were men, too."

And an administrative assistant noted:

I worked in the municipal government for a department called Environmental Protection, Water Resources, Traffic and Roads. We had female secretaries and other female workers for each section, and the bosses, they were men. All the management positions were filled by men. They were members of the governing board. They were all men except for one woman.

Mechanical jobs—for example, driving tractors or operating other heavy machinery at the agricultural cooperatives—were usually done by men. A few women in my sample, however, performed hard manual labor because, as one gardener said, "We didn't have a lot of technology . . . . The tractor was old, and remodeled, and didn't work all the time." And another gardener commented:

The greenhouses had an area of 5,000 square meters each. We had eight of them. That was a lot of work. . . . Most was manual labor, especially the heating system. . . . We had to fill the [fire] kettles from the top [with] wagons. Each held about one ton [of coal]. We had to shovel the coal into the wagons by hand. . . . Then we had to pull them to the lift to take them up and put them over a [fire] kettle. We pulled a lever and the coal fell into the fire. Often we had complications . . . [the coal got] stuck. . . . We used a lot of brown coal and those are huge clumps and they would not fall through. We had a long iron stick and we had to stoke the coal until it fell through.

Because nondomestic work was publicly recognized as a valuable contribution, the women in my sample conveyed a sense of pride, strength, and practicability about it. For most, the gendered aspects of their work place were of little concern. Indeed, many said that their job had been their choice, or close to what they had wanted to do. They had mostly felt comfortable and secure in their knowledge that they did their jobs well, were financially independent of their partners, and managed to combine home and work life satisfactorily most of the time.

Most women I interviewed had both family and work lives. The role of "housewife" was not considered an alternative life role. But they wanted more flexibility in their daily lives, because to have "one is too little, [while] both are [sometimes] too much" (Becker-Schmidt, cited in Hagemann-White, 1997, p. 557).

CONCLUSION

The socialist system did not entirely succeed in translating its *theoretical* claim of gender equality into the *reality* of everyday life. However, it did succeed in redefining women's primary social roles by fully integrating them into the labor force, promoting further education and job training, and establishing a comprehensive child-care system and other services that assisted women and their families to cope, albeit imperfectly, with paid work and domestic responsibilities. These structural changes forged a new self-understanding for most women, but occupations remained gender segregated.

Despite its goal to control work and family life, the state did not succeed in strictly regimenting it. This was particularly true during the last decade of the GDR's existence, when East German women improvised to cope with everyday difficulties. They creatively bent the Communist Party's rules or evaded them altogether, if those rules complicated their lives.

The next chapter addresses the challenges that East German women face in reunified Germany with regard to their occupational status. It explores how the abolition of the planned economy and the introduction of West Germany's free-market economy have affected their occupational choices and opportunities.

NOTES

1. In 1989, 91 percent of the women of working age in the former German Democratic Republic (GDR) worked outside the home; while in the Federal Republic of Germany (FRG), 54 percent of the women of working age worked outside the home (see Haller, 1992, p. 15).

2. Mecklenburg-Vorpommern, where my interviewees lived, is a predominantly agricultural state.

3. The women I interviewed could be divided roughly into two groups: (1) rural women and (2) urban women. It was generally more difficult to win the confidence of the rural than the urban women. But once that was achieved, the rural women described their circumstances in a very direct language, leaving little doubt about how they felt about their circumstances. Urban women, on the other hand, used more tentative language. Generally, rural women did not feel as comfortable as urban women about reflecting on their circumstances and "digging" at deeper levels and pondering alternatives.

4. The income scale was taken from the *Staatliche Zentralverwaltung* (Government Central Administration) of the former GDR (Winkler, 1990, p. 88).

A comparison of average incomes in 1988 shows that East German women earned about 75 percent of what men earned in the former GDR (*Bundesministerium für Frauen und Jugend* [Federal Ministry for Women and Youth], 1992, p. 51).

5. In the former GDR, the high schools consisted of the *Allegemeinbildenden Polytechnischen Oberschulen* (general educational polytechnical high schools), including grades 9 and 10; and the *Erweiterten Allgemeinbildenden Polytechnischen Oberschulen* (extended general educational polytechnical high schools), including grades 11 and 12 (Winkler, 1990, p. 41).

6. East Germany's model for gender equality was the first Constitution of the Soviet Union (1918), which stated that "Women in the U.S.S.R. [are] accorded equal rights with men in all spheres of economic, government, cultural, political and other public activity."

West Germany's model for gender equality was the United States, which, in 1918, had not yet granted their women the franchise and, to this day, has not added an equal rights amendment to its Constitution (cited in Shaffer, 1981, p. 9).

The equal rights paragraph in the GDR constitution declared: "Men and women have equal rights and equal legal standing in all spheres of social, political and personal life. The furtherance of women, particularly in regard to vocational qualification, is a duty for society and for the state" (cited in Shaffer, p. 12).

7. On April 10, 1974, the equality clause in the GDR Constitution was amended to read:

Article 20, Paragraph 2: Men and women are equal and have the same rights in all areas of life—social, state, and personal. It is the goal of this state and society to ensure the advance of women especially with regard to their professional qualifications.

Article 24, Paragraph 1: Each citizen of the German Democratic Republic has the right to work. (Cited in Horn, 1992, pp. 101–102)

8. According to Assmann (1987, cited in Horn, 1992, p. 101),

[t]he marxist-leninist ideology, as interpreted by the Socialist Unity Party (SED), defined equality as freedom from exploitation, as worker ownership of the means of production, and as participation of all citizens in developing the social and cultural spheres of society. . . . "In the socialist states, equality of all citizens in all spheres of life is the law, which is inviolable, and laid down in the constitution."

9. Katha Politt (1997, p. 162) asserts that individuals in the United States are blinded by the dominant ideology in a similar way because: "people fail to see how unequal women are, or they see it but rationalize [it] as the result of women's own choices and capacities" (cited in Rhode, 1997).

10. Of those who made up the other half in my sample, some did not address this topic, and others believed that state policies had failed to live up to their theoretical claim.

11. Clara Zetkin worked all her life to realize the demands of Marx and Engels vis-à-vis the "women's question." She fought for the right of women to work (many non-Marxists at the time tried to prohibit women from working outside their homes), and tried to organize women in order to improve their conditions in life. She believed in the ideals of socialism, and believed that women and men must unite to fight capitalism (Elsner, 1982, pp. 158–171).

August Bebel's (1910) *Woman and Socialism* and Engels' (1962) "The Origin of the Family, Private Property and the State," as well as Marx and Engels' *Manifesto* (1964), all argued that once the means of production were socialized, class consciousness achieved, and women integrated in the work force, the oppression of women would end.

Lenin wrote,

Notwithstanding all the liberating laws that have been passed, woman continues to be a domestic slave, because petty housework crushes, strangles, stultifies and degrades her, chains her to the kitchen and to the nursery, and wastes her labor on barbarously unproductive, petty, nerve-racking, stultifying and crushing drudgery. The real emancipation of women, real communism, will begin only when a mass struggle [led by the proletariat which is in power] is started against this petty domestic economy, or rather when it is transformed on a mass scale into large-scale socialist economy [and women are freed to participate in the productive work force]. (Lenin, 1951, p. 56)

12. The East German government had at least three other reasons for integrating women into the work force: (1) after World War II, East Germany carried a double burden of rebuilding the country and making reparation payments to the Soviet Union for the latter's wartime losses. Reparation payments to the Soviet Union included "equipment, livestock and other material resources as well as labor"; (2) 2.7 million people fled to the West between 1949–1961; and (3) the fact of slow technological development with a simultaneous shortfall of skilled labor (*Defense Diplomacy*, Special Report 1989, p. 33; *Institut für Angewandte Sozialwissenschaft*, 1990, p. 1).

13. For additional information on how East German women's socialization in the GDR entails both opportunities and risks for their occupational chances in reunified Germany, see Nickel (1993).

14. The proportion of women who worked in the former German Democratic Republic was high even by international comparison. In 1989, 91.2 percent of women of working age were employed. This figure includes female trainees and students (Winkler, 1990, pp. 62–63).

15. See Gysi and Meyer (1993) and Trappe (1995a, 1995b) on the socialist construction of the worker/mother and her role in the family, partnership, and marriage.

16. See Trappe (1995a) for an analysis of how social policies influenced different cohorts of women to employ specific strategies to meet the demands of paid work and family obligations. Also, see Roemer (1995) for a comparison of biographies of East and West German women who were born in 1949.

17. A Louis Harris and Associates Inc. survey, conducted with the Whirlpool Foundation and the Families and Work Institute, found that a majority of women in the United States provided half or more of their families' income. This finding matches the data collected by the U.S. Labor Department (Mathews, 1995, p. B13).

18. In this regard, see Stein and Wetterer's (1994) comparative study of East and West German university-educated women.

19. By guaranteeing women's rights, the government, which considered women a political risk factor, hoped to secure their political and ideological loyalty and not only integrate them in the work force but also to increase their commitment to the Party and other mass organizations (Penrose, 1990, p. 64).

20. The sentiments of the East German women who joined the Party in the hope of building a better society were most eloquently expressed by Doris Lessing (1997) (cited in Sichtermann, 1998, p. 17): "Today it is all incomprehensible that communism offered a generation a degree of certainty of a peaceful society, particularly after the Second World War when poverty and exhaustion were ever present and warm shelter and food could not be taken for granted."

Helga Schubert (cited in Haller, 1992, p. 59), an East German psychologist and author, said: "As long as communism was an idea, a utopia, yes, it was OK. But it lost its innocence as soon as it was associated with power."

21. This perception has not been borne out in reality. See chapter 8 for statistics on income differences between East German women and men. What can be said is that the gap in income has been of a lesser degree in the GDR than it is in reunified Germany.

22. Of those, 60 percent worked between 25 and 35 hours. The work hours of the other 40 percent varied. Some worked fewer, some more hours (Winkler, 1990, pp. 83–86).

23. Suggesting a norm that holds cross-culturally, the Whirlpool Foundation conducted a survey of 6,781 women and men in Britain, France, Germany, Italy, and Spain and found "that 6 out of 10 women chose to work for money, but that 48 percent would still work if money was not an issue. 'Assumptions that women work for just extra cash, and that having a family means giving up a career just don't hold for today's women in Europe,' a representative for the foundation, Francesca Rennix, said at a conference in Brussels" (*International Herald Tribune*, 1996, p. 5).

Further, a survey of 1,502 women conducted in the United States by the Louis Harris and Associates Inc., the Whirlpool Foundation, and the Families and Work Institute found that "56 percent of American women do not want to give up either home or work duties despite severe time pressure. The percentage rises to 60 percent for women under age 35" (Mathews, 1995, p. B13).

3

Work Life under Capitalism

INTRODUCTION

After German reunification, East German women spent inordinate amounts of energy coping with the transition from state socialism to capitalism. German reunification had obliterated, overnight, the taken-for-granted predictability of daily life and cut to the core of women's material and emotional existence. Nevertheless, most women were determined to deal with the new conditions and corresponding difficulties. They mixed determination with a sense of humor, and many smiled at the naivete, trust, and innocence with which they had embraced the new system.

In this chapter, I examine East German women's efforts to adapt to a radically different work environment in the new social market economy.[1] I analyze the *structural* and *gender* barriers they encountered in their search for paid work. Some barriers were unique to women, others not; but all tended to shift women's focus away from the labor market and back to home and family, establishing a clearer and more hierarchical division of public and private labor. The women I interviewed addressed four interrelated aspects pertaining to their employment: their occupational status after reunification; the structural barriers and gender bias they encountered in the labor market; and their efforts to preserve their professional *identity*. Their experiences reflect their struggle against the imposition of traditional roles to preserve their autonomy, employment status, and access to resources.

WOMEN'S OCCUPATIONAL STATUS AFTER REUNIFICATION

The employment situation had changed drastically for most women I interviewed. Whereas *all* 52 women had been employed under state socialism, in reunified Germany 27 (52 percent) were employed; 14 (27 percent) were enrolled in retraining/job creation programs sponsored by various government agencies and, thus, officially counted as employed;[2] 3 (7 percent) had retired; 7 (13 percent) were unemployed; and one chose to stay at home. Over half of the women had experienced unemployment at one time or another during the first five and a half years after German reunification. Of those, half had been unemployed for longer than three years.

A survey conducted by the Ministry for Family and Children in Bonn produced even more extreme findings. By 1995, *two-thirds* of formerly employed East German women were unemployed.[3] Of those, 77 percent constituted the long-term unemployed (Atkinson, 1995, p. A25).[4] Hahn and Schön (1995, pp. 107, 113), who define "long-term unemployment" as being out of work for longer than a year, found that in contrast to men for whom older age was a significant factor with regard to long-term unemployment, women experienced long-term unemployment at any age.[5]

Thirty-three women (63.5 percent) in my sample discovered that the education and training they had received in the GDR were defined as useless by prospective employers in reunified Germany. Consequently, the same number of women felt that their professional choices had diminished considerably. Only 5 women (10 percent) said they had better choices after reunification.[6]

NEW STRUCTURAL BARRIERS AND GENDER BIAS

Searching for paid work under competitive market conditions was totally new for East German women. Most had encountered various structural obstacles and gender bias in their search for paid work. Hardly anyone knew what exactly the new labor laws were and what exactly constituted discrimination. The legal system, like all other social institutions, was new, unfamiliar, and overwhelming.

Workplaces were eliminated at a particularly high rate in traditionally female sectors—kindergartens, child-care centers, cafeterias, retail stores.[7] According to one educator, "[German reunification] was very bad. . . . One was practically thrown out of work." And a gardener explained: "There was immediately a dismissal boom. Women out! Women back in the kitchen. . . . That is how it is over there [West Germany], that is how they wanted it to be here. That was immediately obvious."

A child-care worker, too, recognized early on that women would be especially vulnerable in the newly established capitalist system:

[In 1990] I said, "now sales assistants will be dismissed *en masse*, and teachers, too." Those are [the women] you see in retraining classes today. We had so many child-care centers and kindergartens. Today, there are very few left, also because there are hardly any children born now.

Women who had previously worked in the agricultural sector were particularly hard hit by unemployment after many of the agricultural production cooperatives closed down or were restructured and privatized. According to the *Bundesministerium für Frauen und Jugend* (1992, p. 49), women made up about 60 percent of the unemployed in the agricultural sector. In my sample *all women* who had previously been employed in the agricultural sector were unemployed. In this regard, a technician who had worked for 32 years in a state-owned agricultural cooperative said:

[In] ... our village ... everything has been destroyed, everything. They used to have so many cows and pigs. Now all the buildings are empty. And the land does not belong to the people anymore. Before [reunification], everyone was a member of the agricultural cooperatives and owned a certain number of shares. But now it has been given back to private owners. Now they use part of the agricultural land for recreational centers and to build golf courses. I feel so sorry for the people who worked the land.

A cattle breeder who had raised cattle at a state-owned agricultural cooperative observed, "The agricultural sector has taken the hardest hit. You felt that almost immediately. Everything was privatized. There were some in our agricultural production cooperative who tried to privatize. Some succeeded, but many did not."

No sector of the economy escaped economic restructuring, downsizing, and privatizing. Women were more likely to lose their jobs than men. In January 1995, the unemployment rate for the state of Mecklenburg-Vorpommern, which includes Güstrow, the hometown of the women I interviewed, stood at 17 percent (*The Week in Germany*, January 27, 1995, p. 1). In March 1996, it had increased to 18 percent (*Schweriner Volkszeitung*, March 3, 1996, p. 5).[8] In Güstrow itself, a steady increase was observed in the proportion of women among the unemployed. In August 1990, women made up 41 percent of the unemployed, in December 1991, they made up 54.8 percent, and in December 1992, the rate had climbed to 61.0 percent (Falk and Hohmann, 1993, p. 7).[9] A teacher echoed the sentiments of many, when she said, "I can say with certainty that women are affected more by unemployment than men, and this trend is on the increase. Men find new jobs more easily because they are more mobile, more flexible. The assumption [of employers] is that men perform better because women have family responsibilities."

The language many women used to describe the collapse of the work structures they had known for most of their lives conveyed a sense of doom and demise: Shops were "destroyed"; state enterprises "killed"; agricultural cooperatives had "died." The words of one interviewee who had worked in the retail sector of a large state enterprise exemplify how many expressed what they were experiencing: "After the *Wende* [turning point],[10] our production and trading cooperative was divided into two sections. One division became a bank, the other a trading company. . . . The bank was taken over by a [West German] bank in Kiel . . . but they let the trading company *die*."

And a teacher explained her experiences in similar words: "My husband was part of a group of veterinarians. I think there were nine of them in our community. But it was *destroyed*."

The words chosen by these East German women to express their experiences were so poignant, precisely because paid work had been their primary *identity*. And this identity had come under assault as a result of the restructuring of the economy after German reunification.

Getting Fired: A New Experience

Getting fired from a job simply did not happen in the GDR. For most women, the experience of dismissal was very painful. They felt betrayed, in part, because of the way the dismissal was handled. Pregnant women and mothers with small children felt particularly vulnerable because the GDR law that had granted them protection from being fired was abolished (Haller, 1992, p. 66). Unfamiliar with the new labor laws of the West German system, and with no procedures in place to explain the situation to them at their places of work, they felt at the mercy of their supervisors. Moreover, most superiors lacked any experience of dismissing people from their jobs with whom they had worked together often for decades. Frequently, women were just handed an envelope. They were confronted with a reality for which they had no precedent, no context and that, consequently, was a *life event* of immense proportions. A gardener recalled:

Well, a meeting was called for all members [of the agricultural cooperative] and there we were told that dismissals were imminent. . . . Then we got blue letters. And one letter came flying over to me, very elegantly. I said, "Well, of course!" Then [the supervisor] said, "Well, you know, . . . you are a single woman with no children." I said, "I see, that is really great, those of us who don't have children can starve or what? . . . I have to live somehow. I have worked here for 14 years and . . . now I get a kick in the ass."

One educator described how deeply shaken she was when she received her notice:

And one day—it was exactly June 12, "Teacher's Day" in the GDR—I was called to the town hall. At that point I had worked 25 years as a teacher. I thought they wanted to reward me for 25 years of service. I had always worked well. I thought, perhaps I'll get promoted or something like that, but I got my dismissal notice instead. There was no warning, nothing. At that time, it was still inconceivable to be dismissed—[to receive] a notice of dismissal! It was as if a hammer had dropped on me, because I just did not expect [to be dismissed]. I actually thought I was irreplaceable because of my education, because of my commitment.

And a nurse explained: "[The thought] just did not want to go into my head. . . . You know, we had no experience of being unemployed. It did not exist [in the GDR] and that is why the first notice of dismissal was so very painful."

Dealing with Social Insecurity and Stress

The new capitalism in the West is characterized by a sense of pervasive social insecurity (Sennett, 1998a, 1998b).[11] This assertion found support from 37 employed and unemployed women (71 percent) in my sample. The establishment of West Germany's capitalist system in the GDR magnified the feeling of insecurity. Only 5 women (9.6 percent) said that they felt as secure as they did in the GDR. And 43 women (83 percent) said that stress had become a major factor in their lives as a result of having to live with uncertainty and ongoing, fast-paced social changes and economic decline.[12]

These perceptions are compatible with the results of a general survey conducted in 1996. The vast majority of East German women and men in that study defined the general economic situation in reunified Germany as "bad" and "very bad."[13] Economic uncertainty and social insecurity explain, in part, why East German women's desire to work outside the home has remained as strong as that of East German men, and why women's focus on finding work and succeeding professionally has intensified (*Schweriner Volkszeitung*, March 8, 1996, p. 3). In addition, paid work is a primary part of East German women's *identity* that they wanted to restore. The remarks of a white-collar worker echo the sentiments of many: "I literally threw myself into the work. I wrote applications, applications, applications. . . . I also took a temporary job, not only because of the money, but because I needed to get out, I needed to get [back into a job]."

And the remarks of this teacher were also shared by many: "It is a continuing [source of] stress, I search and search and search [without much success]. . . . Had I known that I would not be employed as a teacher anymore, I would not have had a second child. Somehow, you give up on yourself."

All 52 women considered paid work essential because it brought them "peace of mind." Most were not prepared to stay at home. As a matter of principle, and for economic reasons, they did not consider it an option. The prevailing viewpoint among East German women in all age groups is that work is very important.[14] Most women I interviewed could not conceive of being permanently without paid work. Their upbringing and education in the GDR had emphasized work outside the home, and it was very evident that they liked it. They wanted to be financially and socially independent of their partners; they had always been and refused to imagine it otherwise because, according to one white-collar employee, "It is so important that one stands on one's own feet in life. . . to have a profession."

And a textile worker noted:

I find it very important that women work outside the home [not only because of the money]. Women need . . . to exchange ideas, and not just wait at home for their husbands, who are also stressed when they come home. One needs [to talk] woman to woman. Where I work we are all women, we know exactly the problems of the other family. . . . We grew up next to each other. That was nice, very nice.

Social-emotional independence from their partners was as important as financial independence for many women I interviewed. Thirty-five women (67 percent) said that they had enjoyed the support and relationships they had built with their coworkers in the past, and enjoyed being part of a cohesive group at work that shared leisure activities such as going out to eat, to the theater, and the movies. It was an important part of their lives and they wanted to continue it. But searching for a job in reunified Germany posed new and previously unknown barriers.

Searching for Paid Work

East German women realized quickly that in reunified Germany the status of breadwinner was accorded to men. Men's income is considered the family income. Women's income counts as *additional* money, even though in reality this notion is not substantiated.[15] Women are regarded as "naturally" dependent because the family household and not the state (as was the case in the GDR) is the provider of individual social security. The family household, *normally* headed by the male, is the "key unit of economic, social, and moral importance," which stresses the significance of "the monogamous relationship and the [importance] of women's domestic role within it which has particular consequences for the choices open to women" (Rai, Pilkington, and Phizacklea, 1992, p. 5). Consequently, the social space in the reunified Germany is more sharply defined, organized, and divided for women and men who, as a result, are expected to take on more distinct responsibilities in the private and public domains, respectively. And many women in my sample still struggled to deal with this new reality. Many reflected in the same manner as a shepherd, who said:

I really do not understand this. A father can look after the children just as well as a mother. So when a woman is employed and she has a husband who is unemployed, then he can look after the child. I don't understand why [employers don't get that] and still prefer to employ men. I really don't understand that.

And many voiced the same thoughts as this self-employed interviewee:

[Today,] it is easier for a man to find work than for a woman, because [in the West German system] fewer women work outside the home. That is how it is over there. A woman belongs in the kitchen with the children, and that is her work. Well, if she has time left, she can get some education. And many [West German] women seem to be satisfied with that choice. But not East German women. We don't know [that life]. We went to school. After we finished school, we got trained and found a job, and everyone had work. That's how it was. And that is why unemployment is now so *depressing*.

Increasing unemployment, the closure of many child-care facilities, increased child-care costs, and a renewed emphasis on traditional gender roles made it difficult for many women to hold on to the idea of combining work and family responsibilities. According to the *Deutscher Gewerkschaftsbund* (DGB) [Federation of German Trade Unions] (1995), the overall unemployment rate for East German women remained persistently at *twice* the rate for men; skilled women workers were less readily considered; and the willingness to take on female trainees declined markedly. Employers were reluctant to consider women with children, and women even charged that some employers asked them to undergo sterilization to be considered for employment (cited in *The Week in Germany*, June 2, 1995, p. 5). At a meeting on International Women's Day in Rostock

(GDR) in March 1996, Annette Niemeyer, from the *Independent Women's Union*, said,

The social development [in reunified Germany] clearly takes the direction of convincing women to accept exclusively the role of mother, homemaker, and appendage to men. Our critique [is especially directed] toward the employment offices which not only let women be pushed out of the labor market, but actively support it. (*Schweriner Volkszeitung*, March 9, 1996, p. 19)

The structural barriers that East German women confronted in reunified Germany clashed with self-concepts and experiences they had acquired in the GDR.

Gender Discrimination in Job Ads, Applications, and Interviews

The gendered barriers in reunified Germany were unexpected and surprising to many East German women, because they were neither subtle nor hidden. The Hamburg Institute for Human Resources and Labor Studies identified help-wanted advertisements as an important source of gender discrimination and showed how particular notices had clearly violated the 1980 "Amendment to the EU [European Union] Labor Law for Equal Treatment of Women and Men at Work." This law states that "job advertisements should be written in a gender-neutral language" (*Bundesministerium für Frauen und Jugend*, 1992, p. 57).[16]

The Hamburg study found that ads that addressed primarily male job seekers were on the increase. Of the "over 13,000 ads for skilled workers and management positions [the institute examined in 1994], 41 percent used the masculine form, . . . six percent . . . used 'veiled male-directed formulations.'" Half addressed both genders and applied the male and female forms. The feminine form was used in only 3 percent of the ads.[17] The Hamburg Institute for Human Resources and Labor Studies concluded that if companies do not address women, they won't apply (*The Week in Germany*, September 22, 1995a, p. 5).

If job ads presented a serious barrier to East German women's occupational opportunities, the job application process presented another. The competitive labor market in reunified Germany requires that applicants, in addition to specifying their professional skills, disclose their private lives, that is, their age, marital status, and number and ages of children. In addition, they have to attach a passport-size photograph of themselves. A gardener said:

The entire family situation has to be included in the job application: whether I am married or not, how old I am, how many children I have, the ages of my children. And . . . you can't be older than 28, at most 30. And if you have not written down [the information], then they will ask you *if* you get an interview. . . . And a photograph has to be included. That has to be. They don't look, first and foremost, at whether I am qualified for the job, but the way I look. It doesn't matter whether I have a super brain. If they don't like the way I look, they throw my application out.

Women with dependent children and those who were of childbearing age were particularly vulnerable. Some underwent sterilization to safeguard their jobs, or to increase their chances of securing one (Pinzler, 1996, p. 22). Thirty-two of the 37 women in my sample who addressed the subject of children and job opportunities had concluded that their children were a handicap in obtaining work. One nurse described it as follows:

A woman can get pregnant. A man cannot. It is unfortunate that today a woman is only hired if she has undergone sterilization. I know it from a very reliable source. That is simply how it is. That is Germany. No one would say it publicly, but it is suggested to a woman [when she is interviewed for a job] and put under tremendous pressure.

Employers in reunified Germany clearly assume that children and the home are women's responsibilities. Recently married women said that employers told them they might get pregnant and, therefore, represented too much of a risk for a company to invest in. This reflects the traditional assumption that marriage must lead to children, and children must lead to women staying home. In the words of one white-collar employee, "When you get married [the company thinks] 'she could get pregnant, and then she will take time off. And we have to pay for everything.'" Women who had small children were told that their children might get sick, and, therefore, they were too unreliable as workers:

A woman with children—who will employ her nowadays? [Employers] ask, "how many children do you have, how old are they?" They go by age, don't they? If you have three children, no company will take you. . . . They figure, "If she has so and so many children, she will miss work so and so often because her children will get sick" (a salesclerk).

One of my interviewees, herself an employer, said:

I have employed a young woman who has a three-year-old child. I said to her, "Why don't you have a job yet?" [She is] intelligent, beautiful, has a wonderful education and training. "Well," she said, "because I have a three-year-old daughter." That would never have happened in the GDR. And why not? We had kindergartens and day-care centers. A woman could participate fully at work.

Women who were single and had no children did not find it any easier to get a job. They learned that employers preferred men because, it is assumed, men have to support their families and, therefore, should have priority. A highly educated biologist with 16 years of experience in in-vitro research remarked that being "single does not help much in the job market. And it does not play a role at all that I have a good education."

Age presented another barrier. Although the issue of age was not unique to women, it became a major obstacle for 25 of the 32 women who raised the issue. The experience of one white-collar employee was typical, "If one looks at the job ads, they look for people who are at most 28 or 30 years old. It says so in the ads." Prospective employers favored young men because they are assumed to be unburdened by family responsibilities and, therefore, cheaper and more reliable, and able to give their best. Employers told some women directly that they were too old. One educator said: "That is actually the worst [thing] to recognize, that [we] still have so much energy and knowledge, but that no one wants [those of us who are over 35] anymore."

And a white-collar employee made sense of her experience this way: "That was always the tone in these job interviews. They wanted somebody with 30 years of professional experience, but to be 17 or 18 years of age" [laughs heartily].

A division manager of a state enterprise recalled:

At the time of the [job] interview, I was 37 years old. Well, they showed me clearly that they would have to invest four years of training in me. Then I would be 41 or 42. By then, they said, I would not have the energy any more to perform adequately for the company. That is what I was basically told. That was not only one interview. I had many, many interviews of this type.

And an educator had to resign herself to the fact that:

I am too old [between 45–54 years]. That is the reality. I see it here in the retraining program. Women with small children do not get jobs because employers think they will be absent from work more often. And the older women do not get jobs because the employers think they will be a liability—they could get sick more often, or can't be dismissed because of labor protection laws.

The understanding that education and professional experiences are generally a plus in women's search for paid work was not easily transferred to the women I interviewed in East Germany. Women with advanced education were particularly suspect in reunified Germany because their status implied collaboration with the old system. Many are now caught in a paradoxical situation: In the GDR, they had to make an ideological commitment to qualify for admission to the higher educational system, but in reunified Germany this commitment is held against them.[18] A highly qualified biologist commented:

It is absolutely of no consequence that I have had a good education (PhD in biology and 18 years experience in *in-vitro* research). [German reunification] was a total rupture. . . . For biologists there are no positions. There are so many of us. [In any case,] they only take people who are younger than 35. I have experienced it at the employment office in Rostock. And [it does not help that] I studied in the [former] Soviet Union. That is considered suspect.

A professor found that:

There is this tendency not to employ any professors from the technical university. They are regarded by many as being part of the "red ivory tower." . . . When my colleagues and I tried to apply to teach at the *Gymnasium* (German high school that prepares students for university), . . . it was clear that they did not even consider us.[19]

An art historian explained:

[East German] academics were thrown out altogether. They were completely put down, [and] the really good positions were taken over by West Germans. . . . Academics were affected very, very badly [by reunification]. Artists were affected very, very badly. I have experienced this myself.

Hahn and Schön (1995, pp. 104, 105), who studied representative samples of the long-term unemployed in East and West Germany, found that "an important feature of the unemployed in East Germany is their above average educational level." Thirteen percent of the unemployed in East Germany (in contrast to 5 percent in West Germany) have graduated from technical and other universities. The status of the women I interviewed followed a similar pattern. Except for 14 (27 percent), mostly older women who had less than 10 years of education, the majority was well educated: 37 women (71 percent) had graduated from high school; of those, 19 (37 percent) had graduated from college and 14 women (27 percent) had advanced degrees. Over half of the women in my sample, representing all educational levels, experienced unemployment at one time or another during the first five and a half years after German reunification.

Dealing with a No-Win Situation

In a climate of rising unemployment, it did not matter what women had to offer the labor market. Any or all aspects of their biography could be, and often were, defined as inadequate: their education, professional experience, newly acquired skills, familial circumstances, and their ages. Simply being a woman put them in a no-win situation, leading them to conclude that women were not employed because they were of the wrong gender. These realities contributed to feelings of anxiety, frustration, anger, and/or depression among many of the women. Thirty-six women (69 percent) talked about experiencing anxiety to various degrees, largely because they felt they had little control over access to, and opportunities in, the labor market. One health care worker said: "I was very depressed. . . . I had the feeling that everything I had done [in the GDR] was for nothing. . . . I was totally destroyed. I had my education, I had my training, I had my job experience. . . . [but] it was really hard [to find a job]."

Twenty-three (44 percent) felt angry about having no choice but to endure humiliating treatment at the unemployment office. They depended on it for unemployment benefits and assistance in their job searches. The experience of one white-collar worker was typical for many:

A little while ago we had a horrendous snow storm and I had to go to the unemployment office because the allotted time was running out. I called them and asked, "Is it really necessary that I come today during the snowstorm? Can I come tomorrow or the day after when the weather has improved?" They answered, "No, you have to come today, otherwise we have to register you as noncompliant and have to reduce your unemployment benefits." I drove there, which took me almost an hour [for a rather short distance]. I got to the office, and the woman looked at me and asked, "Do you still live in West Street?" I said, "Yes." "Do you still have the same phone number?" "Yes." "Do you still have your driver's license?" "Yes." "That is it, thank you." I just lost it. I told this woman, "You can't be serious! [For that you make me come here] in this weather?" That is pure harassment! I have a car, I live in town, but what about the women in the villages who have no car, who have to go [to the unemployment office]. That is pure harassment. It makes me so angry.

The realization that access to paid work was often severely restricted because gender expectations played a decisive role caused confusion and heightened feelings of alienation. One manager who was part of a team that selected new employees observed:

When I sit in on interviews and see how women are expected to sell themselves, how they have to present themselves, I feel terrible! What they must do to themselves to get a job! They have to wear the right clothes, sit the right way. There are so many things now that are expected of women that I think are not natural anymore [and totally irrelevant to the job]. It was not like that in the GDR.

A counselor in a supervisory position who had worked for 31 years for the Department of Health felt that her gender was the deciding factor when a position she was qualified for was denied her:

In 1990 [three months before Germany was reunified], I was still working in the Department for Public Health. But then I was given the job to reorganize the Social Service Department for the county, and I took it. About three or four days before the county administration was to officially take over the Social Service Department, I was asked to come to the county headquarters. I went and I met with three men. They said to me, "*Frau L.*, listen, we think that the job of director for the Social Service Department is a rather difficult position for a woman to assume. We really believe that. Just think about what is left to do, what is left to reorganize. We think that *Herr P.* should become director. You look surprised, did you expect a firm offer?" I was speechless. All I could say was, "I have to go to the post office. They close at 12:00 noon." I ran out of the building. I do not remember how I got home. These were the same men who asked me to reorganize [the entire department]. And they let me do it, they never interfered or complained. Let me put it this way, they let me do all the dirty work. And when the position became publicly a visible position, a man had to fill it. I could have jumped in their faces!

Dealing with a Competitive Work Environment

Not all women described their experiences in the reunified Germany as negative. Although access to paid work was restricted for many, and opportunities were limited, some women retained their positions or found new ones. Nine (17 percent) of the women I interviewed experienced the social changes that came with reunification in a positive way. When the pressure to conform politically was lifted, they saw barriers to professional advancement removed, and found new opportunities for themselves. In the words of one nurse:

Well, yes, I have to say that reunification has brought major changes. . . . I knew that I had reached the limits with my work [in the GDR because I was defined as politically untrustworthy]. And after reunification, so many possibilities opened up, especially in my work [with people who have special needs]. It is extremely satisfying and also surprising.

A bank manager described what she experienced as positive in reunified Germany:

The last five years have been incredibly interesting. I have learned an enormous amount. I have gotten to know great people, and that, I think, is very important. . . . I would not want to miss the last five years. I mean, they have been very, very hard. In addition to being trained as a bank manager, I also continued my economics studies, which I had begun in 1987. . . . In 1991, I would have finished, but then the new state, this new system of law, did not recognize my GDR education.

And a teacher explained how things had improved but also become more complicated:

I am . . . a teacher for the hearing impaired. . . . We were needed. We did not have to dismiss any of our colleagues, quite the opposite. . . . [But] now we have to make really tough decisions about what teaching materials to use. There is much too much choice. The materials we developed ourselves, we basically miss them now. The technological side [for the hearing impaired] is better today. That is a very good thing.

The positive aspects of the new situation at work were mitigated, however, by the pressure to perform and conform to a new set of rules. Working conditions had changed drastically for everyone in East Germany after reunification. According to 34 women (65 percent) in my sample, conditions did not necessarily improve. Many East German women resented the competitive nature of unified Germany. Forty-one women (79 percent) said they found it extremely difficult to work in an economy that was driven by competition and noted that the work climate had become competitive and impersonal.[20] The remarks by a deputy school director were typical:

Now I am expected to deliver, *period*. There is no room for compromise, no room at all. I have to perform and account for it. There is constant pressure because there is competition all around us. . . . My job depends on my performance, they hold me accountable. This type of pressure we did not have in the GDR.

Of the 26 women who were employed, 18 found it difficult to adapt to the West German work style. They felt that the pressure to conform to West Germany's *economic* norms was as bad as the pressure they had experienced in the GDR to conform to *political* norms. Many found that political control in the workplace had given way to economic control. They considered it ironic that the conditions for succeeding professionally in reunified Germany did not differ all that much from those in the GDR. Before reunification, the Socialist Unity Party demanded loyalty and promoted cooperative behavior. After reunification, the boss demanded loyalty and expected competitive behavior. The form and actors (although not always) had changed, but the rules remained basically the same—*nondemocratic*. In the GDR, political nonconformity was sanctioned with demotion or prevention from being allowed to progress in one's career. In reunified Germany, economic nonconformity is sanctioned with dismissal from the job. Many women I spoke with resented the new rules as much, if not more, as the old rules, because the new rules empowered the employer to take away their livelihoods.

Barbara Ehrenreich (1996, p. 80) notes that political "[f]reedom" is [the] official . . . rallying cry [in the West], but *un*freedom is, for many people, the price of economic survival." In the capitalistic marketplace, most workers "can be fired 'for any reason or no reason'—except when the firing can be shown to be discriminatory on the basis of race, sex, or religion" (p. 80). For many workers this means, "If you want to talk [or otherwise critique your boss], be prepared to walk" (p. 80). Reflecting on the new working conditions, a nurse summed up the experiences of many women:

In East Germany, I could not publicly say anything against the Party or the prevailing ideology; it would have affected my opportunities at work. Now I can't say anything against my boss, or I risk losing my job. So, nothing much has changed. I am still careful to whom I say what. And often, I just shut up.

A textile worker said:

In the GDR, I had always voiced my opinion at work [because I knew I would always have work]. I always said what I thought. To be sure, I am not the type who talks without thinking beforehand. But I was less careful than I am now. Before, I felt more at peace [with my situation at work].

A cook remarked:

In the GDR, I could not have said at my place of work that Honecker [party secretary of the Socialist Unity Party] is an idiot. But I could say to my boss, "What you are doing is not acceptable to me." Today it is the other way around. Now I can say Kohl [then chancellor of reunified Germany] is an idiot. But I can't voice any criticism to my boss or I would risk being dismissed.

An educator concluded:

Actually, I see the transformation [from communism to capitalism] as a transformation from subject to object. I am very self-assured. I know what I can do. I know what I am worth, I have clearly demonstrated that. I say that without trying to sound arrogant. I was sought-after as far as knowledge was concerned. But sadly, I had to learn to sell myself short [in reunified Germany]. At first I thought, "They must see what I am capable of. They can't just expect me to exhibit subservient behavior or give up my straightforward outspokenness." But I had to learn that the boss is always right. And I had to learn to keep my mouth shut. I can't really say what I think anymore. And these are the situations when I feel kind of raped.

A former mayor of the city of Rostock (GDR) noted that "[t]he change from a solidarity to a competitive society [has been] the greatest rupture in the East, the repercussions of which are totally beyond [people in the] West to understand."[21] And "for us [East Germans] the situation [in reunified Germany] is like the one of the frog who is being thrown into hot water: the change is so drastic that the situation becomes unbearable" (Weslus, 1994, p. 29).

East Germans avoided competing against each other in the GDR and still avoid it in reunified Germany. In comparison to West Germans, East Germans are still much closer to each other [at work] and privately, more spontaneous, and they do not think, first and foremost, of their own advantage (Richter, Brähler, and Geyer, cited in *Spiegel*, 1995).[22] The solidarity in the GDR was impressive, because the GDR had succeeded in reducing the competitive behavior that is taken for granted in capitalist societies (Wagner, 1996, p. 168). East Germans were more social than West Germans at their workplaces and felt personally more connected to their work, as exemplified by this white-collar worker, who was employed by the city government:

[In the GDR] my work was not just focused on advantages for me personally. When I work I do not only think about what kind of money I can make. I see my work as a whole. I have a typical example. We went to the old federal state [West Germany] to a governmental agency and I was sitting next to a West German professional observing his work. I noticed that he had a very narrow view. He was not interested in what was happening on his right and left. He did not want to know. He got a phone call and someone must have asked him a question. He answered, "I am sorry, this is not my area." And he put the receiver down! I would have said the same, but also asked, "Can I perhaps help you." I would have found out what [the caller] needed and given him the right number or connected him. I think my colleagues would have done the same. That was our style. But now, it is not like that anymore.

A social worker who had welcomed the change and tried to comply with the competitive rules of the market economy nevertheless struggled with the implementation of those rules at her place of work:

I worked again with the same clients [people with special needs]. . . . But the law had changed completely and that was very, very hard because I could not help in the same way as before when very little bureaucracy was involved. . . . When someone came to see me [after reunification], I had to say, "I can help you, but now I have to know whether you can help yourself. Can I see your bank account, your savings?" That was terrible for me. . . . That question was a blow below the belt. I had to base my decisions on their financial situation. . . . I felt horrible. I began to suffer physically. It was a terrible time. I had to quit and find another job.

The competitive work climate also heightened the awareness of gender differences. The response of a manager was typical of what many interviewees expressed:

In the GDR, I felt definitely more equal to men. I find [now] that men assert their power again in so many areas [of daily life], and one has to be really courageous to block that. Otherwise, women would just disappear from the face of the earth. In the department where I work, I am the token woman. I am the only woman in a domain of men. Whatever committee I am on, I am [as a result] the only woman. I have learned that it is very important to be always up to date, to be precise and very concrete, and not permit myself to show any signs of insecurity. I can really say that men behaved differently in the GDR.

Dealing with Longer Work Hours and Longer Commutes

In addition to a competitive work climate, 24 (46 percent) women I interviewed were concerned about work hours. For many, hours had become longer and the work more demanding. Given the high unemployment rates, many considered longer hours socially unjust. It indicated that there was enough work to go around, but that it was distributed unfairly.[23] Almost all women had either friends, former colleagues, and/or other family members who had been or were unemployed at the time of the interview. Of the women who were employed, many felt that they had to remain quiet. They perceived an unspoken, but real threat that there were many well-qualified people waiting to be employed in their place. One interviewee responsible for managing a branch of a large West German bank said:

The workday has become much harder and longer, too. OK, my tasks are totally different from what they used to be. In the GDR, I worked, at times, 10 to 12 hours a day as well. But I was not so terribly exhausted as I am now. My work day generally begins at 7:30 in the morning and I am not home before 8:00 at night. That is my day, every day.

A health care worker noted:

We simply work much more [nowadays], well, at least I think so. During the time I work, I work much harder than I used to [in the GDR]. I am not quite sure why that is so. Well, I think I am in this with my heart and soul. . . . I think that is one reason.

But I also think it is expected that we go to our outer limits. I think that is part of it, too. One has to work harder and better all the time. I think that has changed a lot [since reunification].

And an agricultural worker observed: "We have to work harder, physically harder. Although the work remained the same, what two [people] used to do has to be done by one. I lost seven kilograms (15.5 pounds) in three weeks."

The distance between home and workplaces has increased as well, especially for women who lived in rural areas and had previously been employed in agricultural cooperatives, the majority of which ceased to exist. Getting to or finding work outside their villages presented a particular problem for these women. It meant expending extra time and energy on an already demanding daily schedule. Most did not have a driver's license because in the GDR few owned a car and public transport was mostly adequate. After reunification, women depended on others for rides and on a more restrictive public transport system. Many simply could not afford to obtain a driver's license and to buy a car. Unemployed women struggled to find work along bus routes; or close enough to home so they could ride a bike; or in the vicinity of someone else's work place so they could catch a ride. Often they found themselves caught in a vicious cycle. Without a job, they could not afford a car. And without a car, they could not get a job.

Dealing with a Discriminatory Salary Structure, Mistrust, and Recirculated Elites

Most of the women who were employed said that their earnings were adequate. Still, there was a sense of being treated unfairly, especially by West German companies that paid their employees in the West higher salaries for doing the same jobs. This was hard to accept because the costs of living were the same in East and West Germany. Some women felt discriminated against *twice*: first, because they often earned less than their male counterparts in the East; and second, because they earned less than their female and male counterparts in the West. One interviewee who managed a branch of a West German bank observed:

[If you compare] where we and where our West German colleagues are located in the salary structure, who have exactly the same responsibilities, you notice a significant difference. As a manager of this bank, for example, I fall into the same salary category as the cafeteria staff in the West German system.

The competitive work climate and the ever-present threat to their job security as a result of increasing unemployment prevented most women from discussing issues of compensation openly. The new workplace organization injected a previously unknown distance between, and mistrust in the relationships among, coworkers. Thirty-one women (59 percent) addressed this subject, noting that the relationships among colleagues had changed for the worse, with solidarity and trust among coworkers replaced by competition and mistrust. An administrative assistant reflects the viewpoint of many: "In the GDR, we knew what was going on in the lives of our colleagues; not in detail, but generally we knew each other well. Today everyone keeps to themselves. I have one friend whose colleague does not tell anyone where he went on his vacation. That is something we used to talk about."

Although 11 women (21 percent) maintained that the relationships among coworkers were unchanged, none of the women I interviewed said that her work relationships had improved. Work habits, climate, and relationships in West German work places are more formal than they used to be in East German work places. West Germans keep their private and public lives strictly separate, a "job is a job, and private is private." One West German manager said, "I can't stand this friendly '*Geduze*' in East Germany," referring to the informal "you" (*Du*) and first names that East Germans used, instead of the formal "you" (*Sie*) and last names that most West Germans use. The former creates and maintains closer personal relationships at work, and the latter distance (Brähler and Richter, 1995, cited in *Spiegel*).

Women in my sample said they were more hesitant and careful about what they talked about at work because they did not want to be perceived as unable to cope with their workload or be defined as incompetent for the job. An administrator exemplifies the experiences of many in this regard:

In the Office for Social Services where I was working, I noticed after a while that the way we used to work, hand in hand, was gone. . . . In the process of all these changes, the trusting relationship that we had before among colleagues was gone. I mean, we could talk from the heart about everything; we could be really honest with each other without having the feeling that the other was taking advantage of me. . . . All that has disappeared since reunification.

And a midwife remarked:

Well, at some places of work, they mistrust each other. [People think] "if I do not pay attention, 'mobbing' could occur." You know, these new [Western] phrases? "Mobbing" does really exist. I did not believe it at first. [Mobbing] is psycho-terror: [the attempt] to get rid of you. Every day your boss finds something, anything. That is terrible. That did not exist in the GDR. You could get rid of your frustrations. Nobody dares to do that today because there is the fear that you can lose your job.

Not all bosses were West German, however. After the collapse of socialism, previous East German decision-makers took advantage of their connections with West German business partners, who often disregarded past political and ideological activities of their East German counterparts. To have done otherwise would hurt their business interests. Katja Wolle, a member of the state board of directors of the German Social Democratic Party (SPD) and mayor of a small city near Berlin, commented:

Many former Party functionaries of the GDR have started their own businesses. They preferred to be self-reliant and not unemployed. They mostly had a sound education and often were well connected. They moved seamlessly from the Socialist Unity Party (SED) to the Party of Democratic Socialists (PDS) (Schmid, 1998, p. 29).[24]

In their new roles, former Party functionaries continued to control access and opportunities to paid work, which affected particularly those who had defied the socialist system and had chosen to live "outside" of it. A number of women I interviewed resented the so-called "turncoats," who had supported and reinforced the dictates of the socialist state, and who were all too willing to do the same for the new system. One agricultural worker noted: "Not all have suffered the same consequences. Many who were in privileged positions before reunification retained their positions afterwards. But we little, stupid workers . . . have taken the hardest hit."

A nurse commented:

Dr. K. still has a leading position [at the hospital]. I am always astonished when I hear this sort of thing. Even in the old system I used to say, "You can't entrust a patient to him." [But he got to where he got because] he was so convinced [and loyal] to the state, and the new system values these qualities [as well].

A self-employed woman observed:

Those who work in the new government agencies worked for the [socialist] government before. They were all . . . *staatsnah* [cooperated closely with the socialist state]. They saved their skins very well [after reunification]. And the many unemployed—who became unemployed not because they had done anything wrong—see this [irony] quite clearly. They know that the people in the employment office have been *rote Socken* [red socks].[25] It's doubly depressing to observe that.

And a salesclerk recalled:

When it got to be more and more difficult and there was more uncertainty, and the question was, "who leaves and who stays?," everyone agreed that mothers with small children—and my daughter was small, too—had to go. And now I can say it, it is not a secret anymore: The Party elite, like my boss, kept their positions in reunified Germany.

These experiences led many women to conclude that not much had changed with regard to who controls material and nonmaterial resources. Both under socialism and under capitalism, access to material and nonmaterial resources is controlled by mostly male elites. Often not even the players have changed. Socialist elite members adapted swiftly to the conditions of reunified Germany by discarding one ideological hat and donning another, in effect, leaving the underlying patriarchal power structures undisturbed.

PRESERVING THEIR PROFESSIONAL IDENTITY

Because socialists believed that collective work would lead to social integration and shape people's character, which, in turn, would strengthen the system, no other social system has emphasized nondomestic work for women as much as socialism (Münkler, 1998, p. 26). This very premise was reversed for East German women when Germany was reunified. The stricter gender division of labor took on particular importance because a smooth transition depended to a large degree on women easing the stress and uncertainty for their families and, by implication, for the larger society.

But having been shaped, for 40 years, by a system that valued women who worked outside the home more than women who worked inside the home, none of my interviewees was willing to privilege her mother/spouse role over her professional role. Women wanted to have both, to combine employment and family responsibilities in a more meaningful way. Realizing that they had to rely on themselves, they said, "What counts . . . is health, optimism, and positive thinking," and "I am what I am today, [and] I have achieved [what I have achieved], because I did it by myself. I cannot rely on anybody else."

Most women I interviewed had not internalized their decreased social status as a personal failure, but as the failure of the new political and economic system (Forrester, 1997). Unlike many unemployed in the West, who tend to blame themselves, withdraw, and eventually "disappear" from public view, the East German women I interviewed were relatively free of feeling ashamed about their predicament. Most were determined "to do whatever it takes" and "to go it on my own." They talked with pride about their professional accomplishments in the GDR, and many reevaluated the skills they had acquired and came to recognize them as an asset like this nurse:

We in East Germany have always had this practical knowledge. We have been able to do everything ourselves. . . . And that is a foundation on which one can build other things. . . . We have this foundation. That is simply there. . . . Our everyday lives required us to have flexibility and a certain stability of character. . . . We have always been able to handle what came our way.

A self-employed woman said resolutely:

I have to be very honest. East German women do not have to deny who they are. In many ways we are much more self-confident than West German women. That is my experience. We have been shaped by our life in the GDR. At least I can say that for myself. We get down to the crux of the matter so much faster than they do. At least that is how it was in a meeting in which I participated. They talk too much, they talk around the issues. . . . Somehow, we have difficulties with [that approach]. We are used to acting, not to keep on talking!

One interviewee was in the final stages of opening up her own art gallery. She showed all the skills that are required under competitive market conditions: a willingness to embrace change, take risks, cope with stress and uncertainty, and be flexible (Sennett, 1998a, 1998b, 1998c):

I want to do something that is fun. I am not just in it for the money. . . . I envision a women's art project for the summer with artists from Mecklenburg Vorpommern: Paintings, graphics, jewelry, ceramics, and sculptures. . . . Soon women over 40 years of age can get [government grants] between DM 10,000 and DM 100,000. So we can build something for ourselves: small shops, small guest houses, small businesses. It dawns on people that the big enterprises that were sold to the West for nothing cannot be relied on [for employment]. We have to build a middle class [ourselves]. When I open my gallery, I have to employ someone because I will be traveling around and organizing. That is how I see it. When someone starts something, they will employ one or two people. And we have many courageous people, especially women. If someone opens a small clothing store, she will hire someone who can do alterations. And in any case, we have women who head construction companies with 60 or 70 employees. . . . We are not the sweet, little, fragile females who some want to portray us as. We are courageous women.

The *Bundesministerium für Frauen und Jugend* (Federal Ministry for Women and Youth) (1992, pp. 46–47) found that East German women showed great readiness to acquire knowledge and develop skills involving the latest technologies and a desire to work in nontraditional occupations. An engineer and computer specialist, who teaches at the Technical Center for Women, has learned to debunk many biases and cliches about women and technology: "Women and technology go together very well.[26] Women are more respectful, more critical, have team spirit, and work enormously hard and, most important, *they get it*." Fifty percent of the women who are older than 45 years have taken classes at the Center and have found work again (*Schweriner Zeitung*, March 9, 1996, p. 19).

One interviewee, a manager of a workshop for handicapped people who went to West Germany for additional training in special education, said:

I was the only female workshop manager. All others were [West German] males. How do you think I was looked upon? It took a while for them to register that "she is not that stupid. She actually knows something. She actually knows more than we do in some respects." I had read up on all the recent [West German] literature [that they had taken for granted]. And they thought they knew everything, and could do everything. Well, they were forced to respect me.

There is this general knowledge [that we East Germans have]. . . . We have this practical general knowledge. . . . I can paint, I can plow, I can make butter, and I can bake bread. And that is a basic foundation on which one can build other things. That is also why I can manage this workshop that has many different areas.

We have a printing shop, a painting shop, landscaping division, and assembly work division. I just have this foundation. I would not say I have a very deep knowledge about each area, but I have a sound basic knowledge about each. [East Germans] are practically oriented. And I think that someone who can work practically can build on that intellectually. Anyway, that is how I do it. And my colleagues respect me because they know I have this basic knowledge.

The women in my sample decidedly resisted attempts to shift the *identity* they had acquired under state socialism back to one reflective of an earlier period in German history (or forward to the future?): an identity that reinforces the status quo of traditional gender relations.[27] In contrast to most West German women, the *identity* of East German women is tied very loosely to the socioeconomic status of their husbands. It rests on their own employment status because "this is how young women grew up. We [had our own jobs] and continued to work even when we had a family [to look after]. That is what we wanted."

CONCLUSION

Paradoxically, it is at a time of accelerated modernization and the establishment of democratic institutions and processes in former East Germany that women's employment opportunities are being curtailed. Deeply gendered employment patterns have openly emerged and are arrogantly pursued. The paid work in the mostly female-dominated service sector—for example, child care, health care, elder care, education, food preparation—has been transferred to the private sector where mostly women continue to perform the same tasks *unpaid*. This transfer not only relegates women's work to the social periphery, it hides its importance to the market economy, which favors a hierarchical organization between women and men and thereby reinforces gendered power relations.

As a result, East German women have expended inordinate amounts of energy to survive materially, psychologically, and emotionally in a climate of increasing unemployment, decreased occupational opportunities, discriminatory barriers, and increased social insecurity and stress. Those who are gainfully employed have experienced pressure to perform and conform in accordance with West German norms and rules. They generally work longer hours, deal with discriminatory salary structures, increasing mistrust among coworkers, and a more pronounced hierarchy at their workplaces.

The women in my sample evaluated cautiously and critically the organization of the West German system that had devalued everything they had to offer. They were keenly aware of how precarious women's occupational status becomes when an economic downturn occurs as a result of political and economic restructuring. At the same time they were confident of their accomplishments and wanted their GDR experiences, skills, and knowledge and, therefore, their *identities* to be recognized. They understood that they had to change the existing power disparity to secure equal "access to scarce and valued societal resources—material and nonmaterial" (i.e., income-generating roles, incumbency in elite roles, and time for leisure and personal growth) (Chafetz, 1990, pp. 83, 188–192). Most women face this challenge head on, which has increased tensions between individual *identities* and needs, and the dictates of the market economy. By resisting pressure to withdraw voluntarily from the labor market, East German women have rendered the West German model of women's role in society ineffective for solving the problems of high unemployment.

In the next chapter, I explore *family life* during four decades of socialism and the opportunities, choices, and constraints that East German women were presented with in their efforts to combine paid work and family responsibilities.

NOTES

1. Unlike the United States, which has a free market economy with minimal interference from the government, Germany has a *soziale Marktwirtschaft* (social market economy), in which the government plays a greater regulatory role. Germany's social market economy was developed after World War II and claims to be

a socially responsible market economy coupled with macroeconomic management. This system rejects equally the old-style laissez-faire and government interventionism. It combines the free initiative of the individual with the principles of social progress. The *Basic Law*, which guarantees freedom of private enterprise and private property, stipulates that these basic rights be exercised for the public good. Under the tenet of "as little government as possible, as much government as necessary," the state has a mainly regulatory function of the market economy. (Hoffmann, 1992, pp. 185–186)

2. One instrument the Federal Agency for Labor employs is *Arbeitsbeschaffungsmaßnahmen* (*ABM*), that is, policies to create jobs and integrate the unemployed into the labor market by providing financial incentives to employers. In particular, these policies target the long-term unemployed and those who are young, and/or without training, disabled, and/or older. In 1993, 237,000 work places were created in East Germany through these measures at a cost of DM 12,060,400 in areas such as "environmental improvements, construction, economic infrastructure, social infrastructure, administrative infrastructure, education, science, culture, tourism infrastructure, sport, and others" (*Bundesministerium für Arbeit und Sozial Ordnung* [Federal Ministry for Work and Social Order], 1995, pp. 10–11).

3. According to Seager (1997, pp. 66–67, 118), "Women are typically the last to benefit from job expansion—and the first to suffer job contraction. In most of the industrial economies, unemployment rates for women are higher than for men, and rising at a faster rate. Women are especially suffering the economic contractions in Eastern Europe, where they now represent about two thirds of those officially unemployed."

After the collapse of communism, women made up 62 percent of the unemployed in Bulgaria, 55 percent in the Czech Republic, 66 percent in East Germany, 70 percent in Kirgistan, 71 percent in Russia, and 70 percent in the Ukraine (Seager, 1997, p. 67).

4. For example, there was little debate and no outrage was expressed by German trade unions when, in the southern regions of East Germany, Thuringia and Saxony, almost 320,000 workers—90 percent of whom were women—became unemployed. For generations, they had toiled in the textile mills, producing goods intended mainly for export. By 1991, with state subsidies cut, workers were unable to compete with the low wages of third-world textile workers, and most lost their jobs (Reicherzer, 1991, p. 23).

5. A survey of a representative sample of East German women found that women between 16 and 34 years of age did not give priority to their mother/

spouse roles by withdrawing from the labor market to raise their children. Nevertheless, unemployment was highest in this age group, which indicates the bias of employers against women with family responsibilities. The study also found that women over 34 whose children were self-sufficient "Will do everything to retain their paid work and, if unemployed, will persistently look for paid work" (Holst and Schupp, 1991, cited in Schneider, Tölke, and Nauck, 1995, p. 10).

6. With regard to East German women's changing social status, also see Braun, Jaspers, and Schröter (1995).

7. In this regard, Glazer (1993) observed that "The public/private interdependence can be seen in the process of work transfer in which tasks are moved from the world of paid labor (the economy) to unpaid labor (gender work within the family) . . . as a strategy to resolve the economic crisis of capitalism" (cited in *Footnotes*, September/October 1997, p. 4).

8. In some districts, unemployment had climbed to 25.4 percent, and in the town of Anklam it soared to 27.7 percent (*Schweriner Volkszeitung*, March 6, 1996, p. 1). In December 1997, the unemployment rate for the state stood at 20.5 percent, where it held steady as of April 1998 (Daniels, 1998, p. 21; Drozdiak, 1998, p. A11).

9. In December 1998, the overall unemployment rate for women and men stood at 16 percent in East Germany, and at 8.8 percent in West Germany (*The Week in Germany*, 1998, p. 4).

10. When state socialism collapsed, people in East and West Germany did not refer to it as a revolution, but as the *Wende* (turning point).

11. In this regard, also see Beck (1986).

12. See Parmentier's (1995) analysis of developments in the labor market, and Jansen's (1995) comparative analysis of conditions and pressures in East and West German workplaces.

13. The survey, conducted by EMNID in March 1996, asked East Germans to assess the general economic situation and found:

The General Economic Situation Is:	Age 18–29	Age 30–59	Age 60+
very good	3%	1%	2%
good	24%	10%	13%
bad	**46%**	**43%**	**44%**
very bad	20%	**44%**	39%
no comment	8%	1%	2%

Source: *Schweriner Volkszeitung*, March 21, 1996, p. 5.

14.

Importance of Work

	Age 18–24	Age 25–34	Age 35–44	Age 45–60	Age 60+
work is very important	72.7%	69.5%	76.9%	78.1%	42.7%
important	27.3%	29.5%	18.2%	18.7%	24.0%

Source: Winkler, 1990, p. 63.

15. A survey by the European Women's Lobby found that "three out of five working women in Britain, France, Germany, and Italy take home at least *half* of their family's income" (emphasis added) (*International Herald Tribune*, 1996, p. 5).

16. Gender-specific advertisements for jobs are common practice throughout former socialist countries. "For example, in the Slovak Republic in February 1991, there were 7,563 vacancies, but only 29 percent of them were for women. In Hungary in 1988 and 1989, between 65 percent and 71 percent of vacancies for manual jobs were men-only. . . . Foreign [often Western] joint ventures openly prefer men to women in their job advertisements and many companies specify men for their higher managerial positions. Women in Poland reported that the length of skirt to be worn to interview or the shape of legs favored for the job have been included in some advertisements. The state-run employment agency initially had different departments for men and women which inevitably meant gender-specific job vacancy advertisements" (Einhorn, 1993, p. 134).

17. "Nouns in German are either feminine, masculine or neuter. An *Arzt* (emphasis added) is a male doctor and an *Ärztin* is a female doctor. Gender neutral usage would include both forms (*Ärztin/Arzt*)" (*The Week in Germany*, September 22, 1995, p. 5).

18. Hagemann-White (1997, pp. 558–559) points out that [i]n the course of restructuring, Western standards were applied to both the academy and professional training. . . ."[A]ll of the social sciences, law, and economics (as well as much of the humanities) were suspect as possibly corrupt[ed] by intimate association with Marxism-Leninism. University staff were reviewed as to their previous political activity—in particular, their degree of compliance with the socialist party and state (no one has examined the degree of subservience of West German social scientists to the state). Foundation and appointment committees of established predominantly mainstream, West Germans were set up to restructure these fields."

19. Many university departments and research institutes in East Germany, which had been part of "the enormous scientific and research sectors of state socialism [closed]. These closures are partly accounted for by [the] discrediting of entire subject fields such as philosophy, Marxism-Leninism, and often history and economics, but partly by lack of government finance. . . . A high proportion

of lower-level researchers and university teachers, and almost all administrative and clerical staff in these institutions, were women" (Einhorn, 1993, p. 130).

To integrate East German scientists in the universities after reunification, the federal government established a program. Scientists from the East German Academy of Sciences were evaluated often two or three times with regard to their ideological commitment in the GDR, to gain access to the program. In August 1996, only 30 of the 1,469 participating scientists were offered a full-time position. Others were offered various academic posts for a limited time. The money they received came from the funds of the program for scientific integration, which ended on December 31, 1996. For most scientists, it meant joining the unemployed (Zimmer, 1996, p. 35).

20. See Jansen (1995).

21. Also see Beck (1994).

22. For a comprehensive analysis of East and West German characteristics, see Brähler and Richter (1995).

23. Not only did the unemployment rate increase steadily, so did the pressure to work overtime. In 1995, workers in reunited Germany worked 2.6 billion hours in overtime. The Federal Agency for Labor noted that if overtime hours were reduced by one tenth, 100,000 jobs could be saved (*Schweriner Volkszeitung*, March 6, 1996, p. 1).

24. The Socialist Unity Party (SED) was dissolved and reconstituted as the Party of Democratic Socialists (PDS) after the collapse of socialism.

25. East Germans referred to people who were loyal to the old communist system as *rote Socken* ("red socks").

26. In this regard, it is interesting to note that, according to "Kathy Bushkin, . . . senior vice president and chief communications officer of America Online Inc. (AOL), . . . women [must] challenge the myth that the Internet [is] a male tool. Fifty-two percent of AOL's membership [in the USA] is female" (Peltak, 1998, p. A7).

27. The *BALTIC Women's Center for Education and Information* in the city of Teterow is one example of East German women organizing on a regional level to claim the right to be gainfully employed. With funds from the *Sozialministerium*, the center offers reintegration courses for long-term unemployed women. It provides women with the necessary psychological as well as practical skills to cope. It imparts the necessary knowledge for women's reintegration into the work force. Most important, though, the center tries to raise money and organize projects such as the renovation of buildings. For that, it employs women who have the necessary skills and experience to see the project through (*Beratung und Information für Frauen*, 1995).

4

Family Life in the German Democratic Republic (GDR)

INTRODUCTION

The socialist state influenced almost every aspect of family life through its extensive social policies such as guaranteed employment, financial subsidies, and extensive child and health care provisions.[1] The policies were progressive in the legal sense. In practice, they turned out to be a curious mix of traditional and progressive measures reflecting a complex and contrary belief system rooted in the patriarchal organization of socialism. Legally women were equal to men. They enjoyed the same rights and opportunities. Yet, they were also regarded as essentially different from men. On the one hand, the social policies enabled women, or more precisely mothers, to be fully integrated into the work force and to cope with their work and family responsibilities. On the other, they protected the status quo of gendered power relations, thereby reproducing and reinforcing traditional gender relations also within the family. Inequalities that persisted for women who tried to meet the material, physical, and emotional needs of their families were rendered invisible because socialist ideology denied their existence.

Most women I interviewed accepted the benign functions of the state, but many consciously counterbalanced the state's attempts to exercise influence in their homes. They fiercely guarded their private space where fragments of civil society were kept alive and nurtured, practiced private entrepreneurship, shifted the gendered division of domestic labor, and tempered (but did not abolish) patriarchal structures.

FAMILIES

When Germany was reunified, the GDR had 4.8 million families. Of these, four million were married couples, half of which (49.2 percent) lived in households with children under 16 years of age. About 760,000 families consisted of single parents who were, with few exceptions, women (*Bundesministerium für Frauen und Jugend* [Federal Ministry for Women and Youth], 1992, p. 72).

Marriage patterns and family structure began to change in the early 1980s, when more East Germans decided that it was not essential to get married to live with a partner and/or to have a child. Although most East Germans married once, the trend was declining. In 1975, 29 percent of new mothers were not married. In 1989, that number had increased to 67 percent (Winkler, 1990, p. 28). The change coincided with newly introduced family policies. For example, single (but not married) parents were given priority for available child-care places and paid leave of absence when children became sick. The new policies were introduced as a response to a declining birth rate, not to further emancipatory goals.

For some married mothers these policies caused difficulty because it was assumed that they would interrupt their paid work and stay home with their children until child-care places became available for their children. A post office worker recalled:

It was not easy to get a place in a nursery. I had great problems to get one for our oldest daughter who was born in 1980. Because we were married when our daughter was born, we had to wait. Had I been single, the state would have seen to it that my daughter was accepted immediately because single mothers had to work and were given priority. My husband was also unable to get our daughter into the nursery at his place of work because they, too, had many single parents.

Later, when the same priorities were extended to married couples as well, the marriage trend was somewhat reversed (Winkler, 1990, pp. 105–106).

All women I interviewed valued family highly. This corresponds to representative surveys, which found that 86 percent of East German women, in contrast to 70 percent of West German women, said that "one needs a family to be really happy" (*Institut für Demoskopie Allensbach* [Allensbach Institute for Public Opinion], 1993, p. 55). And 91 percent of East German women and 85 percent of East German men between the ages of 18 and 60 years believed that children were "very important" and "important" for one's happiness (Winkler, 1990, p. 116).

Marriage

Most East Germans regarded marriage as the "normal" form of living together for partners, parents, and children. Both men and women of all ages felt that marriage provided a sense of security for parent-child relationships, and that it improved emotional and material conditions. Other reasons for marriage included love, tradition, access to housing, and financial advantages (Winkler, 1990, p. 105). An agricultural technician said:

I was pregnant with [my daughter] and we decided to get married because we wanted the credit [of 7,000 Marks which the state provided]. We could not just let it go. . . . We had to pay it back, but the conditions were very favorable. I paid 53 Marks per month. It's incredible, really [how low it was].

Marriage was the only way for young people to leave their parents and get housing for themselves. This encouraged many to marry at a relatively young age. The average age for men was 25.3 years and for women, 23.2 years (*Bundesministerium für Frauen und Jugend* [Federal Ministry for Women and Youth], 1992, p. 72).[2] Getting married at a young age may have played a role in a steadily increasing divorce rate as expectations went unfulfilled. Women appear to have looked at partnership more critically and seemed to have had different expectations than men. This may explain why, by the late 1980s, women in the GDR applied for about two thirds of all divorces (Winkler, 1990, p. 111).[3]

Domestic Responsibilities

Many women I interviewed were hesitant to view domestic work as "work." Their ambivalence reflected the classical Marxist doctrine, which maintains that women's domestic labor is "unproductive" labor (i.e., it does not create surplus value) and, thus, is of little or no importance. The planned economy, like the market economy, had ignored domestic work in its public account of goods produced, services rendered, and wealth generated. Consequently, many East German women I interviewed spontaneously assigned little value to their domestic labor, even though it was often physically hard labor. Household amenities, taken for granted in the West, were difficult to obtain in the GDR, and when they became available, they were prohibitively expensive.

Probing the issue of domestic work in more depth, women came to define domestic work as demanding and as vital as their nondomestic work for building and maintaining socialist society. Chronic labor shortage had plagued the socialist state throughout its 40 years of existence, which left decision-makers with little choice but to create conditions that kept women in the labor force and, at the same time, enabled them to bear and rear a new generation.

The state assumed an instrumental role in rearing and educating children by creating a widely spun net of child-care facilities, schools, and youth organizations such as the *Pioneers* and *Freie Deutsche Jugend* (FDJ).[4] A volunteer, who had been active in church and critical of the state, remarked that "The first goal [of the state] was to ensure that all children would become communists. The second [goal] was the commitment of each of us to fulfill that goal." By guaranteeing women extensive social rights, the government integrated them into the work force, and hoped to increase their political and ideological loyalty, and their commitment to the party and other mass organizations. One purpose of this strategy was to bring the family under the control of the state (Penrose, 1990, p. 64).

THE LIMITED CONTROL OF THE STATE

Despite the declared goal of the Socialist Unity Party (SED) to control family relationships, and despite its long reach into family life, the Party never quite succeeded in exerting the power over families it had envisioned. Families in the GDR were not isolated. Most were embedded in far-reaching support networks that extended beyond the individual family and the state. The barter network, through which people had close connections with each other and obtained goods and services of all kinds, weakened the hold of the state on individual families. Because the state could not provide what it had promised, it increasingly lost legitimacy in the eyes of many East Germans. The informal network also weakened traditional gender roles. Women and men depended on each other and often were united against the state. Government efforts to direct family life met with varied and complex responses. Some families lived in open opposition to the state, defying its every rule, as exemplified by this church worker, who steadfastly refused to bow to state demands:

The ideological education [by the state] was at the same time accompanied by the education that took place at home. It became clearer and clearer to me how much parents can influence their children. And the experience and suffering of parents [who defied the system] formed the image our children have of society. Either the children assume their parents' view and say, "OK, I accept it." Or they say, "No, I do not share that view." But parents influence their children much more than any state. That is something I became more and more aware of.

We decided always to be honest with our children. They did not have to be double-faced. That was very common in homes where parents told their children, "You must not say anything in school about what we think and do at home." . . . Children were brought up janus-faced. . . . We said, "We don't do that." What we think and do we say everywhere. . . . And we told our children, "You do not have to be silent about the way we live."

A nurse who grew up in a family that provided her with alternative views said: "I never joined the FDJ [*Freie Deutsche Jugend*; Socialist Youth Program] because my father was always against the state. I was never a convinced socialist. I was always unsure. . . . [even though] in theory [socialism] was very appealing."

Others resisted the state more passively as described by this child-care worker: "Our parents said, 'Socialism is OK, it's alright, but it's not quite the way they tell you [in school], all socialists are [not] the greatest and all the fascists [do not] live over there [in West Germany].'"

Still others reluctantly accepted the conditions as "that was the way it was." A secretary recalls how her family dealt with the situation: "My daughter . . . knew exactly what she could say in school and what she could not. [She knew she could not tell] that we tuned in to watch West [German] television."

A committed Party functionary and educator dealt with the conflict in a similar way:

It was a difficult situation in our family. We could receive West [German] television. And our daughter kept on saying, "Everyone talks about this or that [television] program, and I am not allowed to watch." The pressure became massive. And then I found myself saying, "OK, watch it but don't say anything in school about it."

Almost all women said that, despite ideological, political, and economic restraints imposed on them by the state, they were able to create "a happy family life that was well worth living," as exemplified by a health care worker:

If people now say that we could not live in this system, that is not true. I tell you we did live, and we also took the freedoms we wanted. We said what we thought, we did not conform [all the time]. And except for access to higher education, we did not suffer disadvantages even though some people want you to believe that they were victims of persecution. But that is nonsense. We did live.

A nurse who was critical of the state said:

There is no need to apologize for the way we lived, the way we brought up our children, and for not going openly in opposition to the state. We created our lives in such a way that we were able to live in a somewhat harmonious way. We looked after our children and were happy, despite everything. I cannot understand people who now complain about the GDR, or who paint a glorified picture of "the good old days." I have always looked at the system critically.

And a life-long church volunteer who had lived in opposition to the state reflected:

Our children, as children of a pastor, were generally not given the choice of higher education. There was a certain quota for each district. Two or three children of a pastor were allowed to attend college. Thus, the political functionaries always had two examples and could say, "Well, see for yourself, we admitted two children [to college]. Besides, not everyone can go, and, anyway, who do you think you are?" So we made sure that all our children entered an apprenticeship. We said, "It is good to learn a trade, there is no shame in it, quite on the contrary, it can be very useful."

Families learned to organize life alongside the state, reflecting historical continuity as well as change. Engels' (1962) vision of a socialist society was not realized in the GDR. The individual family continued to have an important function in society. Private households remained private and were not industrialized. And the nurturing and education of the children did not entirely become a state matter. Still, state-run institutions such as schools, child-care centers, and youth groups ensured that socialist values were instilled in most children, even though many families carefully guarded their family space from the intrusion of the state. Many women were critical, and those who rejected the values of the state lived with a persistent underlying tension between the needs of their families and needs of the state.

THE FAMILY AS PRIVATE ENTREPRENEUR

The GDR government provided every family with basic social security, which included guaranteed employment, subsidies for housing, utilities, public transport, child care, free health care, free education, and basic consumer goods. Yet, the state fell increasingly short in meeting the material expectations it had promoted. Conditions were deteriorating, and most women in my sample took it in stride because there was little choice. Individual families stepped in and made up for the state's shortfalls in goods and services.

Family members, colleagues, neighbors, and friends gained paramount importance because they helped provide what was needed and/or desired.

They pooled skills and nurtured personal connections to make up for the state's deficiencies. They created the so-called *niche*, which was made up of trusted individuals who were connected by mutual material and other interests. According to one nurse, "Connections were the 'vitamin B' [during socialism]. They were very, very important." Regine Hildebrandt, minister for Labor, Social Services, Health, and Women in the state of Brandenburg, noted that life in the so-called *niche* was "a life with values that one cannot buy" (Szepansky, 1995, p. 117). Personal ties were as important as money for survival, the enjoyment of life, and the well-being of families.

In the *niche*, East German families effectively created an *informal* economy, a private sector that was tolerated by the state, mainly because the state could not do without it. Gender relations in the *niche* reflected the notion that "gender as a category and set of relationships" was elastic and that gender boundaries were continuously negotiated to respond to changing circumstances and experiences as women and men went about their daily lives (Gerson, 1997, pp. 228–230; Potucheck, 1997). Thus, as one teacher put it, "My husband does the dishes and the laundry, he makes lunch, and takes care of the children."

In general, due to the scarcities of certain kinds of foods, services, and other consumer goods, and because all women (and their spouses) in my sample worked outside the home, men assumed, if not an equal, then a substantial share of domestic chores; that is, took care of children, grew and tended gardens, harvested fruits and vegetables, took care of livestock, and secured spare parts for repairing and maintaining all kinds of household equipment and cars if the family owned one. And many East German women echoed the sentiments of Einhorn (1993, pp. 61–62) that

[women] were situated, through their role as wives, mothers, sisters, friends, at the focal point of the highly valued *niche* society. . . . The centrality of this role, together with the gender-transcending solidarity of the private sphere, seems to have overridden any oppression suffered by women within it.

Getting anything repaired or obtaining spare parts for just about everything was next to impossible in the GDR. This work was essential to the household because new consumer items were very expensive and often entailed long waiting periods. A satisfying standard of living for many required work both *inside* and *outside* the planned economy and good connections. It was difficult to achieve or maintain a reasonable standard of living based on the income of both spouses alone. According to one agricultural worker, it required "working hand in hand with each other."

In rural areas, for example, it was common for East German women to manage, together with their families, private farms in addition to working for pay at the agricultural production cooperatives. They raised their own cattle and tended their own fields to supplement their incomes, as described by an agricultural worker:

[In the former GDR] we raised bulls and pigs. We earned a lot of money [by selling them to the state] and were able to dress four children [well], buy furniture and electrical household appliances. . . . For one bull, we got about five thousand Marks (the annual salary of many agricultural workers was about 6,000 Marks). It took about 18 months to raise it.

Almost all women in my sample who lived in the city had a garden, often located on the outskirts, that provided a weekend retreat in the summer. Many had built a small *dacha* (weekend house) in their gardens where they spent time during the summer because, "during GDR times, a *dacha* was the best thing one could have."

For 24 women (46 percent) in my sample, it was of great importance to be able to produce what was difficult to purchase even during the season: fresh vegetables, fruits, and flowers. Often they raised chickens, ducks, and sheep. Interestingly, most women I talked with did not appear to perceive the work in their gardens, which was done in their spare time, as a tremendous burden. Nor did they view raising their own cattle and tending their fields in such a way. That was something that had to be done, and many associated it with spending time with their families because often the entire family was involved in taking care of such chores. Everyone was assigned tasks, and mostly they derived pleasure from it because everyone knew that extra rewards would flow from it. Surveys show that 85 percent of East German women and 81 percent of men spent their leisure time with "my family and partner"; 67 percent of the women and 66 percent of the men spent it "performing tasks for my family"; and 65 percent of the women and 52 percent of the men spent it "doing things with my children" (The Institute for Sociology and Social Policy in East Berlin, cited in Winkler, 1990, p. 136).

Many fruits and vegetables were not available in state stores during the winter months. To be able to enjoy strawberries in winter, for example, one had to preserve them in jars because freezers were difficult to obtain and very expensive. Because fresh vegetables and fruits were so highly valued, positive feelings were associated with growing, harvesting, preserving, and storing them in the cellar for the winter or special occasions. A health care worker and a teacher described what many others expressed:

I preserved a lot. We were very proud of it, my mother-in-law and I. We really enjoyed going into the cellar. We would stand there and admire our jars [with preserved fruits and vegetables], and get very upset when one would open up (health care worker).

We have a fruit and vegetable garden. We preserved *everything*. We have a greenhouse so we could grow as many tomatoes as we wanted, and cucumbers, too. And we preserved *everything*. We always had what we needed (teacher).

Preserved vegetables, fruits, fresh eggs, and meat could also be exchanged for other goods, knowledge, and labor, that were otherwise difficult to obtain; for example, advice on how to build a house, spare parts for fixing a car and broken household items, painting and repairing an apartment or putting in new plumbing. The "extras" produced from private gardens, fields, and livestock constituted valuable "currency," which ensured a higher standard of living.

Money was important, but good connections and relationships with others were even more important: "I scratch your back, you scratch mine" was the motto many people lived by. Supporting each other also saved time because being part of an elaborate barter network meant that people could rely on obtaining what they needed in a relatively short time. The time invested in growing and preserving food and raising livestock paid off when a new household item or spare parts for a car or a kitchen appliance were urgently needed. Mutual dependence created not only a sense of solidarity, but as one white-collar worker said, it created the feeling that "together we can create something out of nothing." It made possible small dreams, such as repairing a *Trabi* (the infamous GDR car), building a small *dacha*, or redecorating a home, that could only be realized by working together (Wagner, 1996, p. 177).

In the informal economy, women felt equal in status and ability to the men they lived and worked with. Since most of that work was done in addition to their paid work and other family responsibilities, neither could have managed the extra work very well without the other. And both knew that their family was better off if they succeeded in their private enterprise together. Life in the GDR exemplified Sherif's (1967) concept of *superordinate* goals: goals that cannot be achieved by one person alone, but only by working together.

The state's shortfall in providing goods and services also created a common ground for the leaders of the Socialist Unity Party (SED) and the dissident population. Both had envisioned a utopia of a homogeneous and harmonious community. The dissidents wanted to realize the socialist ideals of a community of equality and harmony in which family ties were strengthened and the so-called *niches* fortified to keep the state at bay. The Party leadership was interested in "reducing the complexity of society as much as possible. Plan and control processes tend to increase manifold with a small increase in complexity. . . . The goal was for *Gesellschaft* (society) to become *Gemeinschaft* (community)" (Wagner, 1996, p. 178).

NEGOTIATING DOMESTIC LABOR

Everyday demands made it impossible to strictly adhere to traditional gender roles, and both women and men negotiated their responsibilities within the family. However, these progressive developments within families did not lead to a conscious change in traditional gender relations. According to the dominant ideology, the goal of equality between women and men had been achieved. Gender inequality was regarded as a matter of the past, and open discussions about gender discrimination did not develop. Conventional aspects of social policies remained hidden, reproducing and reinforcing traditional gender relations. Thus, for example, women (but not men, except when they were single fathers) were entitled to one "household day" per month; that is, a day off from work at full pay. Almost all women in my sample embraced the "household day" as an opportunity to get things done at their own pace. A bookkeeper and a gardener explained:

From the moment I worked full-time, I had the household day. That was in August 1975. From then on I was entitled to a household day and I chose when to take it. It was a good thing and very helpful (bookkeeper).

Oh, yes, the household day! That was real nice. I could take it once a month. I was able to choose which day I wanted. I could do things in the house, or go shopping. I mostly used it to go shopping (gardener).[5]

The household day was regarded as a "normal" and welcome practice. Most women in my sample perceived this policy as equitable. They did not see it as an encouragement for women to take on more of the necessary family and housework. The "household day," it can be argued, signified an acknowledgment by the (mostly male) decision-makers that the socialization of domestic work had not succeeded in *praxis* the way Marxist-Leninist theory had predicted. Their solution was to again reinforce a traditional gender division of labor by paying women to perform the larger share of domestic work.

Gendered Division of Household Labor

The time a family spent on housework in the former GDR was considerable and varied. On average, a family would spend about two to three hours a day doing housework. Considering that the average work day was eight and three quarter hours long, this was a substantial amount of time. Many East German men (in contrast to men in other European countries) felt responsible to share in household chores (Winkler, 1990, p. 127). Forty-five (79 percent) of the women I interviewed echoed the sentiments of this salesclerk, who said spontaneously that housework was divided "half and half, [because] how could I have managed everything otherwise?" And, "We do it together [and] divide it according to what each wants to do and what each can do best."

When they described in more detail what a typical day in the GDR had entailed, a clearer gender division of labor emerged. The experiences of women in my sample corresponded closely to the findings of a survey in which 42 percent of East German women said that their spouses/partners "helped often with household chores," 48 percent said that "they helped sometimes," and 8 percent said that "they never helped" (*Institut für Demoskopie Allensbach* [Allensbach Institute for Public Opinion], 1993, p. 51).[6]

The way housework was shared also varied by class, even though officially only one class—the working class—was recognized in the GDR (Winkler, 1990, pp. 127–128). In the rural families in my sample, housework was divided along gendered lines to a greater extent than in urban families, in which one or both partners tended to have higher education. Rural women were often left to do most of the household chores. One agricultural worker said, "I have to say this honestly. Housework is not what men do. Women do it all even though they work full-time as well." Another commented:

My husband comes from a strict Catholic farm family. The tasks are very clearly divided [in that household] even today. The woman is responsible for the housework, the man for the heavy physical labor in the stables and fields. He has his work, she has her work. I did not have the energy to change that. I would have risked my marriage and I thought, "Alright, let him do the things that I can't do, like repairing electrical appliances." I know I should have insisted on much more equality at home, I should have made demands, but I am just not like that, and now I know I can't complain about the situation I am in.

And a gardener reflected:

I decided that I wanted a family and I said, "Well, then I will do [the housework] and that is OK." And my husband told me, "If you had gone to university, then you would never have had time for your family and your children." And that would have been the case. I would have had to have a position somewhere with a lot of responsibility.

Housework was managed in many different ways. Some men assumed the larger share of the chores, but they risked ridicule by people around them as described by this child-care worker: "My feeling is that only very few men take on most of the household chores. I have a brother who does it. He was mainly responsible for the housework because my sister-in-law's job required that she was gone for 12 hours every day. But he was an exception. And many ridiculed him."

Some of the urban women relied on their mothers to help out. One teacher said:

I have no idea what would have happened if I had not had my mother. I managed everything because my mother was there. And I have to say, my entire social commitment and engagement was possible only because of my mother and because of my husband, too. We had great harmony in our family, and we still have it.

Others employed bourgeois methods in a socialist system that "theoretically" did not tolerate any, to cope better with both housework and full-time jobs. Eliciting support for their decisions from other family members, women encountered considerable resistance as recalled by a cosmetician:

I remember asking my mother-in-law if it was alright to hire some household help. . . . I knew that was regarded as exploitation. . . . [She said], "For God's sake, don't do that, dad won't talk to you anymore." You didn't let anyone work for you. That was the attitude. Even if you paid them well.

Still, women in the socialist society did what women in a capitalist society do when they are desperate and can afford it—they hired help as this self-employed woman did:

My neighbor, a single woman who worked night shifts, would come over to help me cut up apples. . . . So I said, "That is very nice of you but you should not do it for nothing." She did not want the money, but I knew it was helpful to her. . . . And it was important to me to have more time. I paid her well, I did not want to exploit her. . . . [Eventually] she cleaned my house. . . . She would come when my husband was not home because he was against it. . . . And then he would ask, "Did you clean windows today?" I would say, "Yes, of course." And he would ask, "When did you do that?" And I would say, "Well, kind of in between other things."

Because socialist ideology did not define housework as productive work, an important part of women's daily reality was made invisible. Housework was considered the responsibility of women to manage with help from family members. Women of all classes relied on family members to perform tasks that were essential to the family, and often the division of labor had to be negotiated. Traditional gender boundaries were thereby crossed, as illustrated by a white-collar worker: "My husband did the dishes and cleaned the floors; I cleaned the windows and did the laundry." And a teacher said:

We shared housework. Well, let's put it this way: The kitchen was my territory, the cellar his; the stroller was mine, and the car was his. But we cleaned house together. My husband vacuum-cleaned and he cleaned windows. And I had the rare luck to find a man who likes to iron. I hung wall paper because I was better at it, and because I am a teacher, I did homework with our children.

A textile worker remarked:

I know many families that are like our family. The men do the housework. My husband did not like to do the dishes, but he was responsible for everything that our children needed. Each of us did [the things in the household] that we liked to do. And the things we both did not want to do, well, we both had to make an effort to get those done.

A teacher said that in her family: "The household was more or less the responsibility of my husband. We did not have a strict division of labor like, I am responsible for this and you for that. Household chores worked well for us because my husband had a much more flexible schedule than I did."

A cook described how her work schedule made it necessary for her husband to assume the bulk of child care in her family:

My husband was always responsible for our daughter. I had to get to work very early in the morning. And in the afternoon, he picked her up. Sometimes I did it. It was a very long work day. I was home at quarter to five. Well, then we looked after our daughter together and got things done in the house.

Men assumed responsibilities such as heating the apartment in winter and the bath water, which was heated up separately. Central heating systems were rare, and were only found in newer apartment blocks. Older houses and apartments had to be heated with coal, which meant that ashes had to be cleaned out of stoves and often carried down several flights of stairs. Wood and coal had to be carried up. A secretary describes what was a typical part of the day for many families: "My husband was very supportive. He had to be. He would heat the apartment before I came home from work. He would heat the bath water, too, so I was able to start taking care of the children."

Another white-collar worker expressed it as follows:

I would come home at about five o'clock. My husband was home already because he used to work at the agricultural production cooperative. I had to rely on him a great deal. He supported me a lot. In winter he had always heated our apartment by the time I came home. . . . Then we would sit down and have a cup of coffee together. And then we started [our work at home]. I would give the children a bath because they had to be in bed early as they had to get up early.

Grocery Shopping

Food shopping was a time- and energy-consuming task. Because of constant shortages and too little storage facilities, "we went shopping every day." All women in my sample assumed this responsibility and went to their local *Kaufhalle* (market hall) or *Konsum* (grocery shop). This deviates from the findings generated by the *Bundesministerium for Frauen und Jugend* (Federal Ministry for Women and Youth) (1992, p. 77), where 43 percent of couples said that they did the shopping together, and 42 percent regarded it as women's responsibility. Only in every eighth household was shopping done by men.

According to 26 women in my sample (50 percent), the choice of shopping facilities was poor. Only 9 women (17 percent) felt that facilities were adequate. For 38 women (73 percent), the availability of consumer goods was a problem. And of the 42 women (80 percent) who talked about the variety of consumer goods, 36 women (69 percent) said it was very much lacking.

Many women used their lunch breaks for shopping, or shopped on their way home, often with children in tow. There was no need to compare quality or prices because "prices were the same everywhere." They were fixed by the state. The quality of goods was about the same in every *Konsum*. The experience of this agricultural worker was typical: "Well, we had a *Konsum* in our village. During my lunch break I used to go and shop. . . . The prices were the same everywhere. . . . Normally one could get what one needed."

The potential for corruption by store managers was always present because of shortages. Store managers were in a position to abuse the system by giving some customers preferential treatment in return for personal favors. Those who distributed goods equitably among their customers were held in high esteem, as described by another agriculture worker:

We had a really good *Konsum*. It was open from 9:00 A.M. to 6:00 P.M. In the villages they usually closed at two o'clock. It was very difficult to get citrus fruits, but not for us. There was always something because the manager always divided it up equitably. Families with three children would get three bananas, and families with five children would get one more. And our community liked the way she did it. We knew she did not cheat on us. . . . And when she had something left over, well, then she would give it to a grandparent for their grandchild.

Since shopping inevitably meant standing in lines, women would head for the most conveniently located *Konsum* or *Kaufhalle*. For some, getting to a *Konsum* or *Kaufhalle* involved little time as was the case for a sales assistant: "After work I used to go to the market to get bread, butter, and whatever else was available. Then I took the bus home." Basic food items were mostly available, "We used to go the *Kaufhalle*. Everything was next to each other there. And I could mostly get everything I needed."

For others, getting to a *Konsum* or *Kaufhalle* was more difficult. It involved more energy and time and the ability to take things in stride as this nurse did:

I did my shopping in our small village *Konsum*. I could get the basics there. In the morning the bread and the milk had not arrived. . . . and I would leave my order. After I had picked up my children [from day care in the afternoon], I would go back and my bag stood there with the bottles of milk. In the summer the milk was often bad because there was no refrigeration and the bread was hard because the room was warm. . . . But we had milk, bread and sometimes rolls, too. And at that time, we did not mind at all.

An agricultural technician explained:

In general, I went food shopping every day. At that time you could not stock up [the way we do today]. I went shopping on my way home [from work]. Then I had to walk up hill, on a sandy path, with my heavy shopping bags and a stroller. I should tell you that our village was about two kilometers (about a mile and a half) from where the *Konsum* was.

And a nurse recalled: "When I finished work, I went shopping and then I picked up my children. . . . I remember that my bicycle was fully packed [with my shopping bags, my two children, and myself]. My mother used to say, 'How can you ride your bike that way [over cobble stones]?'"

Although staple foods were almost always available, to prepare for a wedding, *Jugendweihe*,[7] or any other family celebration was often a challenge, involving "a lot of running around, keeping your eyes and ears open," and mobilizing the network of the informal economy as this secretary did:

I would know someone, who knew someone, who knew someone else whom I could ask, "Do you have a can of pineapples or whipping cream?" You know, we would buy only an eighth of a pound of coffee. It cost 8.75 Marks (or 70.00 Marks for one pound). My husband used to earn 720 Marks a month.

Women had learned to be flexible when they went food shopping. They expected not to get what they had set out to get. Changing meal plans became second nature because more often than not, they would arrive at the head of the line to learn that what they had intended to buy was sold out. And they had to stand in many lines: the meat line, the bread line, the "return empty bottles" line, the milk and cheese line, the fruit line, the vegetable line. As a consequence, according to one agricultural technician: "Grocery shopping was terrible because there were lines everywhere. You had to stand in line. On Saturday mornings one had to be there by eight to get in line to get *not* what you wanted, but whatever was available."

Another agricultural worker said:

On Mondays we had *Warentag* (delivery of goods). People formed long lines to get something of what was delivered. I remember that at first it was difficult to buy chocolate, then fruit, then vegetables. And then it was difficult to get anything. And often only customers with connections could obtain certain goods. It was all handled under the table, of course. With meat it was the same. [In the end] one could only get four or five cutlets. It was rationed.

Food Preparation

Food preparation tasks, too, were readily assumed by most of the women I talked with. This corresponds to findings generated by the *Bundesministerium für Frauen und Jugend* (1992, p. 77). In that study, 74 percent of the women said they assumed the sole responsibility for daily food preparation. Only 16 percent responded that they took turns with their partners or prepared meals together.[8]

Food preparation was a major task before state kitchens and cafeterias became widely available, because women prepared at least three meals— breakfast, lunch, and dinner—every day for their families. They went home during lunch time and prepared lunch for their families, who also came home to eat. If time permitted, they did some housework like laundry or cleaning and then returned to their paid jobs. This was possible because workplaces were mostly in close proximity to home. Later, with the establishment of state-run cafeterias, children were fed in schools and parents could buy meals at their places of work; thus, according to one cook, "We used to eat lunch in the canteen at work. The children got their lunch in school or kindergarten. I did not have to prepare lunch every day. We paid one Mark (less than 50 cents) per meal."

Laundry

Laundry was major work for all women in my sample. It was time-consuming and hard physical labor. Almost without exception, women assumed this responsibility, although partners and spouses helped out. This diverges somewhat from the findings of a study conducted by the Institute for Sociology and Social Policy in [East] Berlin, in which 79 percent of women and 67 percent of men said that they were mainly responsible for doing laundry (cited in Winkler, 1990, p. 128).

Even though statistics show that over 80 percent of couples with one to three children had fully or half automated washing machines (Winkler, 1990, p. 127), none of the women I interviewed owned a fully automated washing machine. A washing machine was a major expense and not easily obtained. Twenty-eight women (54 percent) said that the technology lagged far behind Western technology, and one teacher observed that "There were no real [fully automatic] washing machines." A half automatic washing machine would not necessarily rinse or spin clothes, so those steps often had to be done manually. Many women bought a spinner separately to ease the back-breaking work. A teacher explained what "doing laundry" entailed:

We had a washing machine. But first we had to boil the clothes, and then we put them into the washing machine. You could program how long you wanted it to wash. And then you had to take the clothes out and put them in a tub or sink to rinse them. After that I put them in a spinner that I had. Well, each step had to be done separately. Sweaters I washed by hand. But that was the way we were used to doing laundry.

The experience of "doing laundry" was similar for this nurse: "I did not have a fully automatic washing machine. I had a *BM 66*. You had to take the clothes out, rinse them separately and spin them. We did all that, and somehow we managed it."

And a bookkeeper, recalling the arduous task, lent a helping hand to her daughter:

My daughter has two children and I always saw her in the laundry room when she came home from work. . . . I said, "That has to end. That is too much." I gave her 500 Marks as a present. That was a downpayment for a fully automated washing machine. These are the things that somehow stick in your mind.

Because that was the way things were done by most people, and because material comparisons were mostly made with other socialist countries that were comparatively worse off, most of the women I interviewed did not think a lot about the inferior quality of consumer goods and outdated technology. Consumerism was not part of people's lives and, comparatively speaking, the women did not perceive themselves as badly off.

However, it was different for the families who had relatives in West Germany and/or had access to Western television stations that beamed Western styles of living into their living rooms. They were more aware of the gap in the standard of living between East and West Germans and experienced greater levels of frustration with the conditions as they existed in the GDR and, hence, were more likely to question the legitimacy of the GDR leadership.

The Role of Children in the Family Household

East German children were expected to take care of themselves and were entrusted with household chores. The women I interviewed placed a high value on independence and brought up their children accordingly. One teacher and mother of two said:

We wanted to bring up our children to be independent. They were in child care and in after-school care. They were allowed to go home at about three o'clock in the afternoon and they knew we would be coming home an hour later or so. They did it as of fourth grade. We wanted them to learn to do their work independently of us.

An agricultural worker recalled:

When my children started school, they had to get up by themselves. . . . If they wanted breakfast, they had to make it themselves. They had enough time for that. I did not want to spoil them [by getting everything ready for them]. And, anyway, I had to start work at 5:30 A.M. I had to leave them home alone. But I could totally rely on them without exception.

It was understood that everyone in the family had to contribute to the household. That was the way many of the women had grown up themselves. It was normal for both parents to work outside the home, as described by one gardener: "Both my parents worked outside the home. We had to help at home when we were children. Someone had to do the housework. [Because of that experience] I do not find it difficult to combine a job and family [responsibilities] now."

Another gardener recalled: "My brothers and I, we had to help early on, we had to help a lot. . . . But I had fun doing it, I can honestly say that. [We had to help] otherwise it would not have worked." Their experience had taught them that contributing to the household was a valuable lesson, and they passed that lesson on to their children, who learned to be self-sufficient at an early age, and recognized that their help was needed and valued in the household. One textile worker explained it as follows: "My children are very independent. They do the laundry. If they would not participate [with the chores], our house would look terrible. . . . [But] there [was] always time to play. That is part of it."

A white-collar employee described how she had included her children in coping with domestic chores: "Well, the children would come home and each had their assigned task. . . . [Their responsibilities] depended on what had to be done and on their age. Still, they had time to play. It was not so much that they could not play."

Many East German women had grown up that way themselves. In the aftermath of World War II, their mothers and grandmothers had rebuilt a devastated country and cared for torn families. They had been entrusted with responsibilities as young children by their mothers, who were heads of households because fathers and grandfathers had not returned from the war. Women, like this secretary, remembered that, "My mother was very independent; she had to assert herself. I basically do things the way my mother taught me through the way she lived."

Later these women had the same expectations of their own children. They assigned them responsibilities and expected their children to carry them out. The assignments reflected a traditional division of labor as exemplified by this agricultural worker: "My children had to help. We have four boys and one girl. She had to help in the household, the boys had to go in the fields."

Another agricultural worker said:

Well, yes, my children had to help. Later when my boys were older, they had to help a lot with the outside work. And the girls had to help in the household. They had to do the dishes, and wash clothes and hang them on the line to dry. I encouraged them early on. Otherwise, I could not have done it because we did not have a washing machine that was fully automatic.

The way household chores were assigned suggests that family and gender were mutually produced and inseparably linked under socialism, and that the family was a primary institution of traditional gender socialization.

The bulk of the daily household chores remained women's responsibility, and this tradition was passed on to the next generation.

RAISING AND TAKING CARE OF CHILDREN

East German women, like women everywhere who juggle multiple roles, were at times torn between their work outside the home and the time left to raise their children. Their long work days left too little time to be actively involved in their children's lives. This created what Thompson and van Houten (1970) termed a "multiple position conflict"—not so much on a permanent basis, but at certain stages of their children's lives. The GDR's social policies did not address this conflict because they were designed by mostly male decision-makers who: "set the goals, define[d] the 'socialist norms' and order[ed] the priorities by standards according to which men and women [were] equal, but it [was] women who [were] different" (Scott, 1976, p. 198, cited in Einhorn, 1993, p. 32).

These conditions caused a dilemma few women were able to solve. They tried to fulfill their duties within a male model of family and work life, which left them struggling. One educator and active Party functionary reflected on the dilemma that she faced and was unable to resolve:

What I had always wished was to be a mother who had a little more time. But that was not possible [in the GDR] because the state needed our labor. It was simply necessary. We liked to do it, of course, that was the way we grew up. That is why [in reunified Germany] we fall into this deep hole, because we just can't imagine being just a homemaker and a mother. But I would have liked to see a healthier balance between being a mother and a worker . . . but one income could not have sustained a family. . . . In my family, I earned more than my husband, about one hundred Marks, which was a lot of money for us then. [But had there been more flexibility] my children would not have said, "Mom, we wish you had more time for us instead of giving us presents for Christmas."

And a nurse described how she and most other women felt when faced with having to meet the needs of both their children and workplace:

My children were very, very important in my life. I don't want to say they were most important, but one of the most important things in my life. . . . It was not accepted that a mother stayed at home. [But when she did], it caused surprise. Few women stayed home because it meant a decrease in their standard of living. Many thought it was a good thing to do, but [they] also said they would not do it. We had child care. We could bring our children there. And to stay home the entire day and wash diapers, many women did not want to do that. But [those of us who stayed home for a while] did not have to concern ourselves with losing our jobs, that was secure.

Upon reflection a white-collar worker concluded:

When I think about it all, in some ways I spent too little time with my children, too little time. I hardly remember the time when they were little and when they went to kindergarten. I would have liked to start work later; I really would have liked that much better. I would have seen them in the morning, and I would have come home a little earlier at night. I would have preferred that. I was always totally exhausted. In those days, I slept so well and I only had six hours of sleep on average.

Party functionaries at work and in school, who tried to interfere with private beliefs on how to raise children, created additional stress for a number of women in my sample. For those who had been active Party members, the pressure was considerable. Sometimes these women were not only torn between their work and family roles, but also between the expectations the Socialist Unity Party (SED) had of them as mothers and the needs of their family members, especially when their adolescent children rebelled against the system.

One Party functionary described how she and some of her colleagues were publicly reprimanded during Party meetings for failing to guide their children to meet the preferences of the Party. Party functionaries did not consider reevaluating existing policies for their effectiveness but chose, instead, to blame parents, and mothers in particular. When the state was unable to instill the "right" values, that is, socialist values, in their children, parents would be called in.

One educator and Party functionary uneasily recalled that:

There was always the same sentence and I will never forget it: "Comrade, how do you bring up your child?" . . . [At my place of work] we had to recruit our sons to become [army] officers [and other loyal functionaries of the state]. . . . The idea was to get our children to choose what we wanted them to choose. And this was a point that was discussed over and over at the directors' meetings. And there was this underlying tone like, "You don't bring up your son right if he does not want to become a [military] officer." But that was the point where I put an absolute stop. I became very stubborn. And in any case, when I thought about it, who among my colleagues had children in the army? Very few. That [entire situation] was stressful, too. It was a different kind of stress [from that in reunified Germany].

Irrespective of how the women I interviewed felt about the socialist system, all found their own way of using, as well as evading it, particularly when it concerned their families. Many negotiated a delicate balance between the values they taught at home and the values the state tried to instill in their children. In rare instances, parents found the tacit support from individual teachers who would "ignore" the "deviations" of their students.

Child-Care Provisions under Socialism

The GDR took great pride in its comprehensive net of child-care facilities.[9] Monthly child allowances and child-care facilities were such an integral part of GDR society that it was completely taken for granted.[10] By law, towns, communities, and state enterprises were responsible for creating and maintaining child-care facilities and assisting families in finding a place for their children. Child-care institutions, perhaps more than any other institution in the GDR, revealed a clear gender division of labor. There were no public debates about who was going to take care of the children in the public centers. Women were "naturally" expected to do the nurturing and caretaking work. Among the women I interviewed, only one said that her child was taken care of by a male teacher.

Access to child care varied from region to region but increased steadily. In 1955, 91 children (out of 1,000) had access to infant/toddler care. In 1989, 802 children (out of 1,000) had access to it. Parents did not have to pay for the service, except a small amount toward meals. A similar trend was observed for kindergartens, which provided care for children between the ages of three and six. In 1955, 345 children (out of 1,000) had access, and by 1989, 951 (out of a 1,000 children) had a place in kindergartens. The costs were covered by the state as well, except for a very small meal allowance (Winkler, 1990, pp. 141–143).[11]

One gardener spoke for most when she commented: "For the nursery we paid about DM 30.00 for an entire month. Otherwise, we had no costs. When they went on a field trip, we paid perhaps 5.00 Marks extra. We could easily afford that."

Because parents had to work when children were off from school, "vacation camps" were available. (Children were off from school, on average, for 90 days per year, while parents were off from work 20–25 days.) Every year about 90 percent of the children enrolled in "vacation camps." The costs for parents were four Marks per week (Winkler, 1990, pp. 141–143).

The women I interviewed were generally satisfied with the care that was available for their children. Of the 43 women who addressed the issue, only one was dissatisfied, three said that the system they had entrusted their children to had as many pluses as minuses, and 39 women said that they were satisfied with the quality of the child care as it had existed. A mother of three said: "We had a nursery and a kindergarten at every corner and they were all filled up. I was very satisfied with the quality of the child care I received. They did a lot, and the children learned a lot, especially when they were about five or six years old before they started school proper."

Easy access to child-care centers was important to many because few had a car, work began early, and work hours were generally long. A nurse recalled how she was able to take her children to a child-care center because it was near: "The child-care center was near the [Güstrow] castle. That was on my way to work. It was quite wonderful, actually. I transported both children on my bike. . . . I transported them for many, many years on my bike. I did not have a car or a driver's license."

An agricultural worker described how they handled child care in her village: "[Transportation was not a problem in our village]. We had a community bus. And we took turns driving the children to the Kindergarten. After school, children went to after-school care. In the evening there was a bus that brought them home."

A teacher and mother of one daughter said:

When [my daughter] was small, she first went to the nursery because I had to work. The nursery was in the same house where I worked. That was ideal. . . . When she was three, she went to kindergarten. We had a school bus that brought the children to school and home again in the afternoon after they had taken their nap. When she started grade school, she took public transportation. She would take the bus to school, but it was a bit more difficult. When school was out, she had to either walk home or go into after-school care. She preferred going to after-school care and to do her homework.

Not all women chose to bring their children to state-run child-care centers, however. Their reasons differed, but none thought twice about putting their own and the needs of their children above the needs of the state. Some women were simply unable to get a place for their children. Some felt uncomfortable leaving an infant in a public setting for an entire day. Others thought that the facilities did not offer adequate resources to meet the special needs, such as medical attention that their children required. Some women needed more flexible hours, and one mother said, "I actually felt guilty when I had to leave my children in the nursery from early morning to late evening." A division director of a large state enterprise relied on her mother for child care: "I could have had a place in the nursery. But my mother looked after both of my children until they entered kindergarten. Our older daughter had a skin problem. She was born with it, and she needed a lot of special care [that she could not have gotten in a state-run nursery]."

A post office worker who needed more flexibility because she and her husband worked shifts looked for someone who could accommodate such work schedules:

[Our daughter] went to an elderly woman who also looked after other children. She was flexible, and I would arrange with her when I would bring my daughter. Sometimes I took her in the afternoon and sometimes in the evening. That was, of course, considerably more expensive. But I have to say it was also very good for our daughter. And I think I was lucky with our "day-mother."

A child-care worker wanted more personal attention for her child than the state-run facilities could offer:

I chose private child care. I knew the woman [who took care of my child]. She was a former colleague of mine, who had decided to stay at home. Also, I had worked in a nursery myself. And I did not like it very much for children who were really small. One child-care worker was responsible for eight infants and toddlers. I mean, it was all very clean and orderly, and the child-care workers were loving and gentle with the children. But still, it was not what I wanted. When you have to take care of eight babies, something has to give. I mean, the children got attention and were held, but still, it was not as personal [as I wanted it to be].

And a white-collar worker, concerned about her daughter's health, chose private over state child care: "We knew a woman who was looking after her granddaughter. And [we asked her to] look after our daughter. . . . That was a very nice [arrangement], I have to say that. [I preferred private child care] because [our daughter] got sick easily."

Many women in my sample carefully reflected on the choices they had made in the GDR with regard to rearing and taking care of their children. They almost all concluded that child care and after-school care were absolutely necessary. It gave them peace of mind and allowed them to do their jobs well. The observation by an educator was typical:

I always had the security that my children were well looked after. They had three healthy meals a day. They were well taken care of, and they learned to grow up together with other children. . . . Our children developed real friendships in these schools. [Being in school] was normal for them.

It was clear from these women's descriptions that the child-care facilities were generally seen in a positive light. Women made use of them because they served their needs and the needs of their children. Parents built close relationships with their children's caregivers and the relationship was not perceived as one between the state and the parent, but between the individual caregiver and the parent.

Some women weighed the long-term effects on parenting skills in a society that was structured in such a way that most of the work of child-rearing is assumed by professional educators. These women did not advocate that childrearing be the sole responsibility of mothers or parents. Instead, they supported more choice and flexibility for individual families, because they wanted parents to have more time to practice their parenting skills. A nurse/midwife was concerned because:

As a midwife I could always tell that women were really looking forward to having their babies. But I would talk to them because I noticed that many women did not know how to deal with their babies once they were born. They took them to the nursery early in the morning and to the kindergarten when they were older. And 12 hours later they picked their children up. That was how the state wanted it. The state wanted to control the rearing and education of children. It was all very deliberate. The mother and father were to be involved as little as possible. And when the child became ill one day, and the mother had to stay home, she did not know how to deal properly with her own child. I am not saying this was true for all mothers, but you can believe me, it was a considerable number.

An educator remarked:

I noticed that young mothers did not know how to play with their children or how to occupy them. Children, I am afraid, were becoming more and more marginal in families. Often they were a necessary burden. At least that is how I perceived it. Children were not the center of a family anymore, and that is why little consideration was given to children when there was a divorce [for example]. [People seemed to think], "Well, that is how it is." I don't want to say I was better than other mothers, but I thought about what was in the [best] interest of my children.

An agricultural worker reflected:

I think it would have been better for some families if the mother could have stayed at home without being banished to the kitchen. It would have been better [to have the choice] at least at certain ages of the children. I did not like it when I had to bring the children to the child-care center at six o'clock in the morning. [When they are infants], they are better off in a home atmosphere.

Although the state influenced children's socialization through child-care provisions and an array of financial and material support for families, the well-being of a child was, in the final analysis, the responsibility of the mother: "Yes, I assumed most of the responsibility in our family [and] for our children," was a typical response. Thus, it was mostly women who took off from work when their children were ill. According to a bookkeeper:

When children were ill, mothers would get permission from the doctor to take time off from work. Later, fathers could take time off as well. As the manager, I handled the finances, and dealt with the payroll and that is why I know this. It was mostly women who took off from work when their children were ill. We had to account for everything very precisely. We had booklets where we had to enter sick leave. Each child had a little booklet. It was the mothers who stayed home.

Sometimes a grandmother or a (female) neighbor was relied on, as described by one cook:

You know, [during GDR times] we had real neighborly relationships. When my children were ill, it went without saying [that we helped each other out]. We had a grandmother, who lived in our house. And there was also a young woman, who stayed at home. When my children were ill, they would look after them, make lunch, look in on them, and stay with them. Of course, I was able to take off work without penalties. That was the law. I don't remember exactly, but I was entitled to 10 or 20 days per year to take care of my child. I was lucky with my children. But had it become necessary, I would have stayed home with them.

A dairy technician's description of how she coped when her child/ren got sick was typical of many women I interviewed:

When my son was small, I stayed at home with him when he was sick. When he was a little older, I could leave him alone for a while once I was sure he did not have anything serious. Our home was close to my place of work. I would quickly go home and check on him during my lunch break. And we also had a phone, so he could reach me.

In my sample of women, there was only one father who assumed the primary role for his children because their mother, an educator, who also had a high-ranking Party position, earned more, and was, therefore, less available for family matters: "My husband had more time for our children than I did. When they got sick, he stayed with them. And why did he do it? Well, he earned less than I did. It was a financial question for us."

Even though it was parents' legal right to stay home with their sick children, some, whose children were sick more often, felt ambivalent about claiming this right. They were afraid that they may have been thought of as taking advantage of the system. Sometimes a not very understanding supervisor would remark that, "Your child is ill again!" And, "It is about time that we see you here again." These experiences make visible the gap that existed between the ideal of how women were supposed to meet the demands of daily family and work life and the reality they faced. The socialist ideology did not permit the consideration of alternative theoretical "lenses" that would have exposed the deficiency of its premise, that is, that male experience and male standards of work and family were universal.

CONCLUSION

Socialists regarded the transformation of the family as fundamental for the emancipation of women. However, Friedrich Engels' (1962) vision that, under socialism, the individual family and private households would be "socialized," and that the rearing and education of children would be a public matter, was never realized. The institution of the family was surprisingly resistant to political influences and unexpectedly bourgeois, in the sense that the family remained the primary institution where traditional gender roles were assigned and "masculine" and "feminine" behaviors learned (Mitchell, 1984, p. 212).

The socialist goal to control and influence all areas of social life, including the family, was not achieved either. Although the family was very much within the reach of the state, it remained, at the same time, difficult to penetrate. The home provided the base where family members, together with close friends, established and maintained *niches*, extensive networks where the state was criticized, politics discussed, goods bartered, and information exchanged. The *niche* was "protected" in the sense that the GDR relied for its very survival increasingly on the informal economic contributions produced by individual families, particularly during the last decade of the state's existence.

Family life was not, as is commonly assumed, uniform or monotonous under socialism. Families related differently to the system because each had different needs, wants, values, and expectations. They adopted different strategies to deal with the daily demands of family life, and most were closely connected in the so-called *niche*: the carefully guarded space from which they attempted to keep the intruding state at bay. Each charted its own path to create a family life that was both supportive and satisfying. Most women viewed their roles within the family as significant and valuable, and felt that other family members regarded them as such, too.

The choices open to East German women and their families were limited, shaped by the opportunities and constraints of the social structures within which all women had to live. These structures did not permit real gender equality (equal rank and power relations between women and men), nor did they encourage the development of a gender consciousness. Yet, they were flexible enough to allow modifications in existing gender relations within the family, modifications that were prompted by the demands of daily life that all women in my sample had to contend with: long work hours, household and family responsibilities, shortages of all sorts of consumer items, and participation in the informal economy and *niches*. Hence, traditional gender relations were weakened by countless actions taken by families to meet the needs of their members.

Nevertheless, at their core, familial relations were traditional. Under socialism East German women had to deal with the tension resulting from their *real* struggle to combine family and work life in accordance with the socialist *ideal* of how these two spheres ought to be combined. The *ideal* was based on male experience and male standards of work and family, whereas the *real* was the lived female experience of meeting the material, physical, and emotional needs of their families.

In the next chapter I depict how the struggle for women continued but also changed in reunified Germany. After the collapse of state socialism and the establishment of West Germany's democracy and social market economy, a shift could be observed in the gendered division of labor. Women assumed, once again, more responsibilities within the family, making visible more unequal rank and power relations.

NOTES

1. The state provided substantial direct and indirect material and financial support to families with children, without which women would have found it difficult to raise and take care of their families. It granted a credit of 7,000 Marks to newly wed couples to assist them in setting up their own households. The credit was interest-free and had to be repaid within a period of 11 years. If children were born during that period of time, the credit amount was reduced: 1,000 Marks upon the birth of the first child, 1,500 Marks upon the birth of the second child, and 2,500 Marks for the birth of the third child (Winkler, 1990, p. 149).

Women enjoyed full protection while pregnant. They were entitled to six weeks off work at full pay prior to giving birth, and 20 weeks after the baby was born. They could, if they wanted, take a "baby year" and stay home with their child until her/his first birthday. They could also transfer the year to the father or grandmother of the child. During the "baby year," the state paid a monthly allowance of 250 Marks to the caretaker. In addition, a woman received 1,000 Marks "welcome money" for each birth, which was the equivalent of a monthly paycheck for a blue- and white-collar worker. However, the payment was dependent on regular pre- and postnatal checkups at the doctor's office. If a mother nursed her child, she was granted an additional allowance.

The state also paid a monthly allowance for each child until the child had completed 10th grade. Children who continued their education after the 10th school year received a monthly educational allowance during grades 11 and 12 of 110 and 150 Marks, respectively. Mothers who were students or in training received an additional allowance of 60 Marks for each child. Public transportation from home to school or to work was free for children until the age of six and half price for apprentices and students (Winkler, 1990, pp. 139–147).

2. In West Germany, the age is 28.2 years for men and 25.7 years for women (*Bundesministerium für Frauen und Jugend* [Federal Ministry for Women and Youth], 1992, p. 72).

3.

Filing for Divorce by Gender in the GDR

Year	Divorces	Total Men	in %	Total Women	in %
1960	25,640	11,487	44.8	14,153	55.1
1965	26,576	10,737	40.4	15,839	59.6
1970	27,407	10,015	36.5	17,331	63.5
1975	41,632	14,230	34.5	27,402	65.5
1980	44,794	14,561	32.5	30,233	67.5
1985	51,240	16,316	31.8	34,924	68.2
1987	50,640	15,758	31.1	34,882	68.9
1989	50,063	15,497	30.9	34,566	60.0

Source: Winkler, 1990, p. 111.

4. Children joined the *Pioneers* when they entered school, usually at the age of six or seven. They were encouraged to join the *Freie Jugend Deutschland* (FJD) at the age of 13 or 14.

5. The GDR was not a consumer society, and shopping had a utilitarian purpose. The "household day" offered an opportunity to avoid standing in long lines and/or to get the item one set out to buy.

6. In contrast, 26 percent of West German women said that their spouses/partners "helped often with household chores"; 52 percent said that "their partner helped sometimes," and 20 percent said that "they never helped " (*Institut für Demoskopie Allensbach*, 1993, p. 51).

The same survey also found that 54 percent of East German women who worked full-time do most of the household chores, and only 25 percent said that they share it equally. Of those who were unemployed, 66 percent said that they do most chores, and 13 percent said they share it equally.

Of the women who worked full-time in West Germany, 45 percent said that they do most of the household chores. Of those who were unemployed, 60 percent said that they do most of the chores (*Institut für Demoskopie Allensbach*, 1993, p. 53).

7. *Jugendweihe* was the rite the Communist Party introduced for children in an attempt to replace the Catholic Church's communion and the Protestant Church's confirmation.

8. The division of household labor in the capitalist United States closely resembles the division of household labor in socialist Germany. When a survey by the U.S. Department of Agriculture in 1994 asked 1,100 adult men who lived in a household with an adult woman, "Who usually plans the meals?," 25 percent of the men said that they usually planned the meals, while 95 percent of the women said that they did. When asked "Who usually does the shopping?," 35 percent of the men said that they usually did the shopping, while 90 percent of the women said that they did. When asked, "Who usually prepares the food?," 25 percent of the men said that they usually prepared the meals while 90 percent of the women said they did.

The study further showed that (a) younger men were more likely than older [men] to be involved in planning meals; (b) men from households with incomes near the poverty level took part in planning meals almost three times as often as men from high-income households; (c) in homes where the woman was employed full-time, the men were twice as likely to participate in planning meals (Harnack et al., 1994; USDA Continuing Survey of Food Intakes of Individuals, 1994. Cited in *Washington Post Health*, 1998, p. 5).

9. Child-care facilities included:

- day nurseries for infants and toddlers;

- kindergarten for children between the ages of 3–6;

- after-school care for children in grades 1–4; and

- summer camps and other facilities during school vacations (Winkler, 1990, p. 141).

10.

Child Allowance as of 1990 in East German Marks per Month

Number of Children	1	2	3	4	5
Up to the Age of 12	95	145	195	195	195
Over the Age of 12	115	165	215	215	215

Source: Winkler 1990, p. 140.

11. To serve one meal cost 1.35 Marks (kindergarten), 1.60 Marks (grades 1–6), and 1.90 Marks (grades 7–12). Parents paid 0.35 and 0.55 Marks for kindergarten and school, respectively. In 1988, the state paid 1,025 million Marks for school meals, or 80 percent of the total cost (Winkler, 1990, p. 145).

5

Family Life in Reunified Germany

INTRODUCTION

In 1990, shortly after the West German system took effect in the Eastern part of then newly reunified Germany, East German women began to realize that the West German definitions of women's social roles differed profoundly from the ones they had been socialized into. The East German family had become vitally important to decision-makers, because it was considered essential for mitigating the impact of reunification on other levels of society—political, economic, social, and cultural. In January 1991, then Chancellor Helmut Kohl said:

Among all the institutions that provide stability, the family is first. Especially in times of profound change, the family gains significance as a source of human warmth and security. It remains the most important place for personal development and the transmission of values and virtues. It remains the goal of our policy to strengthen the family. (*Bundesministerium für Familie, Senioren, Frauen und Jugend*, 1994a, p. 4)

The tasks involved for women to provide stability in a system that had collapsed and had been replaced by a new and totally unfamiliar one were hidden and unspoken, but included equipping family members with the ability to respond in a stable manner to the demands of the newly established democracy and its market economy. Also, most of the necessary emotional labor to ensure continuity was "naturally" and implicitly assigned to women. For many of the women I interviewed, the focus became, indeed, the daily economic and emotional survival of their families.

The (mostly male) East and West German elites had given top priority to maintaining social peace during the transition from socialism to capitalism. They expected East German women to make crucial contributions to ensuring peace, and women readily reorganized and adjusted the lives of their family members to ensure stability in the day-to-day routines at home and, by implication, in the larger society. Although women's work was indispensable to the ruling elites, it received no recognition and has remained *invisible*.

With the establishment of West Germany's political and economic system, West German law and policies took effect in East Germany, providing (or withholding) resources in such a manner that the existing power positions on all societal levels remained intact. The capitalist elites of reunified Germany reinforced more traditional gender relations. From their vantage point, it was a necessary step for "helping" East German women to adapt to the West German model of family life and their role within it. As a consequence, women's social roles, status, and space were reduced.

THE FAMILY

In reunified Germany, like many other industrialized countries, there is a lively debate about what constitutes a family, what values it should hold and what responsibilities it should assume.[1] It is generally accepted that "family" is not a "natural" phenomenon that exists outside the wider economic system. Rather, "family" is shaped by and dependent on the socioeconomic and political conditions of the wider society. Therefore, it is important to understand that familial forms are historically changeable, shaped by culture, dependent on the environment, and resistant to politics (Kaufmann, 1995, p. 7).[2]

Since the 1950s, for example, single-parent households have increased and marriages have declined. More women have entered the work force, which has led to changes in relationships between women and men. In reunified Germany, 1.6 children (statistically speaking) live in a household as compared to two to three children in the 1950s. Life expectancy has increased, changing the relationship between young and old (*Bundesministerium für Frauen und Jugend* [Federal Ministry for Women and Youth], 1994, p. 34).

According to Kaufmann (1995, pp. 1–3), tension has always existed between those who conceive of family as a private matter and those who conceive of it as a public matter, particularly when the need arises for financial or other assistance. Some see an incompatibility between the interests of the state and those of individual women. For the state, the function of the family is to guarantee progeny, whereas for individual women who strive for emancipation, family obligations often foreclose opportunities.

Reunification of East and West Germany complicated the matter because each side held a different view of what family is and what roles women should assume within it. For ideological and economic reasons, family was a public matter in East Germany. East German women were encouraged to enter full-time employment, and the state provided comprehensive financial and other services that enabled women to combine paid work and family responsibilities.[3] Through these policies the state secured the next generation of socialist citizens, not only in terms of numbers but in terms of socialist norms and values through its comprehensive child care, kindergarten, after-school care, and educational systems.

In reunified Germany, the state considers family largely a private matter; nevertheless through its social policies the state influences the choices that are open to women. Germany's Federal Ministry for Family pursues policies that are based on five principles (*Bundesministerium für Familie, Senioren, Frauen und Jugend* [Federal Ministry for Family, Seniors, Women, and Youth], 1994b, p. 1):

1. Family policies must result in more social justice for families;
2. Family policies must make a contribution to eliminating the existing contradictions between the demands posed by paid work and the needs of families;
3. Family policies have to become visible in the everyday lives of families;
4. Family policies have to promote a partnership between men and women; and
5. Europe has to become a Europe of families.

Based on these principles, the policies of the federal government aim to make it easier for young people to decide to have a family and to rear children. They ensure social recognition of families, strengthening them and granting economic support, and ensure that children develop positively, personally and socially (*Bundesministerium für Familie, Senioren, Frauen und Jugend*, 1994b, p. 4).

However, the principles and stated goals of these policies are not easily translated into everyday life. In West Germany, the rearing and well-being of children as well as their positive development have not been so much the responsibility of *parents* as of *mothers*. Child care, private and otherwise, is, by any measure, inadequate. In 1986, only 4.6 percent of the children between one and three years of age had access to child care in West Germany.[4] The gap between the government's principles and policies and everyday life becomes clear when one considers that in 1992, single parents (85 percent of whom were women) reared and supported their children under these circumstances of constrained child-care resources (*Bundesministerium für Familie, Senioren, Frauen und Jugend*, 1994b, pp. 12–18). Combining continuous paid work and family responsibilities is difficult and sometimes impossible, diminishing the choices available for women.

In 1986, the West German government introduced a federal law for *parenting*, improving it further in 1992. The law was to deal with two important issues: (1) in the presence of increasing unemployment, it aimed to expand upon the choices available to women, who often felt constrained to choose between having children and staying at home if their economic circumstances permitted, or not to have children; and (2) to deal with the chronic shortages of child-care facilities and personnel.

The new law, which the government refers to as one of the core elements of Germany's family policies, provides incentives for parents, more precisely mothers, to stay home with their children and for parenting to be publicly recognized as work. Parents can leave their paid work and take *parenting vacations* for up to three years.[5] During this time, their jobs are protected (although not necessarily the same position, and, in the case of larger companies, not necessarily in the same location). Also, parents are entitled to social benefits, including unemployment benefits and health insurance. For two years, they receive a monthly "parenting allowance" of a maximum of DM 600 per month (about $330).[6]

These policies are considered a success by the Federal Ministry because they: "are in accordance with the wishes of parents. This is demonstrated by the fact that 96 percent of the parents took advantage of the *parenting allowance* and 94 percent of the *parenting vacation*" (*Bundesministerium für Familie, Senioren, Frauen und Jugend*, 1994b, p. 14).

Claudia Nolte, federal minister for Family, Seniors, Women and Youth in the Kohl government, conceded that "unfortunately men much too seldom take *parenting vacations*," indicating that these policies, in contrast to their intention, have not necessarily "promote[d] partnership between men and women" (p. 14).

THE IMPACT OF STRUCTURAL AND INSTITUTIONAL CHANGES ON EAST GERMAN WOMEN AND THEIR FAMILIES

German reunification has shaken, and sometimes shattered, what East German women had learned to expect of their lives. Once the process of reunification was underway, there were no options for turning back, only for going forward at what many experienced as breath-taking speed. The impact on all family members was enormous. With the establishment of the West German system in the East, the political, economic, social, and cultural conditions of the German Democratic Republic (GDR) were declared invalid, and many women felt that their experiences—and to some extent, they themselves and their families—were declared invalid as well.

German reunification meant that nothing could be taken for granted: There was a new government; a new legal system; a new economy; new municipal, state, and federal bureaucracies; new shops with new goods; new housing and working conditions; new schools; new public transport routes; new approaches to managing just about everything. As a result, a new family structure with new routines, responses, rules, and behaviors emerged as well.

For many families, long-term thinking and planning were put on hold. The focus was "today," perhaps "tomorrow." Everyone had to react to the unfamiliar: The children reacted to the new school system, the new hours, the new books, and sometimes new teachers. The parents reacted to the new working conditions if they had work, and to unemployment if they had lost their jobs, and generally to the new everyday environment and its demands. Every family member also reacted to the reactions of other family members. Uncertainty and stress became a permanent presence. Friends, colleagues, neighbors, and members of the larger family reacted to the new conditions as well, and many could not provide support for others. Relationships were put to the test. Some held up under the strain, others fell apart, as expressed by an art historian, who lost her job and became self-employed in reunified Germany: "So many things are happening. Marriages fall apart. Husbands [and fathers] are gone the entire day [sometimes week] and women have to build their own lives somehow. . . . One has to go very separate ways."

Because all systems had changed—social, economic, political, cultural—many day-to-day activities in public and in private changed as well, and it was mostly women, including those in my sample, who assumed the responsibility of "cleaning up," "sorting out," and "putting things back together" to make society function again under the new conditions.

For example, under state socialism all bureaucratic matters were taken care of at the workplace. In reunified Germany, it was left to each individual to deal with the many different institutions and bureaucracies. In my sample, mostly women took on this arduous and time-consuming task because "it had to be done," and most found the West German bureaucratic approach alien and utterly frustrating. This teacher expressed the view of many: "[There] are all these changes in government agencies. The *Amtsdeutsch* (bureaucratic German)! Good God, one can hardly translate it [into spoken German]. . . . But one has to. . . . it was imposed on us. . . . [That language] was not our mentality."

Of the 32 (62 percent) East German women who raised the subject during the interview, 29 concluded that a democratic society is a bureaucratic nightmare. An endless number of new forms had to be filled out to satisfy the new legal requirements of registration at the municipal, state, and federal levels, at the workplace or unemployment office, and at insurance companies, banks, and schools. Often women took on this task because, according to a teacher who lost her job: "I am now unemployed and have more time than my husband who is still working." And a shepherd who was unable to keep her flock of sheep said:

Men see it differently from women. Most of the time it is women who do all the running around from one bureaucracy to the next. My partner does not understand what is involved trying to get all the paperwork sorted out in reunified Germany. Men don't even think about it. That is how it is in my experience. But then, they don't have to think about it either because they say, "She can do it, I have to go to work. All she has is housework and the child." But men do not really know the work that is involved. Many men make it easy for themselves.

Going from one government authority to the next was time- and energy-consuming, made even more stressful because often bewildered civil servants were still learning the rules of the new system themselves. A midwife who became the chairperson of the work council at her hospital remarked:

In my new job, I have to deal with an extraordinary amount of new laws. Bureaucracy did not become less cumbersome [after reunification]. Well, how do you go about it? Thank God, we had a partner hospital [in West Germany]. I was able to call, at any time, a very nice and committed woman, who helped a lot. . . . But the [number of] people one could call got fewer and fewer, and one really had to deal with everything oneself.

Those who were at the receiving end like this administrative assistant said: "I had to register here, and have my name deleted there, and go to the next government agency and register anew. I had to run around a lot. My husband was unable to do it because of his job. It all fell on me. I used to make this long list to make sure I would not forget anything."

And a teacher, trying to help parents navigate the new and unfamiliar new bureaucracy, recalled:

In my job [as a teacher for the hearing impaired], I assisted many families to make sure they would receive the financial assistance they were entitled to. During parent-teacher meetings the main concern for parents was, "How do we do it with all these forms?" To fill out these [unfamiliar] forms was really hard in the beginning. I think it is fair to say that we have a difficult time managing the "paper war" that has rolled over us from the West.

The insurance system, taken for granted in West Germany, turned out to be an overwhelming task for many East Germans, increasing an already high level of stress. East German women never had to deal with a multitude of competitive companies and their numerous and unfamiliar offers. It simply did not exist under state socialism. They found it difficult to relate to the many and varied insurance offers, yet they knew it was necessary for the well-being of their families. Not being used to Western sales tactics by mostly West German agents, a number of East German women echoed the sentiments of this health care worker who said that, in hindsight, they were ill advised and easily taken advantage of:

Everywhere there were suddenly banks and insurance companies, and tax advisors. It was like an invasion that rolled over us. We did not know any of that. It was imposed on us. There were certain things we had never heard about. And many of us who wanted German reunification then had second thoughts.

Banks presented a similar problem to many. Not only were there suddenly many different banks, but each offered many types of accounts, all unfamiliar. Yet, in reunified Germany no family could do without having a bank account. East Germans were used to receiving their monthly salaries in cash or perhaps in a checking account. Private credit was an alien concept. People rarely took out credit in the former GDR, and no one had ever used a credit card.

Often women made decisions on the basis of insufficient knowledge because they lacked an experiential context in which to locate the information. The high school system, for example, changed from a one-track system to the West German three-track system, establishing clearer class distinctions again. In fourth grade, children are "guided" to prepare for either an apprenticeship (*Hauptschule*), a technical college (*Realschule*), or the university (*Gymnasium*). After reunification teachers and parents had to "sort" through the new requirements and register all children from the fourth grade onward into three different high school tracks that are often housed in separate schools. Some mothers told me that the context was so alien to them that it was difficult to relate to it and think through the consequences for their children. As a result, often they were dissatisfied with the process and the outcome.

A number of women had to assist their aging parents who felt at a loss because they could not orient themselves in the context of the new social service bureaucracy. They did not understand the bureaucratic West German language and depended on their grown children to claim the state assistance they qualified for and needed. Some women felt so overloaded, frustrated, and exhausted with the new processes that they decided to support their parents themselves.

In doing many of the hidden, unpaid, but vital tasks so their families and the larger society could function under the new conditions, the majority of women I interviewed told me that they began to realize, ever so slowly, that women's public and private work was taken for granted and, consequently, not valued during the transition from socialism to capitalism. They had readily assumed the extra unpaid work to help everyone adjust to the new system, but they had not expected to be handed the bulk of it. They had viewed it as a temporary and not, as it appeared, a permanent situation. They had expected that a democratic society was more just and that such a society would enable them to continue their paid work and better combine it with family responsibilities.

The women were holding on to the socialist definition of women's role in society. They perceived their lives in reunified Germany as encompassing *simultaneously* paid work and family (unpaid) work, and in that order. It was still a deeply internalized norm. Family and work life existed not separately, but together. The West German concept of prioritizing one over the other made no sense to them because "Each woman, just like each man, has only one life and she can't design her life in accordance with two different plans. For all women, just like for all men, professional recognition and a harmonious family life go very closely together" (Schröter, 1995, p. 143).

But German reunification had brought irreversible change, particularly with regard to their roles in the family and at the workplace, which they had earlier learned to combine so matter of factly. The perception of most women I interviewed was that, in the former GDR, their income-generating work roles had played a positive part in how they were defined within the family. In reunified Germany, by contrast, that role was often taken away from them, influencing how they defined themselves and, in turn, were defined by other members of their families. In the former GDR, women's income was regarded, by all family members, as indispensable as that of their spouses. In reunified Germany, that reality was seriously undermined.

In the GDR, women's social security derived from their own paid work and state financial assistance. In reunified Germany, social security derives primarily from the institution of marriage. And because some men were not able to shoulder the sole responsibility for the economic well-being of their families, women have had to deal with the resulting frustration as well.[7] One agricultural worker who had lost her job described it this way:

Now I am home and I am dependent on my husband. And now it all starts. [He says], "Now I am the only one who has to earn money for everybody. It is about time that you start earning some money again." Well, that is what we were used to. I have to say that it is rather stressful at home. We have had a few crises because the sala-ries that men get are not all that good either. When we total up our rent and utility bills, that adds up to more than the money that is left to live on.

And a self-employed woman explained:

[In the GDR] when a marriage was in crisis, one did not have to stay in it. A woman could say, "Good bye, I'm leaving you." She was financially independent. But that is different now. One is dependent. One accepts much more. [In the GDR] I felt more equal. And besides, one should not accept everything [a husband demands]. But now I am much more dependent. I have to say it that way. I accept much more and overlook things. That was not the case before, [when it was] not as extreme as it is now.

The Effect of Women's and Men's Unemployment on the Family

Without exception, all women in my sample included in their descrip-tions of changes in family life the subject of unemployment or potential un-employment. Employed women were very cognizant of living in an environment of social and economic uncertainty, because all of them knew someone who was, or had been, or was going to be out of work in the near future, as exemplified by this agricultural worker, who participated in a job retraining program:

In general, there is constant anxiety. My husband is already tense because he is not sure what is going to happen. He works in construction and they are facing another crisis. [At his place of work] they are talking about another wave of dismissals. It is this uncertainty [that concerns us].

All the women I interviewed had directly or indirectly experienced the tension and suffering in their families that unemployment statistics do not convey. They all seemed to be bracing themselves for coping with that even-tuality. The worst part of being unemployed, they told me, was not that their social status changed drastically, but the negative impact it had on the people around them, especially on their children, but also on other family members, friends, former colleagues, and neighbors. Unemployment often meant a drastic decline in a family's standard of living and nine women (17 percent) witnessed family members or friends descending into alcoholism and/or behaving in a physically and verbally violent manner, as described by a nurse who had lost her job:[8] "Because of unemployment, alcohol consumption has increased. And then there are drugs. There are so many [drugs] on the market now. Women also drink. It is this hopelessness. They don't know what to do. They feel they are not needed anymore."

An educator married to a physician described how alcoholism played a major role in undermining her husband's job prospects, and ultimately their marriage:

I have to say that my husband is an alcoholic. He lost his job before I did. That was in 1990. I was dismissed in 1991. When he lost his job, he could not fathom it. He could not understand why [his employer] did not want him any more, even though it was written down in the letter: "Dismissed because of alcohol problem . . . not responsible on the job."

A health care worker explained: "Many [unemployed men] drink. Some have always done it, but after reunification they were simply axed. [In the former GDR] no one could fire them. Now they are dismissed immediately."

And a agricultural worker participating in a job retraining program recalled the fears she endured when her husband became unemployed:

When my husband lost his job, I was very afraid that he might start to drink. Many, many [men] among our friends started to drink. Their marriages have fallen apart. They just gave up. We had good friends, good acquaintances. I don't know what would have happened to us if we had not had them.

Unemployment caused stress in the family, no matter who was unemployed or why they lost their jobs. Yet, it was the women who felt they were better equipped to hold it all together. A number of women I interviewed felt that they could deal better with being unemployed than their spouses, because they were better able to cope with stress. They felt that their identities, in contrast to men's, were grounded more equally in both the public and private spheres and, therefore, were not as fragile as men's identities.

These perceptions verify that although the traditional gender division of labor may have shifted somewhat in the family during the socialist era, basically it persisted. Thus, in reunified Germany, where men's work is predominantly perceived as nondomestic and women's work as domestic, which includes the bulk of emotional labor, the lingering perceptions of traditional gender relations from the socialist era have been reinforced and, in the words of one self-employed woman: "Now men perceive themselves as the breadwinners again." A salesclerk who had lost her job recalled how she experienced her husband, who lost his job as well:

To live with a man who has no work is more nerve-racking than to live with my unemployed self. I have experienced unemployed women as much more flexible [than men]. Women have started to write a village chronicle or have written about historical buildings. They don't just sit there and brood. Unemployment is very, very difficult for men.

A dairy technician who was participating in a job retraining program also reflected on the difference between women and men who are faced with unemployment:

Men suffer more than women when they are unemployed. In many respects, we have learned to live with it. Unemployed men are the worst thing there is. They need work. Women tend to meet other women. They do things together privately. They look after each other's children, and they start building something up for themselves.

Still, many women voiced dissatisfaction at having their social space reduced to the family, and some unemployed women struggled with the feeling of being seen by society "as not good enough." Bertram's (1996) study yielded similar results. In her sample of 410 East German women, all experienced unemployment as completely or partly stressful. They suffered from the pressure that unemployment had imposed on them. Many, especially younger women, had too little income, were "sitting around," and were bored. They suffered from the feeling of not being needed anymore and being isolated. Among the unemployed women I interviewed, some avoided contact with former colleagues, neighbors, and friends, which increased their sense of isolation.

A child-care worker, living in a large apartment building, observed:

Somehow I noticed it myself. I am preoccupied with myself. Sometimes I think I should speak a word with a neighbor. But everybody is doing their own thing now. I think it has a lot to do with being unemployed; you feel written off. Some people can't handle the situation [of being unemployed], and, [in any case] everybody reacts differently. Some [unemployed] are very angry, some are ashamed, some are in denial and pretend everything is just fine.

The actuality or threat of unemployment was present in the families of all the women I interviewed. Upon reflection they realized that this had caused a latent, but persistent stress that many absorbed, dealt with, and struggled to change, while at the same time keeping every family member "afloat." In the perception of most, the social changes had not been for the better. East German women did not, as many West Germans had assumed, welcome the opportunity to concentrate on family and household because it did not relieve them of the burdens they had carried under socialism. The new burden was often as heavy, if not more so, because it remained unarticulated, unproblematized, and utterly invisible.

Children of Two Societies

Next to unemployment, the greatest concern of the East German women I interviewed was the adjustment that their children had to make, because, in the words of a gardener, who was also the mother of a seven-year-old girl and an eight-year-old boy, "[reunification] is very difficult for me, but for all children it is even harder." In reunified Germany, children had become the sole responsibility of individual families again, and more precisely of mothers who were expected to ease the adjustments their children had to make with little support from the larger society. The world that was familiar, predictable, and secure had disappeared quickly, and many children absorbed the uncertainty, stress, competitiveness, and hostility that permeated the larger environment they lived in. An administrative assistant and mother of two girls said: "I noticed how my daughter has put up pictures of her childhood. She looks at them. [She says], 'It was so nice, then.' It was the security [she had which is gone now]."

An agricultural worker, a mother of three girls and two boys, said:

At first my children could not deal with the changes [in reunified Germany] because we had them brought up differently. We taught them that they could achieve a lot for themselves by being part of a community. . . . and that, even though we do not have a lot of wealth, they can still support others. That is simply what they have been taught.

And a child-care worker and mother of two teenage boys was concerned because:

Even the children among themselves have become so much more competitive. I don't know, it seems that the *Wende* (turning point) has brought this on. The children here actually say something like, "You come here and take away the work from my parents" [to children who have moved into our community]. Where do they get that from? It has to come from their parents, who must say this at the dinner table. Otherwise, children would not say that to each other.

The changes experienced by children at home are compounded by changes that take place in school. The same teachers who had taught them in the GDR to reject capitalist norms and values now teach them to embrace those norms and values as good and desirable. A survey found that 35 percent of East German pupils had difficulties with the new school system, because they were overburdened by the new conditions in school (Misselwitz, 1991; Schröder, 1991; cited in Schmitz, 1995, p. 126). "The cozy intimacy they once felt in a tightly regimented society" was replaced by a confusing new set of rules and expectations (Drozdiak, 1997, p. A15).

Children reacted to the new situations in various ways as did their parents and people around them, who felt ill at ease in the new society that valued *competitive* behavior and put them "in a state of continuous latent and acute stress" (Schmitz, 1995, p. 126). Many children felt anxious and often aggressive, rarely at ease and comfortable. A nurse, and the mother of four grown children, echoed the concerns of many:

The children are affected the most. You can see it. They are the most disadvantaged because they experience close up when their mother loses her job or their father his. And then [they live through] all the fights that follow from that. "This you can't afford and that you can't afford." It is the tension and irritability. It's the children who feel it the most. It is not at all surprising that *crime is on the increase* and that we have so many children with behavioral problems.

A number of children experienced the harsh reality of social inequality when, for the first time, they were not allowed to participate in social events or school activities because the financial situation of their parents did not allow it. A mother of three school-age children who was participating in a job retraining program described the reality her children faced: "When the children go on a field trip with their school and we have to pay DM 400, we [can't pay it]. It would undermine our existence."

A salesclerk, a mother of a teenage girl and two teenage boys, said "The children go to school and when you are unemployed long term, they see what others can afford and you can't, particularly when one child has more than another child."

And a former computer programmer and mother of two teenage sons asked: "Can you imagine what it is like in a family in which both parents are unemployed? When a child is being told [all the time] 'We can't afford this, and we can't afford that.' That is very, very hard on them."

The future of teenagers was of particular concern to many women I spoke with, because "too many parents were involved in dealing with their own situations" and were at a loss about how to deal with the problems their teenagers faced. Some interviewees suggested that when women were employed, they found it easier to respond to the concerns of their children and to deal more calmly with family problems because they could more easily separate important from unimportant issues. In brief, they were generally better partners and mothers because they felt more equal within the family and society (Schröter, 1995, p. 143).

But reunification changed all that and, as a result, many parents cannot give their children and teenagers the support they need. Moreover, youth programs that had been an intricate part of children's ideological and moral education in the former GDR were eliminated and not replaced in reunified Germany, leaving a huge vacuum causing many women to worry about the vulnerability of teenagers who might drift into crime or be attracted to radical right-wing groups.[9]

A self-employed cosmetician and mother of two grown children voiced the worry of many when she remarked: "Today's youth have no moral side. What kind of ideology do they have? The socialism we preached to them was bankrupt, [and what] did we replace it with?" A midwife and a mother of a grown son and daughter reflected:

We have enormous problems to solve in reunified Germany: [We need] compassion, work, and no hatred. [In the GDR] you would join people at the table and talk. Nobody is open and honest today, or only seldom. And the racial hatred! It does not matter where you go, you see swastikas [everywhere]. And very small children are involved in [neo-Nazi activities]. That is very, very troubling.[10]

One mother, a post office worker, described the difficulties that were typical for the majority of those who tried to provide their children with a meaningful future, only to encounter structural barriers that could not be overcome by their individual efforts:

At the time of reunification, my son was still in school. Then he started his apprenticeship. But he was only placed [in the program] because I worked in the post office. He finished his apprenticeship and was told he could continue to work, but that did not last. He became unemployed. Then he was employed for a while and had to leave again. It is really difficult. I am not sure what is going to happen.

With very few chances in the job market, many young people have grown *alienated* from society and turned to, and often found support and recognition in, groups at the fringes of society.[11] Some have drifted into the drug culture, which was of great concern to nine (17 percent) of the women I interviewed. A salesclerk and mother of two teenage sons who had lost her job in reunified Germany worried that:

Young people are especially prone to taking drugs. They go to the discos. They just want to try a cigarette and then they get hooked [on drugs]. It is often because the parents are unemployed and start to drink. These young people don't see anything else. They don't have a family anymore in that sense. And they want *recognition* in their peer groups, and they often find it in the discos. That is where they hang out.

Almost all the women I interviewed, including those who had rejected the system of the GDR, were critical and concerned about the failure of capitalist society to protect its youth. They felt that even though the socialist collectivity was far from ideal, it provided an important measure of social security for all children and youth. With the disappearance of the collectivity, children and youth were left largely unprotected. It was a job many women felt went beyond what an individual family, or more precisely what individual mothers, could handle. One 17-year-old teenager put it this way: "Before, we used to talk about books and theater, but now the only subjects anybody cares about are jobs and money. . . . There's a lot more death and crime than we used to experience. I have the impression that an entire country has lost the ability to laugh and enjoy themselves" (Drozdiak, 1997, p. A15).

Because of the situation their children were facing, many women in my sample came to regard the West German system as indifferent, if not hostile, toward children. Schmidt (1994, pp. 39–40) points out that, "cuts in social expenditure follow[ed] a very old pattern" in reunified Germany. Public funds that have benefited children and their families are cut first. Politicians have lost credibility, especially with women, because they speak of policies for families, but fail to make children and families the center of the political debate; instead, they use women and children conveniently for political speeches and declarations (pp. 39–40).[12]

When West German values that had tempted many young East Germans (because they had been beyond reach in the GDR) did not live up to what they had promised, East German youth found themselves wedged between two systems, neither of which offered a future perspective they could embrace. Indeed, many East German youth, and many women in my sample, found confirmation of what they had once been taught about Western capitalism: *that it inevitably results in unemployment, exploitation of working people, poverty, drugs, crime, and other social ills.*

Capitalism's Indifference to the Needs of Children

Because children and young people were not a primary concern of Germany's political and economic elites, most women experienced the decision-makers as indifferent, eager to shift the cost—economic, social, psychological—of raising children in the new Germany to families, and to mothers in particular. Women were expected to make up for deep cuts in public funding for child care and education, which had resulted in the closing of many child-care, after-school care, and youth facilities and programs, and in increased fees for those centers that remained open.

When I asked East German women to evaluate their dependence on the state for their own and their children's welfare in the GDR, many of them were somewhat astounded by the question. They said that they did not view receiving state benefits for children and families as being dependent on the state. They argued that, through their work—domestic and nondomestic—women had generated at least half of the existing wealth over the last 40 years. They considered it only fair that women and children share in the redistribution of that wealth, and did not consider benefits an interference in their personal freedom as it is often interpreted from a conservative Western perspective.

Most East German women did not agree with the Western notion that children should be the sole responsibility of the individual family. They tended to believe that the larger society should share in the responsibility for caring for its children.[13] They thought it only fair that the state, private institutions, and enterprises should be required to share in the responsibility of guaranteeing the well-being of all children. Having children, they argued, is more than an economic issue. There must be a recognition of the work of parents by the state, employers, bureaucracies, and other institutions, because the well-being of children is in the interest of everyone. "After all, they represent our future," said a white-collar employee and mother of four grown children. A secretary and mother of two small boys commented: "Now comes this [attitude] from West Germany, . . . 'Why should I help finance child care and kindergartens, why should I be concerned about other people's children?' How democratic is that? How just is that?"

A nurse and mother of three grown sons and one daughter observed: "Private companies should be friendlier toward children. As soon as [companies] find out a woman has children, they throw out the application. Women do most of the work [of bringing up children], and companies should not be allowed to punish them for that."

And a teacher and mother of a five-year-old girl and nine-year-old boy remarked: "What I experience as intolerable is that this state [reunified Germany] is hostile to children. I know that there were many things that were bad [in the former GDR], but for children [society] did a lot of things."

However, one mother, a former agricultural worker, was relieved to have the choice to stay home with her disabled child. She found that the benefits for the disabled had improved vastly since reunification, expanding her choices and making financially possible what was not possible in the GDR:

It is as if somebody has taken a burden off me. I am relieved because I can admit to myself, "I really do not want to work right now." I would feel very uneasy if I had to work. It was such a pressure. I did not have a life. Now I can go into town and stop and look and stroll along. I did not know what that was. It was always quick, quick, quick. I went quickly into town, quickly shopping, quickly back home again. I have to learn to do things more leisurely.

The same mother also spoke of the urgent need for decision-makers to recognize that family situations differ and that, consequently, a diversity of needs and expectations exists. She wanted to see more choices for women so they can decide for themselves how much time they want to spend with their children, how many hours they want to work away from home, how much energy they want to expend in either domain, and how much public assistance they need. She said:

I believe that everyone has to be given the chance to gather experiences they think they need. For some the priority is family, for others paid work. I do believe that paid work is important, though. That way one is integrated into the larger social environment and not limited to the boundaries of the home.

While charting a path for themselves and their families in reunified Germany, East German women rejected the West German model that makes women predominantly responsible for family and children, because it conveniently ignores the diverse and changing needs of women over their lifetime. It is a model based not on women's experience but on men's experience of family and paid work life.

Declining Birthrate

To meet their own as well as the needs of their families in an unfamiliar and uncertain socioeconomic—and in what many perceived as an unfriendly—environment for children, many East German women decided against having any [more] children. Between 1989 and 1992, the number of births decreased in East Germany by about half, and in 1995, the East German birthrate was 40 percent below the West German birthrate (Kaufmann, 1995, p. 5; Nauck, 1995, p. 180).[14]

In the state of Mecklenburg-Vorpommern, where the women I interviewed live, the annual birthrate dropped from 23,000 to 9,000 (60 percent) between 1989 and 1996 (*Schweriner Volkszeitung*, March 5, 1996, p. 4). Almost all the women I interviewed addressed the decline in the birthrate because they were either personally faced with making a decision of having a (another) child, or had a family member or friend who was. One mother of a six-year-old son, who had lost her job and participated in a job retraining program, said:

Well, clearly, now the tendency is to say, "We do not want any children in the foreseeable future. You could feel it after reunification. [Everyone said,] "If you decide to have a child now you might as well take a rope." That is how people felt. In our village we have had only two births since reunification [five and a half years ago]. There was an enormous social insecurity. [Women said,] "If I get pregnant now, I'll lose my job." And those who had children said, "No more, that is it."

A midwife and mother of two grown children observed:

For me the rupture in the rate of birth was shocking. It was terrible to realize that the birthrate can be steered to such an extent by the state and financial considerations. One could actually influence [through policies] that children were born in the former GDR because mothers were given a lot of support! There was child care and kindergartens. Now it is the reverse.

At the beginning [in reunified Germany] it was very extreme. [Women would say,] "Children? Not in the foreseeable future." One thinks about it longer. Do I want a child? Or is it better not to have [another] one?

A self-employed mother of two grown children noted:

Women at child-bearing age say "no" to children, at least for the foreseeable future. That is the terrible thing today that hardly any children are born. I think it is changing but only very little. Our family was still very lucky. Our daughter had a child in 1990. But [my daughter] said very clearly to me, "Well, mom, had this happened a year later, he would not have been born." She works in intensive care in shifts. And the [hospital] told her straight out that she could not be absent if her child gets sick. That is just not possible; she would lose her job. And she is the breadwinner in the family.

My son looks upon [having children] in a very critical way. He has a girlfriend but children are a taboo subject. They see it very differently [from my generation].

And a teacher and mother of a nine-year-old boy and a five-year-old girl said: "I would not have had a second child had I known that I would not get work as a teacher anymore, or any [other] permanent job in reunified Germany. I would not have done it, period. Somehow you give up on yourself in reunified Germany when you have children."

The instant and steep decline in the birthrate is an indicator of the profundity of social change East German women have experienced. It also symbolizes the space where women could assert control. In the GDR, it was the norm to have children. Ninety percent of all women had at least one child.[15] The state provided a job as well as child care. Unlike in reunified Germany, in the GDR, children and paid work did not present themselves as alternatives.

Some women, however, looked critically upon the GDR social policies that granted working mothers, and mothers in job training and studying at universities, preferential treatment. They commented that these policies were not designed to further women's emancipation, but rather to respond to a declining birthrate because East German women had chosen to have fewer children in spite of those policies. One health care worker, whose children were born in the early 1960s before these policies had been implemented, remarked:

Yes, the birthrate has dropped very much [in reunified Germany]. It was kind of an insurance in the GDR [to have a child]. When a girl became pregnant, she just had to say, "I need child care, I am single." Some took advantage of the system. Even when the father was present, many did not marry him. So they were single, and single parents had priority over married parents [when there were not enough places for infants], because it was assumed that in a married household, there was still one earner [if the other had to look after the child.] [Young mothers] could get an education and training as well. They received their diplomas even if they had to be absent often because they could get extra tutoring. Sometimes the young women would say [to us older women], "You are envious of us, because your generation did not have all these privileges when your children were small." But that is too simple.

The sentiments expressed by this interviewee reflect the dilemma that neither state socialism nor capitalism has been able to solve. The organization of work and the needs of children are fundamentally incompatible and women are expected to handle it in a harmonious way. When they claim the help they are entitled to, they are suspected of taking advantage of the system. When they drop out of the work force, they are perceived as inadequate. In the final analysis, family policies under socialism (like under capitalism) have been progressive only to the extent to which they have served to maintain the existing power relations and, therefore, the patriarchal order. In other words, the way women combine paid work and family is judged through the lenses of male experience and principles of family and paid work life.

Mothering

Few areas have been as closely scrutinized by West Germans (of both genders and every political color) as East German women's choice of mothering their children. This "debate" illustrates that:

Motherhood is not a static concept nor is it a homogenous category. . . . The word [mothering] evokes a multiplicity of meaning in [both Germanies], meanings that have evolved within a variety of scientific, legal, social, cultural, political, religious and economic perspectives. Moreover, these meanings are constantly changing, shaped by structural elements and also through the individuals and collective, conscious and unconscious work of mothers themselves. (Apple and Golden, 1997, p. xiii)

The East German women I interviewed resented West Germans for applying their standards in evaluating how East German women mothered their children. They disliked vigorously being put in a position of having to justify why they brought up their children the way they did. An educator and a mother of one son and daughter echoed the sentiments of many when she said:

[East German women] always had to manage both family and job responsibilities, and, by and large, we managed it well. But now we are accused of having neglected our children. But that is not how I see it. I can say that my son has not missed anything. We always did a lot with our children. East German women accomplished a lot. I have to say that I feel better when I contribute my share and I am not dependent on my husband.

What this and other interviewees rejected was the West German way of child rearing. Hays (1996, pp. 6–9) termed it "the ideology of intensive mothering," where the mother perceives herself (and is perceived by others) as "the central caregiver," who gives "copious amounts of time, energy, and material resources [to] the child," and subscribes to a method of child rearing that is "child-centered, expert-guided, emotionally absorbing, labor-intensive, and financially expensive."

Most East German women I interviewed saw mothering differently. A teacher, who found it difficult to find a full-time position because she was the mother of a small daughter and son, remarked, "Well, children demand a lot of your energy and time." And an agricultural technician, the mother of a three-year-old girl, explained:

I think you have to have really strong nerves to be a mother full-time. . . . The little one wants attention the entire day. I am really glad that I have half a day away from her. That is the way it is. It does not satisfy me [to spend the entire day with my daughter]. I would be much more impatient [if I had to be with her] the entire day. It would not be for me, not the entire day.

Most of the East German women I spoke with felt that it was an affront to even suggest that their style of mothering was not characterized by love, but by duty and obedience to the state. In this regard the remarks by this educator, mother of a son and a daughter, were typical:

I believe that the reproaches West Germans heap on us now for bringing up our children in a socialist way are really exaggerated. The women in the GDR love their children as much as the West Germans love theirs. I still believe that the time we spent purposefully with our children was as effective as the eight hours that mothers spent with their children while doing all kinds of other things. Or, what is often done nowadays, and worse [than the socialist upbringing], is that children are allowed to sit in front of the television. I see that as a real problem.

Another educator, who also was a mother of two children, felt very strongly when she said:

I want to make one thing very clear. We worked a lot in the GDR and we did good work. Now we are being criticized [by West Germans] for the way we worked. I have heard it said very often that East German mothers are *Rabenmütter* (cruel mothers) because we have taken our children to child-care centers. But when I look back now on how our children were cared for in the GDR, and on how they are cared for [in reunified Germany], and at the opportunities they had then, and what we [as a society] do for them now, I am convinced that our children did not suffer any damage, quite to the contrary.

Now children are often left to their own devices. One can't judge [the situation in the GDR] in such a sweeping way. We are now in a totally new situation. [Many] women are at home. And many [West Germans] tell us, "Well, you can't ask for anything better. At long last, you have time for your children." But that is not at all how it is, but no one wants to talk about it.

A director of a child-care center and the mother of three grown children commented:

I find it very hurtful when I hear [from West Germans] that [East German] mothers are all *Rabenmütter*, who have given away their children [to the state]. We have nurtured our children and done many things with them. We have had time for them. And it was not always easy to bring them to child-care centers when we had to go to work. But I think that we felt secure in the knowledge that they were well taken care of. Our children were not damaged because we worked.

And a division manager, single mother of two daughters, recalled: "At a meeting between East and West German women, one West German woman said to me, 'Well, I had two children, how could I have gone to work?' And I answered, 'but we had to, and we managed alright.' Well, in her eyes I was a *Rabenmutter* (cruel mother)."

Many women readily admitted to feeling doubtful sometimes about the time they had available to nurture their children, but upon reflection, they generally felt good about how they had handled family and occupational obligations. Hans Eberhard Richter of the Sigmund Freud Institute in Gießen (West Germany) pointed out the advantages of East German women's approach to rearing children (*The Week in Germany*, January 27, 1995, p. 6): "[E]ast German families were [not] "damaged" by full-time employment for women and state-run child care facilities. Eastern German children seem to have been punished less and to have been less subject to their parents' ambitions for them than western children."[16]

Similarly, the repeated charge by many West Germans that East German parents left it to the Party to bring up their children, by subjecting them to the state-run youth institutions, like the *Pioneers* and *Freie Deutsche Jugend* (FDJ),[17] was rejected by many East German women as too sweeping and simplistic. A computer programmer and mother of two teenage boys said that: "In the former GDR, our children were in the *Pioneers* and child care. Today they sit in front of the television. What is the difference? They are bombarded with ideology [in both cases]. I did not like the former and I do not like the latter."

And an educator and mother of three grown children who had no objections to the ideological content of either the *Pioneers* or FDJ said:

We had the *Pioneers* or the FDJ. But the children were looked after. Things that happen today did not happen then. Twelve and 13-year-old children did not attack women and steal their purses. I don't think we had that much violence in the media either. I think they show so many terrible things on television. [Now] you can watch cartoons on television at seven o'clock in the morning! There is shooting and aggression. I think it is terrible! I always ask, "Where does all the aggression come from that children harbor [nowadays]?" It all goes against the grain. It was very different in the GDR. And that has nothing to do with nostalgia. [As a teacher and mother,] I simply see how different it is.

A number of women said that the charges made by West Germans are un-informed and stereotypical. Quite a few families were not comfortable with the content of what the *Pioneers* and FDJ programs had to offer, but they al-lowed their older children to participate because they did not want to subject them to the pressure of being outsiders and gave them a voice in the deci-sion-making process. One post office worker and mother of two girls said:

We talked [with friends] about whether we would let our daughter be a *Pioneer*. I mean, in the final analysis everyone had to decide for themselves. And the children can't decide [for themselves] at that age. They are only seven years old. They be-came *Pioneers* in the first grade. And in seventh or eighth grade they were asked to join the FDJ. . . . We [belonged to the church] and we said, "she can only do one thing." Our daughter was very self-assured. She was not bothered by [the fact that she was not in the *Pioneers*]. When children are very sensitive, it was more difficult [to keep them out of the *Pioneers*].

And a mother of four children who had actively opposed the state all her life through her work in the church remarked:

We decided that [our children] would not join the *Pioneers* because they were small and we disapproved of the ideological content, but we let them decide whether they wanted to be in the FDJ. By then they were about 13 or 14 years old and peers were very important to them. They decided they wanted to be part of the FDJ.

An educator, the mother of one daughter, said:

I can truly say that I was satisfied with the care and education my daughter received. Perhaps we were lucky. We had a nice kindergarten teacher. Because we were members of the church, my daughter also attended religious school, and went to music school. She had other contacts, not just in the [state] school. She also went to *Pioneer* afternoons once a month.

The preferred West German model of "intensive mothering" raises the question of whether it constitutes a more loving approach to rearing chil-dren than the East German approach. Are children better off with mothers who have internalized the "ideology of intensive mothering" and who be-lieve that only they can meet the needs of their children satisfactorily for 24 hours a day, every day, and who feel guilty when they are unable to live up to that standard? Is a society that relegates everything that has to do with rais-ing children to the private sphere, that is, to mothers, a more caring society?

East German women reject the "intensive mothering" approach that the West German system tries to impose on them, because it is symptomatic of what they dislike about the new social system: a strict division of labor, where mothering is relegated to the private sphere representing values and beliefs that are in opposition to the public sphere. In unified Germany, the public sphere emphasizes individual, competitive, and impersonal relationships, while the private sphere emphasizes collective, cooperative, and personal bonds (Hays, 1996, p. 153).

The women I interviewed were not without criticism about the state-run child-care system in the GDR, but they were generally satisfied with the care their children received. On a day-to-day basis women did not look upon child care as dealing with "the system." Instead, they evaluated the quality of care by the relationships they had built with individual caregivers and educators who looked after their children. Mostly, women felt that their children were in good hands, that the children were comfortable, safe, and well looked after while they were at work. One agricultural worker and mother of three observed that:

I was satisfied with the quality of child care in the former GDR. You can sense it today that the children are not going to preschool and kindergarten. They fall behind in comparison to those who still go because parents can't give them the intensive attention and education they got there.

And a director of a child-care center, the mother of three grown children, noted:

Child care has been totally devalued [in reunified Germany]; I have experienced that. The idea of privatizing child-care centers has not worked out. One [child-care center] after the other fell apart. [This was] partly because we had fewer and fewer children. The birthrate declined. Today [child-care centers] are only a third of what they used to be.

In capitalist Germany women are expected, once again, to work out of love and duty to their families. To ease the burden for families with young children, many grandmothers quietly and invisibly stepped in and assumed the work, unpaid, that was once provided and paid for by the state. One grandmother who chose early retirement in reunified Germany spoke for many when she said:

Today young families cannot do without the help of grandparents, precisely because employers don't care anymore. Child care is not available or is too expensive. Parents have some rights to take time off when their children are sick. But that support falls away after a certain time and, besides, [parents] always have in the back of their heads, "There are many waiting [to take my job]."

The church in reunified Germany has also fulfilled some of the needs for child care. Some women welcomed the new institutions, others objected to the religious content. For some the private alternatives were affordable, for others they were beyond their financial means. One grandmother, who was self-employed in reunified Germany, welcomed them as a positive develop-ment saying: "[My granddaughter] will be a year and a half next year. We have a wonderful child-care center nearby where she will go. It is run by the Catholic Church. That is ideal. It offers child care for toddlers and has a kin-dergarten and a school."

The policy-makers of reunified Germany speak of "parenting," but sup-port an ideology of mothering that assigns the rearing and well-being of children to *mothers*. They seem oblivious to the work that grandmothers have assumed to make up for the shortfall in child-care facilities. Pol-icy-makers brought about structural changes that have made it difficult and often impossible for East German women to combine continuous paid work and family responsibilities, that have diminished women's choices and op-portunities, and that have strengthened the traditional gendered division of labor.

Shrinking Family Time

Paradoxically, most East German women I interviewed said that they spent less time with their families in reunified Germany than they did in the GDR where they held full-time jobs (i.e., a 40–43 1/2 hour week), per-formed household chores, grew their own food, raised cattle, had fewer household amenities, stood in long lines for buying groceries and other goods, and often owned no car.

In reunified Germany, many previously employed East German women were unemployed or worked shorter hours. Many families did not grow food or raise cattle because, in the words of one agricultural worker, "It is not worth the effort anymore to raise cattle. We can't earn any money with it." Another commented that, "We grow lawns where we used to grow vege-tables and fruit because everything is available in stores now." Many had ac-quired fully automated washing machines and freezers, and some had bought dishwashers and a car. Grocery shopping was often done once a week instead of every day, and waiting in long lines was a thing of the past.

Why, then, was there a persistent perception of having less time with the families? The reasons are multiple and *complex*: More women than men seemed to absorb the larger part of the "fallout" of reunification in their families and in the wider circle of relatives, friends, and colleagues. In addition, women seemed to endure more physical and emotional *stress* while trying to survive in a competitive labor market that made clear that their labor was not needed anymore. They experienced a profound lack of social security and predictability in everyday life and worried unabatedly about their children's, their spouses', and their own futures. If they were employed, they coped with more demanding work, longer work hours, and longer commutes. In addition, husbands/partners were often gone, not only for the entire day, but for the week. By 1991, "20,000 East Germans a month [sought] work in the Western part of the country, . . . and many more commute[d] weekly to the West" (*Financial Times*, March 6, 1991, cited in Einhorn, 1993, p. 131).

It may not only have been their busy schedules that caused such a toll on women emotionally and physically and left little time for families to be together, but also the fact that women's work was not valued, invisible, unrewarded, and unarticulated in reunified Germany. A manager observed:

Despite all the responsibilities I had [in the GDR], I had more time than I have now. It is the time now that actually kills me. I cannot plan long term with a goal in mind. Everything has to be decided on the spot. And what I plan for tomorrow, I won't be able to realize because something unexpected will interfere with it.

A former agricultural worker who managed a cafeteria in reunified Germany commented:

I have to say that we experienced great changes in our family life. It has become much, much more stressful. My husband has always worked in shifts. [In the GDR] he worked an early shift one week, a late shift the next, and a night shift the following. He also worked fixed hours in each shift. But now, when he is off from [his shift] work, his colleagues call him in because something has happened. It is very stressful now. [Before reunification] we had time for each other. When I look at our situation now, I have to say that we do not have time. I work as well. And I also keep thinking, "I hope I won't lose my job." You lose credibility in the eyes of the people now when you don't have a job. That is how it is: work, work, work. Money, money, money, and families are neglected. I don't think we are better off in the reunified Germany.

And a sales assistant explained: "I have to say that in the GDR, I somehow did not have significant personal problems. I did not get up with fear and worries [as I do now]. I knew that I had work, that I had money, that my child was safely looked after."

A former division director in a state enterprise who was managing a branch of a West German bank in reunified Germany reflected:

[In the GDR] the entire social environment was very different. We felt secure, safe. It was a given, because of the roles the state and the family assumed. We simply did not have to worry like we do today. The mere thought that something could happen to me [is unbearable]. It would be a catastrophe for my daughter.

And a self-employed artist explained:

Ideally, both parents should feel responsible for their children, but the burden is now different for many women. The men, if they are employed, often have to drive long distances. And quite a few men come only home to sleep if they come home at all. Sometimes it is a weekend marriage. [In the GDR] a lot more was done to support the family. And women whose husbands are hardly at home have no choice but to accept being a housewife and mother if they have children as well.

Many women were keenly aware that those who have earning power also command more control. Because money is so highly valued in capitalist Germany, family relationships have not remained immune to its influence. With more money comes more choice on how to spend leisure time, which is not necessarily with the family anymore as was the case in the GDR. Although none of the interviewees said that they felt oppressed by this situation, they nevertheless noticed, as did this gardener, that "We don't do as many things as a family anymore," that leisure-time choices depend on financial means, and that their financial means had diminished. They reflected on what it has meant for women when they become economically dependent on one person, usually a spouse or partner, as did this self-employed artist, who had lost her full-time position in reunified Germany:

Family has become something totally different. It is often such—and I meet hundreds of people because of my work—that family members live *next* to each other, and not *with* each other anymore. Each goes her/his own way. The husband who has kept his job [now] pursues new leisure-time activities in his new team or new club. They spring up everywhere. The woman is somehow becoming a *Hausmütterchen* (the little woman at home). She has to assume this totally dissatisfying role to survive. The man has the power in the relationship. There is little doubt about that. And that has been quite a learning curve for many women. Apart from a few exceptions, all women worked during socialism. It is very difficult to handle the reality that when you want to buy some new clothes for yourself, you have to ask your husband whether you can have some of the money he has earned.

The structural difficulty for women to be gainfully employed has reinforced the gendered division of labor in the home and the workplace, and the way leisure time is spent. This division protects the status quo of gender relations within government, business, church, union, and other sectors. The (mostly male) elites of reunified Germany are aware that society and their individual lives function as smoothly as they do because (mostly) women perform annually an estimated 53 billion hours of *unpaid* labor—household chores; raising children; taking care of sick, elderly, and handicapped people; and volunteering social services. In contrast, about 43 billion hours of *paid*, nondomestic labor are performed. In 1982, the value of women's unpaid work for the Federal Republic of Germany was estimated to be worth about 1.08 billion Marks, adding up to 68 percent of the gross domestic product (GDP). Officially, however, women contribute only 2 percent to the GDP (*Bundesministerium für Frauen und Jugend* [Ministry for Women and Youth], 1994, p. 41).[18]

Interestingly, of the women I interviewed, 20 (38 percent) said spontaneously that reunification had not changed much in the way they divided up domestic (unpaid) work with their spouses/partners. One agricultural worker, who had lost her job in reunified Germany and attended a job retraining program, explained: "We have always done everything together. When I came home from work, we took care of our livestock and everything else that needed attending to, including the household. And that is still the way today."

Another agricultural worker explained: "We have always done everything together. If one wants to enjoy the weekend, one has to work together. I have never had problems in this regard. And I have been married for 18 years."

And a shepherd who also had lost her job in reunified Germany and was attending a job retraining program said: "My [partner] does as much as I do at home. That is the type of person he is. Otherwise, I would not be with him. We have equality [in our relationship]. And when I don't wash the dishes, well, then he will do it."

Five (9 percent) women felt that they had a more equitable division of domestic labor in reunified Germany, because of the household amenities that were available. However, the detailed descriptions of 27 (52 percent) women of their daily life in reunified Germany reveal a clearer gender division of domestic labor. And the extent of that division seemed to be related to women's own as well as their partners'/spouses' paid job situation. One agricultural worker, who had opted to stay home with her child who had special physical and mental needs, explained:

We have a different division of labor, that is for sure. But I have to say also that my husband believes that a woman belongs in the house. . . . that way he can concentrate on his job. And that is the way it is in our household now. I have accepted it for now, and I think that it is OK. In any case, we did not really have a choice because I am unemployed, and if I was not, I would not earn as much as he does. And that is important, too.

A sales assistant remarked: "[Now] women do the housework [again]. . . . I keep my partner's back free even though I work [outside the home] as well. I do everything now. He does not concern himself with housework at all."

And a former agricultural worker attending a job retraining program had resigned herself to the situation, which she perceived as inevitable: "Well, yes, housework! I do it, the largest part of it, anyway. That is just how it is now. I understand, too, why it is this way. [My husband] is on the road the entire day and I do the housework and the children. Well, yes, everything has changed [since reunification]."

A survey commissioned by the city of Güstrow—where the women I interviewed live—to study the situation of women found that when both partners worked outside the home, household chores were divided equitably (Falk and Hohmann, 1993). Another study found that when partners define each other's employment as "breadwinning," it influences the way they define gender boundaries and gender difference and the strategies they adopt to share family responsibilities. They tend to be nontraditional (Potuchek, 1997). In homes where women were employed full-time, men were twice as likely to participate in planning meals (*Washington Post Health*, 1998, p. 5). Spouses' resources, gender role ideology, stage in life, and employment schedules, play a significant role in the division of household chores (Presser, 1994, pp. 348–364).

When women were enrolled in retraining or continued educational programs, the division of labor in the household shifted as spouses/partners left more chores to women (Falk and Hohmann, 1993). These findings suggest that spouses/partners did not regard retraining and further education as valuable as paid work. Unemployed women took over most household and family responsibilities, usually with little choice in the matter. This suggests that when women do not have income-generating work roles, particularly if they are unemployed over an extended period, a return to traditional role relationships occurs. This new everyday reality influences how the future generations of boys and girls are socialized. They will "naturally" learn to expect a stricter gender division of labor in the home (Falk and Hohmann, 1993, pp. 63–64).

Many East German women expressed deep dissatisfaction with having few or no choices but to accept the bulk of family responsibilities in reunified Germany. This reflects, above all, the clash between two ideologies of what women's primary responsibility should be. Most East German women I spoke with held on to the model they had internalized in the GDR, where women's nondomestic work roles were highly valued and publicly recognized, and women's domestic work, although important to the functioning of the state, was assigned a lesser value. They charged Germany's democratic leaders with hypocrisy because, "They try to ban women to the kitchen to eliminate competition," while they themselves pursue power, prestige, and money. What men in reunified Germany do not understand is that East German women do not want to return to the home. They want a different, a better way to combine family and work life.[19]

CONCLUSION

The East German family became vitally important to decision-makers during the transition from socialism to capitalism because women were expected, within the family setting, to soften the impact of the transition on all other levels of society—political, economic, social, and cultural. Thus, women were assigned significant, albeit invisible and unrecognized tasks of ensuring political and economic stability. They assumed the task by maintaining stable day-to-day routines within their families and, by implication, within the larger society as well. In the process East German women realized that, contrary to their expectations, the West German system had reduced their social roles, status, and space to the home and family, thereby reinforcing more traditional gender relations, tilting the gendered balance of power decisively in favor of men again.

Although unemployment had far-reaching consequences and all families were directly or indirectly affected by it, women shouldered the larger burden. In its wake social problems, such as alcoholism and violence within families, surfaced and women were expected to deal with that, too. Thus, it was mostly women, including those in my sample, who assumed the responsibility for "cleaning up," "sorting out," and "putting things back together" to make society function again under the new conditions. The caring and emotional labor was assumed to be "naturally" theirs. For example, they dealt with their children, who were responding to the uncertainties and insecurities of the larger environment because government resources to help ease the transition for children and teenagers were cut, and child-care and youth centers were closed. At the same time, East German women's style of mothering came under attack from West German women and men.

Often East German women's choices were reduced to assuming more of the household chores and child-care responsibilities.

West German capitalism pursued the same overarching goals that East German socialism had pursued: reinforcement of the *patriarchal* organization of the German family and, consequently, the larger society as well. This guaranteed the continuity of the existing positions of power of the predominantly male elites. This, then, explains their efforts during the transition to redefine East German women's primary roles as being responsible for home and children again, and women's reactions to resist such redefinition because it increased their already *unequal rank and power positions* within the family and the larger society.

In the next chapter, I examine the material well-being of East German families in the GDR in an effort to better understand why women generally considered socialist society a *more equitable society* than capitalist society, even though material wealth in the GDR was not equally distributed.

NOTES

1. On the question of what a family is, what responsibilities it should have, and what values it should hold, see Baca Zinn and Eitzen, 1996; Cherlin, 1996; Collins and Coltrane, 1995; Eichler, 1997; Eshleman, 1997; Gillis, 1997; M. Johnson, 1997; Root Aulette, 1994; Skolnick, 1996.

2. In this regard, on May 15, 1996, the International Day of the Family, the secretary general of the United Nations, Boutros Boutros-Ghali, released the following statement:

The family, as one of the most vital social institutions, links the individual to society. It had to adapt to fast and far-reaching changes occurring around the globe. These changes impact on the material conditions of all humanity, and affect values and beliefs. Changes have occurred with regard to what support—economic, social, intellectual—families and their members expect from each other, and what family members can give to each other. (*Vereinte Nationen Informationsdienst, Internationales Zentrum Wien*, May 1996)

3. East German women value family life highly. In a representative survey conducted in March 1992 by the *Institut für Demoskopie Allensbach* [Allensbach Institute of Public Opinion Surveys] (1993, p. 55), 86 percent of East German women, in contrast to 70 percent of West German women, agreed with the statement that "one needs a family to be really happy."

When asked to rank sources of a person's happiness, East German women scored issues of family and friends consistently higher than West German women. It is noteworthy, however, that they also scored higher than West German women on issues of professional work and success. When asked "If you had to be without your family and friends often, would you be unhappy . . . ?," 79 percent of East German women, in contrast to 67 percent of West German women, said "yes" (*Institut für Demoskopie Allensbach*, 1993, p. 61). To the question "Do you think that a woman needs children to be happy," 60 percent of East German women, in contrast to 33 percent of West German women, answered "yes." Eighteen percent of East German women and 41 percent of West German women answered "no" (p. 69).

East German women also may value family relationships more highly because under state socialism, the family represented a highly regarded sanctuary where the all-pervasive state could, for the most part, be kept at bay. Within the family, the state could be safely criticized without fear of sanctions. Family relationships and close circles of friends were carefully nurtured, allowing family members and friends to freely articulate their antipolitical ideas. Thus, family and friends constituted a kind of alternative civil society. They constituted the cell where the roots for a peaceful revolution took hold. Traditional family relationships were valued highly precisely because they were officially disapproved of.

4. In recent years, kindergarten (nursery school) places were available for 70 percent of the children, but rarely did a child get in before s/he was four years old. Less than 12 percent of the children could stay in kindergarten for lunch. After-school care was provided for only 2 percent of the children between 6 and 15 years of age. And few corporations offered on-site child-care facilities or had places in public child care centers (*Bundesministerium für Frauen und Jugend* [Federal Ministry for Women and Youth], 1994, p. 81).

5. Many Western women raising children feel ambivalent about how to express what they are doing. They know that raising a family is work and that it is not only important, but necessary labor for any society, even though society does not pay women for what is generally viewed as "nonwork." At the same time, many feel guilty when they do not like those conditions because they see society as critiquing them for failing to fulfill what is supposed to be their "natural" role.

The language of the Federal Ministry for Families [Seniors, Women and Youth] reflects this ambivalence. On the one hand, the policies are intended to emphasize that raising children is *work*. On the other hand, the time and energy spent to do so is termed *parent vacation*.

6. As of January 1994, every parent is entitled to a *parenting allowance* of a maximum of DM 600 per month if the income does not exceed DM 100,000 for married parents and DM 75,000 for single parents. If it does, an adjustment is made accordingly. If another child is born during the period when parents are receiving a *parenting allowance* for the first child, they are entitled to receive the same amount for the second child. For twins or triplets, the money is doubled and tripled, respectively (*Bundesministerium für Familie, Senioren, Frauen und Jugend*, 1994a, p. 14).

7. Although only a minority of the women I interviewed spoke directly about their husbands' frustrations and feelings of being overwhelmed by the expectation to be the sole providers for their families, many hinted that they knew someone in their family or a friend, or both, who was in such a situation.

8. In Güstrow, a women's shelter opened in January 1992. It had space for 25 women and their children. By May 1992, it was filled. The shelter took in five more women and, throughout the year, the number did not fall below 30 women (Falk and Hohmann, 1993, p. 31).

9. See Prantl (1998) for further insights into feelings of powerlessness among Germans in the face of right-wing violence.

10. See Prantl (1998).

11. For approaches to how to solve problems of alienation among young people, see Ballauf (1998).

12. In September 1995, Ingrid Stahmer, member of the Social Democratic Party (SPD) and minister for Social Affairs in Berlin, announced a trend that was observed on a larger scale: "*nearly half* of the recipients on public assistance in [Berlin were] under the age of 25" (emphasis added) (*The Week in Germany*, 1995a, September 22, p. 5).

13. This response resonates with the ideas put forward by Hillary Rodham Clinton in *It Takes a Village: And Other Lessons Children Teach Us* (1996).

14. In 1949, the Federal Republic of Germany (West) had 316,000 more births than deaths. In 1965, there was a baby boom when 421,000 more births than deaths were registered. This trend was abruptly reversed in 1975, when, as a result of the availability of birth control pills, the birthrate dropped 175,000 below the death rate. Since 1972, there have been more deaths than births in the Federal Republic of Germany (*Bundesministerium für Frauen und Jugend* [Federal Ministry for Women and Youth], 1994, p. 35).

15. Seventy percent of East German women of child-bearing age had their first child before the age of 25 (the average age was 22.9 years; the average age for getting married was 23.2 years for women and 25.3 years for men). Many East German women bore their first child while still in training or studying because they knew that having a child would not influence their work (Winkler, 1990, p. 27).

16. For more on this topic, see Ehrenreich (1990, p. 82).

17. Children joined the *Pioneers* when they entered school, usually at the age of six or seven. They were encouraged to join the *Freie Deutsche Jugend* (FDJ) at the age of 13 or 14.

18. See the video, "Who's Counting? Marilyn Waring on Sex, Lies, & Global Economy" (Bullfrog Films, 1995) and Waring (1999).

19. See Gerhard (1990) for additional data on East German women's quest for equality in reunified Germany while resisting total assimilation.

6

Material Conditions under State Socialism

INTRODUCTION

In the GDR, the executive branch of the Socialist Unity Party (SED) held all the political power aimed at controlling both women's and men's lives through ownership of the economy. Policies were designed to persuade particularly mothers (not single and older women or fathers) to fulfill both their *productive* and *reproductive* duties in accordance with the Party's political and economic goals.

Through these policies, the Party leadership linked women's material well-being to their income-generating work roles, and severed the link between women's material well-being and the social status of men. As a consequence, East German women developed a strong sense of self from the secure knowledge that they had adequate (if not equal) access to economic resources, and were able to provide for themselves and their families. In my sample, all women of working age were gainfully employed and most had internalized the view that their labor was needed and valued, and that it was essential for creating a sound material base for their families and for society in general.

For most women, material well-being did *not* mean the ability to consume and accumulate material wealth. A consumer culture and private property did not exist in the GDR. Material well-being meant to be able to provide a comfortable home, to put healthy food on the table, to ensure a good education for their children and, in general, to create a happy family life. This definition of material well-being constituted the basis for East

German women's sense of equality within the family and the larger society. One educator said: "In the GDR, women were more emancipated. I felt that I was equal to men because I had my own income; I contributed half of what my family needed. I was not perceived as a lesser person."

Most women considered the social benefits provided by the state as their right. However the standard of living that East Germans created and maintained for their families did not derive from their income-generating work roles and state benefits alone. In addition to their daily occupational and family responsibilities, women applied their skills and energies to help establish an informal economy to compensate for the shortcomings of the state's planned economy.

The state, being the sole employer, provided the basic material well-being. It guaranteed employment, but kept incomes relatively low. It provided a myriad of social benefits such as affordable housing, health care, child care, and a monthly child allowance. It also subsidized food, children's clothing, energy bills, and basic consumer items. Thirty women (58 percent) in my sample said that they "felt socially secure in the GDR," had "peace of mind" in their daily lives, and "no one fell into a deep hole," because a family's basic material needs were taken care of. A health care worker explained: "The GDR was very socially minded. You could not find anybody without a home, or who was sick and could not afford [to get medical care], or families without child-care places. We paid very little rent [for our apartments]."

One agricultural worker described the financial support she could rely on as follows:

We got a monthly child allowance, clothing allowance, heating allowance. It added up to about 400 Marks per year. It varied. But we had social security. [We had] health care and hospital stay. We were eligible to go to a spa when our children were sick. That was all paid for. Parents did not have to pay anything.

Ironically, heavy state subsidies did not prevent—indeed, may have helped speed up—the decline in overall material well-being. State funds had to be shifted away from making available consumer goods and from repairing or renewing the infrastructure to supporting the state's comprehensive social programs.[1] As a result, shortages in consumer goods increased, leading East German women to improvise, compensate, and "make do" with whatever was available. They discarded nothing and preserved everything. In the words of one agricultural worker, "We learned to make something out of nothing." And a nurse said:

The good side was that we did not throw anything away. We were prudent with the things we had. Today, I feel sick when I observe the attitude of some people toward material resources, whether it is paper or anything else. We used to write on every newspaper margin because we either could not get paper, or it was very expensive. In our workshops we reused old envelopes because envelopes were so expensive.

Over time, anything beyond basic necessities that East Germans wanted or desired required ingenuity. It also required the creation and maintenance of a carefully spun net of personal connections with people who could provide access to material goods and expertise. It required being embedded in a barter system that was often more important than money. According to a drug store manager: "We saved our money because there was nothing we could spend it on [in the GDR]."

The deterioration in the GDR's overall material conditions was slowed by women's skills at improvising, by their resourceful creativity to deal with unexpected situations, and by their willingness to sacrifice. These traits carried greater weight and credibility when goods became scarce than conformity and activities that were in accordance with state rules. Asserting the Party line was not particularly effective because everyone was aware that even many Party functionaries had grown wary of them and were dependent on others to maintain or improve their material well-being. The GDR's economy was kept afloat, and the patriarchal structure remained intact, in part, because of these contested female characteristics (Kaufmann, Schröter, and Ullrich, 1997, p. 14).

The incongruities between the reality of women's daily lives and the official rhetoric slowly but steadily undermined the legitimacy and political goals of the Party leadership. Some women, like this book dealer "felt really uneasy with the way things were going," because it became obvious that the Party leadership "would not deviate from its planned course" and "was oblivious to everyday realities." In other words, although "social security was a given in the GDR, the state could not really afford it anymore." A church worker explained: "The state paid for everything. [But] these are also the reasons why this state collapsed. The state was a barrel without a bottom. Where can you take it from without stealing from anyone? No one wanted to look at that [reality] until it was too late."

A bookkeeper reflected:

I have to say that I liked the GDR system better than [the system of West Germany], with the exception of how we handled the entire area of social benefits. That was without equal. [Those entitlements] most likely were not necessary. I think it would have been good for young people to work for the things they got for nothing. The GDR gave them loans when they got married. And when they had three children, they did not have to pay a penny back. And that was not exactly a small amount of money they received.

A secretary described why she regarded the GDR's economic system as untenable:

Bread was heavily subsidized by the state. A loaf of bread cost only 50 *pfennig*. Many East Germans believed that it was wrong and that the price of bread should have been increased because people bought it to feed to their pigs. At the other end [of the price scale], we had to pay 7,000 Marks for a color television.

An educator responded in a similar vein: "We can't subsidize and subsidize. That is why the system collapsed in the end. We did not recover the cost of the things we sold."

Throughout the 1980s, the state of the economy became increasingly difficult to ignore. Discussions took place in private, but in public the seriousness of the economic conditions continued to be denied and, thus, were not fully comprehended by many people as expressed by one bookkeeper:

I don't think most of us understood the real state of our economy. I received my monthly paycheck, so did my husband. It somehow all worked. We were happy when everything bloomed and grew and we had a good harvest. Our lives revolved around that. We lacked insight into the real state of the economy. I think we really did not understand it.

Increasing incongruities gradually undermined the legitimacy of the socialist leadership, and eventually the system they had created and sustained—at all cost—faced its demise.

Income from Paid Work

For most East German women, material well-being was determined by their monthly paychecks, and although women's paychecks generally did not determine the household income, they were vital in securing a comfortable life style for their families (Winkler, 1990, p. 117). The monthly income of the women in my sample ranged from less than 400 Marks to 2,999 Marks, with the majority clustering in the lower range, between 400 Marks and 1,299 Marks.[2] The women's relatively high levels of education and training—19 women (37 percent) had between 13 and 18 years of education and training[3]—had not translated into higher salaries. This indicates that a gender-segregated labor market persisted under state socialism, resulting in a gender gap in earnings.

The increase of women's participation in the GDR labor force was not identical to their increase in earning power: Of East Germans earning 1,700 Marks or more (the highest category of monthly earnings in the state statistics), 15.7 percent were women and 84.3 percent were men. Of East Germans earning 400–500 Marks (the lowest category of monthly earnings in the statistics), 63.1 percent were women and 36.9 percent were men. These differences in earnings, despite high levels of education and professional training,[4] can be demonstrated to have existed, with some variation, in all areas of the GDR labor market (State Central Administration for Statistics; cited in Winkler, 1990, pp. 88–89).

Although a gender gap in earnings clearly existed, the state generally kept salaries low for a majority of both women and men. Families needed at least two incomes to make ends meet. This gave the state the intended structural advantage of maintaining greater control as all workplaces were provided by the state. This gardener explained: "During GDR times, the salaries were very low and were regulated by the state in such a way that both [partners] had to work to make ends meet. And it worked, more or less."

A teacher remarked: "We could not afford to stay home with our children because if we had done so, we would have foregone almost everything. The money that men earned was just about enough to buy groceries and the bare minimum you needed to survive."

And a book dealer who had retired in 1988 said:

In the GDR, many still worked when they were officially retired. It was possible to stay on in the work force. Our pensions were very low. [By continuing to work] we had a pension plus an additional income. [And many] started only then to put away money for the later years because our salaries were not high. When I come to think about it, I made 415 Marks in 1973. And that was considered good money. But it really is not that much. Today you just laugh about [that amount].

By pursuing such a wage policy, the GDR government not only maintained tight control over individuals and their level of material well-being, but also succeeded, to a certain degree, in accomplishing two of its goals: It equalized people's standard of living and it reduced, but did not eliminate, the gender gap between the majority of women's and men's earnings. Because the state kept monthly incomes relatively low for the majority of East German workers, the women I interviewed generally perceived themselves to be as well off as the next woman *or* man, as exemplified by this division director:

The social cohesion was there. No one was envious of the other. . . . We all earned about the same money. [In capitalist Germany] you are forbidden to tell anyone how much you earn. You even have to sign that you will not talk about it [at your place of work]! That is something that did not exist in the GDR.

Most women I interviewed did not regard the gender gap in earnings as significant because, generally, East German women and men relied on each other to contribute financially to the material well-being of their households. Neither was able to do as well without the other. In the GDR, women compared themselves materially neither to East German men nor to West Germans, but predominantly to other Eastern European countries, as expressed by this teacher: "Our eyes were turned toward the East." Compared to other East European countries, most perceived themselves to be living a comfortable life.

State Housing Policies and Material Well-Being

Because the state controlled not only income, but also access to, and prices for housing, food, clothing, health care, child care, elder care, and all kinds of consumer items, the basic cost of living was covered by the wages people earned. But the state fell increasingly short of providing access to consumer goods and services, and those it did provide declined in quality.

Housing, for example, was cheap in the GDR, but difficult to obtain because the state was the sole, and inefficient, provider.[5] To find adequate housing was a major issue for most women I interviewed.[6] It was especially difficult for young couples, separated, divorced, and single people, because housing policies were designed to give priorities to families with children, thereby providing incentives to young couples to start a family early, and to stay together. According to a post office worker:

It was very, very difficult to find an apartment in the GDR. There simply was no housing available. And we could only apply for an apartment when we were married. And then it was normal to wait for five to 10 years to get it. And when we finally got an apartment, it was inadequate because in the meantime we had children.

Indeed, it was common for young couples to live with their parents for a considerable length of time and then accept whatever housing became available. Many interviewees shared the experiences of this nurse:

My husband and I lived with my parents in a two-room apartment. My father worked shifts, my husband worked shifts, and I as a nurse worked shifts. My mother was surrounded by sleeping people. . . . We did not want to live with my parents for a long time because of the tensions that inevitably arose, but there was little and no choice, really.

Also, because more women than men asked for their marriages to be dissolved, more women had to cope with the burdens caused by the housing shortages.[7] Often, couples, like this nurse and her husband, continued to live together even after they were divorced because housing was not available, so "I moved with my children to the upstairs rooms. I can't tell you how difficult it was."

For single women, it was equally difficult to find housing, as illustrated by this agricultural worker:

[It was difficult to get an apartment] because I was single. I have to say it honestly, I got very upset about it. In the beginning, [the housing authorities] did not come straight out with it. They accepted my application and they said, "Well, that can take three to four years. The housing situation is not too good." [The state] built [apartment] buildings, but they built next to nothing for single people. They built two-, three-, four-room apartments for families.

And when housing was allocated to single women, it was of poor quality, as described by this gardener:

I had one room in a bungalow that belonged to the garden production cooperative. It was a terrible hole. The walls had such big gaps that I could put my hands through. The windows did not close tight. The entire building was sagging. When I stood straight up in my room, I could touch the ceiling with my palm without standing on my toes. I hasten to add, though, that I paid only 10 Marks rent per month. I did not pay for electricity, water, or anything else. I only paid for the bed I slept in.

Available housing rarely met the needs of the tenant/s, because it was inadequate both in size and amenities. Although amenities improved somewhat over the years, private bathrooms, showers, central heating, warm water, and telephone outlets could not be taken for granted in GDR apartments, inevitably increasing the work load for many women (Winkler, 1990, pp. 125–126).[8] And while the older generation of East Germans, generally, had lower expectations of quality housing, younger people voiced dissatisfaction more often with the government's design of living space, the bureaucratic and financial obstacles that were put in their way when they wanted to remodel old apartments, and the inadequate consideration that was given to the needs of individual family members with regard to quantity and quality of private space (pp. 126–127).[9]

Many took it in stride and made do with what they felt they could not change. A teacher remembered:

We lived in the school for the hearing impaired [where I worked]. It is a huge structure. It had classrooms, group rooms, social rooms, a cafeteria, and apartments for teachers, which consisted of two rooms with shower. When my daughter was born, we got one more room. . . . We lived from 1965 to 1978 in the school because we could not get an apartment. My daughter practically grew up in the school.

And a post office worker recalled: "[In the apartment block where we lived], we had two rooms for a family of four, and no private toilet. We had to go down one floor and share one toilet with two other families. We moved when my child was already seventeen [years old]."

Because the state was unable to meet the demand for housing, people decided to build their own houses, which the government quietly tolerated. But construction of private housing did not officially exist under socialism, and consequently, the necessary infrastructure and process for such an undertaking also did not exist. Thus, building a house was financed mostly by private savings and sometimes government loans. It was next to impossible to get high-quality building materials. It was possible only if one was part of an extensive network of people who could obtain what was needed and who had the expertise to build a house. Such an enterprise required the active support and skills of all family members, a circle of friends, and colleagues who were willing to provide their free time. A teacher describes what was typically involved:

In the GDR, we had money because there was not much we could spend it on. So we saved it. In any case, if we wanted to build a house, money did not get us what we needed. [We had to have connections because] without connections we could not get cement, chalk, or stones. Without connections, there was nothing we could have built.

And a secretary remembers how every family member was involved in obtaining building materials:

[Our family] became champions in construction. We built a garage and a *dacha*. We kept our ears and eyes open to find out where we could get construction materials. We used to cut these stones that were made of a concrete mixture. They used to come in huge blocks. They were never cut to size. They were this length and that length. They really were pieces of scrap. Still, we used them.

Building their own houses was often the only way for young couples to leave their parents' apartments and get space that met their needs. Initiative, organizational skills, pure determination, and a willingness to live for years under trying circumstances were crucial in undertaking such an enterprise, as exemplified by this nurse:

[It was impossible to get an apartment when we got married], so we began to build our own house. First we built a kitchen, a huge kitchen with a family room. Then we built the bathroom. We put new windows in and new stoves, too, so we could heat the house. Upstairs we built rooms and a small kitchen for my mother-in-law. It took us almost 10 years to build the house. . . . We did not take out any loans. We built when we had the money. And because I did not work [outside the house], money was always tight because my husband earned between 600–700 Marks a month.

A teacher recalled her doubts to take on the responsibilities that came with building their own house:

[Seen from today's vantage point] building a house was cheap during GDR times. . . . But at that time, it was expensive [considering how cheap rent was]. We obtained a [government] loan that cost us 50 Marks a month. Our employer [the state] gave us 10,000 Marks. . . . Still, I always resisted the idea of building a house. I thought, "Oh God, you have to take care of all the workers!" That was not easy [because of all the shortages]. It was expected that I prepare breakfast for them in the morning, make lunch, and prepare supper in the evening. Today one does not do that anymore. . . . Well, the people who built the house were usually friends and acquaintances. [Often] they would come after work [and on weekends]. That is how we built houses, on our own initiative and time.

To own a house was a purely utilitarian matter in the GDR. It was not an investment or status symbol because in the planned economy, the capitalist concept of private property and a corresponding real estate market did not exist. Hence, with regard to material wealth, for example, ownership of property, women perceived themselves as equal to men because, in accordance with the dominant ideology, everything belonged to the people, that is, the state. According to one health care worker:

It had no meaning in the GDR to think in materially [competitive] terms. . . . Today people ask, "How many square feet does your apartment have?" "Do you own a house?" These are now standard questions. [In the GDR] no one would have asked such a question, no one. What we wanted was a four-room apartment when we had two children. . . . and central heating, because most apartments still had a stove with which to heat them. Central heating was an incredible thing [to have].

East Germans who built or bought a house did not own the land their house was built on. In a sense, they did not own the house, either. They often had little or no control over who would occupy the house besides themselves. The state housing authority had the final say in how much space was allocated per family, as the experiences of this post office worker illustrate:

[We looked for an apartment for a long time]. Then we were somehow offered this house and we bought it because we could not get an apartment. [We did not want a house], we wanted an apartment. [But we did not live alone] in our house. We only had two rooms and a kitchen. By then we had our daughter, too. . . . When one of the women who rented part of the house died, we had to fight to get her space. In principle, we owned the house, but the town of Güstrow decided who got how much space. We could not say we wanted to use the space in our house for ourselves. We had to fight to get two more rooms.

A woman, an official from the town government, came over to check how much space we had. We did not have a bedroom. . . . [In one room] we had a foldup bed and a crib [for our daughter]. The other room was both kitchen and living room. Well, and because the woman [from the town government] seemed to be having one of her good days, she let us have the other two rooms. We had to fight to get more space in our own house! In the GDR five families lived in this house. And three families used one toilet.

But that is how it was. The people from the state could do what they wanted. For instance, once a woman wanted to rent an apartment in our house. We preferred for her not to move in, but she moved in anyway because the state had given her permission. There was nothing we could do about it. We wanted the space to build a [private] bathroom and a room for our older daughter, and a bigger bedroom for ourselves [but there was nothing we could do].

The housing availability in the GDR remained insufficient throughout the socialist era, and existing housing fell into disrepair over time because the state did not raise sufficient funds to keep it in good condition.[10] The deterioration of apartment buildings was further accelerated by the lack of central heating systems. Apartments were often heated with brown coal because it was cheap and plentiful. But it burned fast and caused severe pollution. With no, or minimal, standards for protecting the environment, chimneys spewed out dark smoke. Over the years the soot attached itself in thick layers to the inside and outside walls of buildings thereby hastening their decay. Many building facades started crumbling, giving entire city blocks a dark appearance and affecting not only people's standard of living but their health as well.

The state's decision to subsidize rents and utilities instead of increasing them to generate resources for maintenance and improving existing housing, led to a decline in both the quality and the quantity of housing. This further increased the overall dissatisfaction with the state's performance, because tenants considered the maintenance and improvement of state housing the responsibility of the state.

The deteriorating condition of state housing stood in a curious and stark contrast to the privately built *dachas* (small weekend houses). Many East German women agreed with this nurse who had built, equipped, and enjoyed caring for her garden *dacha*: "During GDR times a *dacha* was the most wonderful thing you could have. We could not afford to travel, but we enjoyed our *dacha*."

These *dachas* were often located at the outskirts of the city, not far from the apartment buildings in which most women and their families lived. Together they cultivated their gardens and spent summer evenings and weekends in their garden *dachas*. In contrast to state housing, they regarded the gardens and *dachas* as personal achievements and possessions even though in reality, the state owned that land as well. The garden *dachas* provided private spaces for enjoying activities with family and friends. They kept the state at bay and provided many families with the space to generate extra goods and/or income.

EVERYBODY NEEDED EVERYBODY ELSE TO IMPROVE THE QUALITY OF LIFE

Most women I interviewed had become astute and prudent navigators of a system that tightly controlled access to material goods. Income and family size determined how much money was spent on necessities such as shelter, food, and clothes; how much was left to spend on "luxury" items; and how much needed to be generated in the informal economy. Almost all women in my sample persistently worked at equipping their households with "luxury" items to ease their work load at home, despite exorbitant prices and long waiting periods for such goods. Purchasing "luxury" products such as refrigerators, freezers, washing machines, and cars, required constant vigilance, perseverance, the help of family members and friends, and plenty of time and energy.

One child-care worker described what transpired when such products became available:

[This is what it was like] to buy a freezer. Everyone knew when freezers came in. Half of the work force left. That is really true. [We were standing in line] across the marketplace and around the church. We went to work at seven in the morning and said, "I have to take time off, . . . and I don't know when I'll be back. I want to buy a freezer." I stood in line in January [to sign up for one]. In September, it was finally delivered. We bought it without ever having seen [a model] beforehand. When we signed up for one, the [salesperson] would roll a dice to decide whether we would get a big or a little one. We bought *everything* without ever seeing it beforehand.

A salesclerk recalled:

We bought this television set in 1988. We had to wait seven and a half months for it. And every week we went to the store twice to check whether we had moved up on the list. We were supposed to get it for Christmas, but that did not work out. Then we were told, "When the next delivery comes in, you will get it." But I still did not get it. And I kept on checking. And one day, when another delivery was made, I was told, "Come in tonight." We paid 4,900 [East German] Marks for this little television. Today it costs less than 500 West German Marks.

And an agricultural worker recalled:

In 1980, my parents bought a *Trabi* [the infamous GDR car]. It cost 12,000 [East German] Marks. There was a waiting period. No one really knew how long it would take. For a *Trabi* one had to wait about 10 years. By the time it was delivered, you had saved up enough because we earned a good salary. And our expectations were not as high as they are today.

Essential consumer items were bought whenever they became available, whether they were needed or not. When women had no use for the available goods, they circulated them in the network of family, friends, and colleagues. There was always someone who needed a particular item. Maintaining and/or improving one's material well-being could only be achieved with—never against—one another as explained by this white-collar worker:

When we saw a line, we would just join and ask, "What do they sell here?" And usually [the person ahead of you] would say, "Don't know." And when you went with your husband or your grown children, you would say, "Get in line behind me." Because each person could only buy two bed sheets [for example, and when there were two of you, you could get four sheets]. And you could buy only three undershirts in one size. My husband needed size six and my son size four. So [when two of us lined up], we could get three in size six and three in size four. And we would tell the others [that undershirts were being sold]. And if you got a size that did not fit [any one in your family], you would buy it anyway and exchange it with someone else who needed that size. Because of that, we had a large circle of friends and acquaintances. Everybody needed everybody else. That is how we used to support each other.

There was true solidarity in the GDR. For example, when I went shopping and I saw cucumbers, which were difficult to find, I would think, "Well, if I can get two or three, I will bring one for Mrs. M. and one for Mrs. S.; that will please them. And others would think of me in the same way.

If a consumer item or service was unavailable, East German women produced it themselves, as described by this textile worker: "We had to improvise [in the GDR]. I used to make trousers and dresses myself." And, "We used to do our own hair for years. It began among colleagues. We would do our own perm, 'home perms,' we called them. We did it for each other, and we did it for years." East German women bartered their goods and skills in extended networks. Some women sewed, others knitted, yet others produced what was needed from whatever they could lay their hands on. One nurse recalled:

When we used to get second-hand clothes from West German relatives, we took each piece apart, altered it, and sewed it back together again. We used to unravel old woolen pullovers, and knit them anew. What West Germans discarded, we would reuse. And when we could not use it ourselves, we would exchange it with someone who could use it.

Within the network, women and their families pooled a host of abilities and goods to improve material conditions: They preserved fruits and vegetables from their gardens, raised livestock on their private farms and sold them to the state or to private customers, designed and built homes, wallpapered and painted apartments, and offered their engineering and architectural skills and designs.

These activities (performed in addition to paid and family work) have remained utterly invisible, particularly to the eyes of many Westerners who stereotypically perceived East Germans as having passively relied on the state to provide for them. Many women stepped in where the state fell short, created opportunities and took matters in their own hands. They relied on their own initiative and energy, on the support of husbands/partners, family friends, and other members of the wider network that was nurtured over years. Embedded in the larger community, confident about their abilities, with an astute perception of what was possible within the constraints of the existing conditions, and determined to improve their material well being, women took on the extra responsibilities with an entrepreneurial spirit and results. One nurse recalled:

I tried to increase the money for our household. We had a huge field, so I learned how to plow it with [the help of] a horse. . . . And because I knew very little about how to plant anything, I got a book and followed the instructions very precisely. . . . We also had pigs and rabbits because I was partial to rabbits. I started breeding them. And we had geese, chickens, and ducks.

I grew a lot of vegetables. And because the politicians realized that the state could not produce enough for the stores, they turned to private growers. There were places where state [officials] would come and buy [from the private growers] fresh vegetables, fruits, eggs, and rabbits, so people who lived in towns would get fresh produce. We took that chance to earn some money.

So I worked this very heavy clay soil and grew a lot of vegetables: lettuce, beans, and also apples. [All that] I sorted by size. That and the rabbits helped a great deal to provide for our household.

A child-care worker, reflecting on how she tried to improve her family's material well-being, said proudly:

Our garden was beautiful. And many people came to buy fruit. We grew fresh fruit and vegetables that were quite rare during GDR times; except for . . . carrots, cabbage and apples, there was little else you could buy. Plums were already considered a delicacy. And when you wanted grapes and peaches, you had to stand in line. And bananas! Well, we used to say that bananas are bent because they had to get around the GDR. We had all sorts of jokes to cope with the situation.

A teacher recalled the fruits and vegetables her family grew and preserved because they were not available in state-run stores:

In our garden we had strawberries, vegetables, and fruit trees. We grew onions and everything we thought we might need. . . . We tried to grow asparagus as well. It was a rarity. We hardly had any lawn. And we preserved everything. I mostly did it at night. When I came home, my husband had brought from the garden whatever was ripe and it had to be taken care of straight away. Because I had connections, I eventually got a freezer. I froze everything, [which was easier] than preserving it in jars. I used to cook a lot of jam.

A salesclerk reflected on her daily schedule as follows:

Somehow I managed to have a garden as well. I used to make butter, nothing much, but we had to have some. We had fresh carrots and strawberries. I used to preserve fruit and vegetables in the evening. I did a lot at night. When should I have done it otherwise? On the weekends I wanted to be with my children.

Through their private initiatives and entrepreneurship, East German women (and men) exposed the inherent weaknesses in the rigid economic and political structures of the GDR state. Because private initiatives could not exist in a socialist system, the Party leadership pretended that they did not exist. They tolerated them because they needed them. Private initiatives served the interests of the (mostly male) elites by covering up, to some extent, the state's ineffectiveness and inefficiencies. The Party leadership tolerated tacitly that East Germans built their own houses and developed an informal economy, because it allowed them, for a while, to keep up the appearance of legitimacy inside the country, but most important, to the outside world. This legitimacy was achieved to a considerable extent on the backs of East German women, who bore the "extra load" to maintain and improve the material conditions of their families, and by implication, the material conditions of the country.

THE PERSISTENCE OF CLASS IN THE GDR

Although there was a perception among the women I interviewed that wealth was, generally, more equally distributed in the GDR than it is in reunified Germany, there was also an awareness that the class system had not been abolished under state socialism, as demonstrated by this agricultural worker:

I am sure we had [at least] three [different social] groups [in the GDR]. There was the lower class, the upper class, and the middle class. That is how I divided them up for myself [because officially we only had a workers' class]. Those who were at the bottom [of the social] ladder [in the GDR] are at the bottom of the ladder in reunified Germany. I come from a family like that. I grew up [at the bottom], and it was very difficult to climb up even when you wanted to [but officially no one acknowledged that]. I always did everything by myself, [in contrast] to my friend, whose parents had only two children [and helped them out a lot]. Both parents worked [all their lives] in good positions and today they have a good pension.

One clear manifestation of a class system was the existence of a two-tier shopping structure: the state stores and *Intershops*. Everyone had access to state stores, but only a selected few had access to *Intershops*. The state stores provided staple foods that were subsidized, accessible, cheap, almost always available, but rarely of the best quality as explained by a biologist:

Bread was always very, very cheap, but the quality was not that good. Everyone said that bread should have been priced higher. But the real issue was to show that our system was different from capitalist systems. The state leadership wanted to be sure to document that things were better here, and the price of bread was a tabu subject.

And a teacher said:

Bread was very cheap. The staple foods were cheap. But all other things were very expensive. For the expensive items we had *Delikatläden* (delicatessen) and the *Exquisit* (gourmet) shops. Only the upper classes could go there to shop. But rent was very cheap, electricity was cheap, and water was cheap. Everyone had an apartment and everyone had food to eat. Those things the state could afford, but everything beyond that was considered luxury and available only to a few privileged Party functionaries and foreigners.

The Party controlled and granted access to special material resources for select groups of East Germans. To gain entry to *Intershops* required Party loyalty, that is, active work on behalf of the Party, and/or Western currency. The latter could also be obtained from West German relatives who would come and visit or send money.

According to one self-employed woman:

Some East Germans had access to *Intershops* because they had West German relatives who sent West German Marks to them. Also, those in high Party positions had access, because it was primarily for those who worked on behalf of the Party that these shops existed. Right here you can see the double standard. [I had access when I had West German Marks, even though I opposed the system.] Our state wanted this money. It was foreign currency. That is how Margot Honecker (wife of the Party secretary) [could afford] to fly to Paris to see her hairdresser. That was money with which the powerful elites speculated. It was important to them. Had we looked closely at this, we would have had to realize that the GDR was for sale. I think that even if we had not gone into the streets [to force an end to the socialist system], it would have collapsed anyway because we lived far beyond our means.

A teacher described how she was unexpectedly and starkly confronted with the divisions the leadership had created between people while taking her class on a field trip:

We had *Intershops* in the GDR. There we could buy Western goods with Western money. I remember passing an *Intershop* with one of my classes [during a field trip]. I am not quite sure how it happened, perhaps one of my colleagues went in. In any case, all the children followed. There they stood and took a very deep breath. Oh, it smelled so beautiful! I am sure, you [from the West] never notice it, [but] the soaps, the washing powder, the cosmetics, they all smelled so pleasantly. When we went into a GDR drugstore, there were none of these fragrant smells. The children got their money out and wanted to buy something. They were so excited. Then I noticed how many had never seen an *Intershop*, and we had to tell them, "You cannot shop in this store with the money you have. You need to have different money for that."

Some women adhered to their personal principles, choosing consciously to forego access to material privileges. Under no circumstances were they prepared to work actively on behalf of the Socialist Unity Party. Others forewent material privileges because they had relatives in West Germany, and working actively for the Party would have obligated them to sever all ties with their West German relatives. Others were members of a church, and would have had to denounce their church activities, in which case, their children could not have been baptized, take communion, or be confirmed. They chose their church over material privileges and consciously emphasized the creation of what they called "nonmaterial wealth" for their families and the community they lived in. They deliberately chose to live in opposition to the system. They felt rich in a spiritual sense and had consciously decided that they could live without material privileges. A church worker remarked:

[Our family] did not experience the daily pressure [as much as many others did]. Because of our faith we lived in great freedom. I really believe we experienced life differently from many [other East Germans]. For example, people used to let themselves be put under pressure because no bananas were available. Well, my attitude was, "I do not need bananas." Of course, we had many contacts within the GDR and beyond its borders. As Christian [leaders in our church] we always received visitors. These visits were purposeful, done with great awareness. Our visitors used to say, "If they don't let you get out, then we will come and visit you." You have no idea how important that was [for us].

Others, however, had chosen active memberships in the Party because they believed in the socialist principles and later felt they had earned the material privileges it brought them. No matter what views they held, most women thought that special expertise and knowledge, not Party loyalty, should have led to influential positions and material advantages because it would have served their country better in the long run. Some people had pledged loyalty to the Party because they were convinced about Party principles and goals, but most had joined because they were opportunists. One teacher noted:

Party bosses did not have to know a lot. To get a good position, it was enough to be a loyal Party member. That is what counted. . . . For example, when a teacher in our school was mainly working for the Party, he was guaranteed a good salary. Teachers who were very knowledgeable in their fields and who had a sound educational background and were good teachers, their work was not [regarded] as important. . . . That is how it was during GDR times. Those who articulated the Party line got paid well and could soon afford to buy a car [or other luxury items].

And a nurse explained:

My brother was a roofer and put a roof on a *dacha* for a [well-known] journalist who used to announce the political information on state television. My brother told me, "You would not believe what kind of *dacha* he has. And that is not his only one. He has several like that. He has a swimming pool in his garden." Those were the rewards [the Party leadership] kept us deliberately in the dark about. We were never able to see how privileged some Party members really were. And when someone told us, it was difficult to believe.

For a number of women, material advantages, and thus a privileged status, came in the form of care packages and/or Deutsche Marks sent by their West German relatives. These families had carefully nurtured fragile family connections over two generations and often under difficult circumstances.[11] West German care packages and currency provided these East German families with goods that were unobtainable for most other East Germans. One educator's description was typical for those who felt enriched by the support they received from West German relatives:

It always was a great celebration when we received these incredible parcels from West Germany. The clothes were second-hand, and sometimes a piece of soap and chocolate was included. We would all gather around the parcel in great expectation.

Once a year the aunt of my husband, *Tante Bärbchen*, would send a "West parcel" to us. And it smelled wonderful! I am still waiting to experience that smell again, but I never have [since Germany was reunified]. I think that smell is always present now, but we can't perceive it anymore. But at that time our apartment was full of this incredible fragrance. And the happiness it brought! It is difficult to describe. It was much deeper than it is now when we give each other presents. [It was amazing] to see things we had never seen before, things that really surprised us. Today we know these are perfectly normal things. But for us they were not normal at the time.

There was always a can of mushrooms in the parcel, not of the best quality, really. Still, we would save it until Easter and then eat them with the greatest pleasure. And we imagined that these mushrooms really tasted like mushrooms. But today we know that they are not all that tasty and that freshly grown mushrooms taste much better.

For us everything [that we received from the West] was a treasure. And the chocolate tasted very different. And the fragrance of the soap! Our aunt always sent a certain brand. And this brand still captures me today. I buy it because of what it invokes. But I know that there are many other fragrances today. But with this brand, I unlodge something in my memory. And somehow I regret that we can not experience the happiness we did then [when a parcel arrived].

146

Regardless of what beliefs they held vis-à-vis the Party, and what their access was to material goods, all women in my sample were embedded in, and relied on, an extended network of people to maintain and/or improve their material conditions. These networks were as varied as the women I interviewed. Networks were also linked across the ideological divide. For example, loyal Party members had to build relationships with private growers, some of whom opposed the system, because the loyal Party members needed the goods that private growers produced, to make up for the failures in the state plan.

CONCLUSION

By socializing private property, creating a planned economy, and implementing social policies, the leadership of the GDR severed the link between women's material well-being and men's traditional breadwinner roles, and linked it to women's income-generating work roles. In addition, the state created an income structure that reduced (but did not abolish) income differences between the majority of East German women and men. This made two incomes essential for securing the material well-being of a family while, at the same time, giving the state greater control over the lives of individual women and men in the workplace. Because paid work was essential, and gave women a large measure of independence from their spouses/partners, women felt that their material contributions were valued both publicly and within the family. As a result, they perceived that a socialist society was more equitable than a capitalist society, even though gender-segregated job sectors and a gender gap in earnings continued to persist, albeit to a far lesser degree than in reunified Germany.

The perception of the GDR as a more equitable society was reinforced further when the shortcomings of the planned economy opened up social spaces for individual action. Many women experienced themselves as able improvisers and as capable as the men they lived and worked with. It was the norm for East German women to work in the planned and informal economies. Many were well aware that the state depended on, and benefited from, their labor, knowledge, and skills, and that private initiatives were tolerated mainly because the GDR elites could not have survived without them.

There was a deep mistrust of the Party leadership, whom women blamed for distributing material privileges to those who were willing to support an elite that was ineffective, inefficient, and corrupt, thereby reinforcing old class structures in the form of Party hierarchies that protected existing privileges and power positions. The Party leadership rewarded their own at the expense of those who had refused to join the Party and, as a result, the Party leadership lost its legitimacy among large segments of the population.

In the next chapter, I provide insights into the conditions surrounding East German women's material conditions in reunified Germany. I examine how these conditions changed when the planned and informal economies collapsed and West Germany's market economy was established, state property was privatized, and a Western consumer society was introduced in the former GDR.

NOTES

1. This must also be seen in the context of increasing military expenditure, typical of the Cold War era. As a country located ideologically and geographically at the epicenter of that conflict, the GDR was a major military spender by the beginning of the 1970s. Whereas in 1965, the GDR spent 3,100 million Marks, in 1975, military expenditure had increased to 9,564 million Marks (SIPRI, 1976, pp. 152–153). By 1985, the GDR's military spending had reached 13,041 million Marks, and by 1988, a year before the collapse of socialism, 15,654 million Marks (SIPRI, 1991, p. 165).

2.

Monthly GDR Income of the Women in My Sample

East German Marks	# of Women*	Percent
less than 400	7	13.7
400–899	21	41.2
900–1,299	14	27.5
1,300–1,599	4	7.8
1,600–1,999	2	3.9
2,000–2,999	3	5.9
Total	51	100.0

*Fifty-one women responded to this question. Thus, the sample size was reduced by one.

3.

The GDR Educational Level of the Women in My Sample

Years of Education	# of Women*	Percent
0–7	7	13.7
8–10	7	13.7
11–12	18	35.3
13–14	5	9.8
15–18	14	27.5
Total	51	100.0

*Fifty-one women responded to this question. Thus, the sample size was reduced by one.

4. In 1989, East German women made up 48.6 percent of university students and 70.3 percent of students at *Fachhochschulen* [technical universities, which includes medical and engineering schools] (Winkler, 1990, pp. 42–43).

5. Irmtraud Morgner, one of East Germany's best known authors, and recipient of the prestigious *Kasseler Literaturpreis* for grotesque humor, immortalized the creativity of East Germans in dealing with the chronic shortages and inadequacies of housing. One of her characters

Herta Kowalczik, the circus artist, nicknamed "hero," enters the communist housing administration. For years she has been on the waiting list for a two-room apartment. "And where are the papers for your husband?," asked the state official. "Missing." "Since when are you divorced?" "Never was married." "Never been married? So you are living together?" "No, we don't. At least not in one apartment. With one man in the same apartment, never!" "And then you dare to apply for an apartment for two people?" "Yes, for the woman in me and for the man in me" (Morgener, 1998, cited in Michaelis, 1998, p. 63).

6. Adequate housing is also a problem for many people in West European countries. In Stockholm, Sweden, for example, the housing agency reported that they had received nearly 67,000 applications for apartments in 1998, but had less than 5,100 available apartments. This means that an applicant waits for about 16 years to get an apartment (Heintz, 1999, p. K8).

7. For divorce statistics, see note 3 in chapter 4.

8. Official statistics of state housing reveal that although amenities improved over the years, they remained inadequate.

Amenities in State Housing

Amenity	1971	1981	1985	1989
Bath/Shower	39%	68%	74%	82%
Inside toilet	39%	60%	68%	76%
Telephone*	6.6%	11.7%	14.1%	17.2%

*Main connections in apartments per 100 households (1970, 1980).
Source: Winkler, 1990, p. 126.

9.

Satisfaction with Housing Conditions
Question: How Satisfied Were You with Your Apartment?

Age Group	Very Satisfied	Somewhat Satisfied	Very Dissatisfied
18–25	37.7%	15.9%	29.4%
25–35	42.2%	23.9%	33.1%
35–45	59.0%	15.5%	15.5%
45–60	78.4%	14.0%	7.6%
60 and over	82.8%	12.8%	3.9%

Source: Winkler, 1990, p. 125.

10. The historian Felix Mühlberg (1998) analyzed *Eingaben* (inputs), which were petitions sent to Communist Party offices, politicians, and local bureaucracies. In these petitions East Germans complained about what did not work in the GDR. By far the largest number of complaints concerned housing conditions. In 1983 about 52,800 *Eingaben* were sent to the government council in Berlin; in 1989 the number had increased to 134,000 (cited in Janert, 1998, p. 85).

11. When the Berlin Wall was built in 1961, communication between East and West German relatives became extremely difficult and, as the years passed, many relationships were severed.

7

Material Conditions in Reunified Germany

INTRODUCTION

Material conditions changed irreversibly for East Germans at midnight on June 30, 1990, when German monetary and economic reunification began and East Germans changed their East German Marks for West Germany's *Deutsche Mark* (DM). Three months later (October 3, 1990), a majority of East Germans voted for political reunification, completing the formal process of integrating East with West Germany. But most East Germans were ill prepared for the social consequences that followed, which for many were "simply catastrophic": Their material conditions worsened and their opportunities were severely constrained (Jarausch, 1995, p. 238).[1]

The West German government pledged huge amounts of transfer investments, averaging DM 150 billion ($107 billion) a year, to change the East German economy from a planned to a market economy (Mitchener, 1995, p. 5). But according to Andre Brie, a member of the Party of Democratic Socialists (PDS), "most of the so-called transfer payments have gone back to the west in the form of highly profitable contracts, and very little has been invested in creating new jobs in the east" (cited in Drozdiak, 1998, p. A11).[2] Lothar Bisky, chairman of the PDS, said that, "Eastern Germany is now 80 percent owned by the west, 15 percent by foreigners and only five percent by ourselves" (cited in *The Economist*, 1999, p. 13).

By 1995, many East Germans were disenfranchised from "their land and responsibility for their livelihoods" (Mitchener, 1995, p. 5). In the process of privatization, the *Treuhandanstalt* (the government trust company) either closed East Germany's state-owned companies or sold them to the highest bidders, which were mostly West German companies (Jarausch, 1995, pp. 234–239). There was no discussion of selling or disbursing shares to the public. As a result, 58 percent of jobs in former East German companies depended on West German investors (Mitchener, 1995, p. 5).

The reorganization of East Germany's economy—from a centrally planned to a competitive market economy—had a profound impact on women's material conditions and opportunities, as underscored by the experience of this textile worker:

Güstrow's *Kleiderwerke* (clothing factory) [a major employer of women] was given to a *Wessi* (West German) by the government's trust company. The new owner had another factory in Hamburg [West Germany]. After he had received a handsome sum of government funds, he shipped all machines from the factory in Güstrow to Hamburg. Then the factory in Güstrow declared bankruptcy. This is only one example. The government trust company tried to find him afterward because he had misused the government funds. Now the case is stuck in the courts. [In the meantime] the [government] money is gone, the machines are gone, and we are left with a wreck [and many unemployed women]. West Germans know their system, they know how it works, [East Germans did not] and that is why this sort of thing has happened [in East Germany].

After reunification, unemployment increased sharply. More women than men lost their jobs.[3] The informal economy that had co-existed alongside the planned economy ceased to exist, thereby eliminating an important social space that many women had created for themselves to improve their material conditions in the GDR. The conversion of state-owned property to private property sharpened the gendered aspects of access to material resources and, thereby, enhanced the gendered aspects of social roles. It pushed many women from the economic center to the margins, from being able to provide for their own and their families' well-being to dependence on partners/spouses, state-financed job retraining programs, and often social welfare. A midwife remembered wistfully how her mother had warned the family about unrealistic expectations and perceptions of the West German economic system and how these warnings had sadly come true:

My mother was allowed to travel to West Germany when she was 65 years old. When she returned [to the East], she often said, "Children, children, . . . not everything that glitters is gold." [West Germans] live such a hectic life. And not everything is the way they portray it on television. We seem more relaxed and at peace with ourselves [in the GDR].

EAST-WEST CLASH OVER CONCEPTIONS OF GENDER EQUALITY

It was the norm for women in the GDR to be materially independent of spouses/partners, albeit dependent on state support. This had shaped their self-awareness and their relationships with men. The majority of women in my sample perceived themselves not different from men, and if not perfectly equal, then close to equal with regard to their ability to provide for themselves and their families. For them, the roots of gender inequality in reunified Germany lie in the lack of access to income-generating work roles from which they would continue to derive their sense of *self*, supporting the thesis that "[w]omen's control of economic resources, especially income, is the most important predictor of the degree of [actual and perceived] gender equality" (Blumberg, 1995, p. 1).

East German women who tried to build relationships with West German women found it difficult to identify with West German women's understanding of what constitutes gender [in]equality. East German women could not understand why West German women focused on [in]equality in interpersonal relationships. For East German women, discrimination was a structural problem, not a personal one with men (Rabe, 1998, p. 14). One nurse said:

When we were able to build our first connections with West German women, I sometimes sat there and thought, "Well, are those the kind of problems they have? Who makes the red cabbage salad for supper?" . . . (Deep sigh). And I was thinking of my job. And when I tried to talk about it, it hardly received any notice. They wanted to let us know all about the difficulties in their [interpersonal relationships] and they thought that it was all so impressive and terribly important. But when I tried to talk about the difficulties about earning my own living, all I got was, "Ah yes, you work [outside the home]. It must be a difficult situation you are in." And that was it. I was sometimes very frustrated.

The change from a planned to a market economy also presented East German women with an unexpected paradox: Their economic independence decreased drastically while, at the same time, the newly established market economy needed them as consumers with disposable incomes. The numerous new media channels aggressively introduced the culture of consumerism in East Germany. Women were bombarded with Western images of Western life styles, femininity, and beauty. In the GDR, consumption was not a social or cultural activity. Consumerism as an ideology did not exist. East German women's *identity* was rooted in their work roles, not in their consumption activities (Bocock, 1993). Consequently, they did not respond to Western visions of material gratification through consumption as the advertising industries had naively believed they would. Western styles of consumption were unfamiliar to them. They did not know the "rules" of the corresponding consumer behavior, nor did they find those rules agreeable. They viewed consumerism with a healthy dose of skepticism.

Moreover, most had little or no disposable income. Without state subsidies, prices for basic food items had doubled and tripled. It was not helpful for the average household that dishwashers, washing machines, other electronic household items and, in general, a host of consumer items had become much cheaper. In addition, many businesses, unfamiliar with free market practices, tried to make a quick profit by taking advantage of the monopoly they had over certain consumer items and overcharging their customers. Because times were so uncertain, four-fifths of East Germans decided to save and not spend their newly acquired *Deutsche Mark* (Jarausch, 1995, pp. 230–231).

German reunification was exacting a price, and how that price was perceived depended on women's everyday experiences.[4] For some, it meant unexpected prosperity, while for many others the price included the loss of, or diminished control over, their material well-being and fundamental adjustments in how they lived their lives.

In reunified Germany, it is not *cooperation* that counts to better one's material well-being, but *competition.* It is not a carefully nurtured social network where skills and material resources are bartered that is important, but access to money.[5] Often, the educational and job skills acquired in the GDR had become superfluous. Moreover, the newly established capitalist system expected East German women to relinquish their aspirations for material independence and to adapt to the new "reality," that is, to let men have priority in the labor market and accept material dependence on their spouses/partners.

Germany's capitalist economy promotes competitive relations in the public sphere and assigns men to fill those roles. Cooperative relations, on the other hand, are limited to the private sphere and women are expected to nurture them. In contrast, in the GDR, cooperative relations were fostered in both spheres. These strictly gendered spaces of West Germany's societal system are accepted as the norm by most West Germans and were installed in East Germany with little or no reflection on their consequences. Therefore, they are resisted by many East German women. Christine Rabe (1998, p. 14), an East German *Gleichstellungsbeauftragte* (equality officer),[6] said:

After 1989, you could read the greatest nonsense in the newspapers about this subject. They published articles that said, "At long last, East German women do not have to work anymore." [What these journalists did not understand is that] East German women want to have a profession *and* a family" [emphasis added].[7]

A majority of West Germans, *feminist* as well as nonfeminist, remained indifferent to East German women's experiences and aspiration to have both economic independence and a family. Eva Kunz, a member of the Social Democratic Party (SPD) and municipal council member for gender equality in East Berlin, said, "It was very surprising to me how ideological the West was and is" (Gaschke, 1998, p. 13). By ignoring or devaluing East German women's experiences and conceptions of how to combine work and family life, many West German women assumed, erroneously, that nothing could be learned from East German women's lives. Therefore, they behaved not much differently from their male counterparts who believed that everything Western was, by definition, superior. Valuable knowledge was not exchanged and, in the words of some interviewees, the "Wall in our heads just became higher."

A large number of East German women in my sample believed that women's and men's social experiences do not fundamentally differ, if they are given the same opportunities and responsibilities. In this regard, they expressed the values and norms they had internalized under state socialism. Thus, paradoxically, they also reflected the sentiments associated with *liberal feminism*. They saw themselves in solidarity with men and rejected the principles of gender difference with regard to being able to provide for themselves and their families. One administrator vigorously disagreed with West German women's approach to gender relations:

[When I am with West German women,] I have the feeling that I have to be against men. That women have to be against men really infuriates me. I don't know if I am emancipated. Most likely not. But I address whatever bothers me. I can say that I am quite fearless in this regard. If I want something changed, I say so. And I say it to a man in exactly the same way I say it to a woman.

Rabe (1998, p. 14) underscores this by insisting that the public and private division of labor (and, therefore, women's and men's social experiences) was never as clearly divided in the GDR as many West German feminists presume it to be: "The notion of West German feminists that GDR women were responsible for the entire family and house work, in addition to their paid work, is too sweeping of a statement. When both [spouses] worked outside the home, then both accepted normally their share at home."

The capitalist organization of reunified Germany has redefined the relationship between East German women and men by separating women's material well-being from their income-generating work roles and state support and shifting it to individual spouses/partners. This has evoked strong feelings of resentment and resistance among many women, and the following reactions were typical among those I interviewed. One teacher observed: "At least we were economically independent [in the GDR]. We may have earned less than men. But still, we were independent. I know many women who say, 'I don't want to live this way.' We do not like the way it is [in reunified Germany]."

And an agricultural worker who had lost her livelihood and enrolled in a job retraining program was profoundly unhappy with the situation she found herself in, commenting: "Women can literally be dominated by men now. At least that is how I see it. Women are dependent, completely dependent. This dependency is terrible."

A cook who found herself in a similar situation remarked:

I don't know. This feeling to ask your husband, "Can I have this; can we afford that? Can I buy this for the children?" For me, it is terrible, because I have always looked after myself, materially speaking. And my husband has made remarks as well. But now I have no choice, I am dependent on him.

In addition, many women still depend on state support. Whereas in the GDR state assistance made it possible to combine paid work and family responsibility, in reunified Germany, state assistance comes in the form of unemployment benefits, retraining programs, or social welfare.

The dissatisfaction with their increasingly dependent economic status has been exacerbated by a shift in their *reference of comparison*. Before reunification, most East Germans had compared their material well-being with that of people in other East European countries. Because East Germans were comparatively better off, they were, by and large, satisfied with how they lived. In reunified Germany, however, East Germans compare their material well-being to West Germans and find that they are mostly worse off, thereby contributing to their feeling of dissatisfaction.

Shifting Frames of Reference

This change in comparative reference caused disorientation and contemplation about the material situation of East Germany. One health care worker explained:

Now we can, of course, see the prosperity the citizens of West Germany have enjoyed. We did not accomplish that in the last 40 years with our work. [Given our different histories,] one can't even compare [the two countries] with regard to material well-being. But we do. We are now part of the West.

The women who had lost their income and were struggling to adapt to the conditions in reunified Germany often perceived themselves as "second-class citizens." They found it impossible to get even close to attaining a West German standard of material well-being because in the harsh reality of capitalism, their skills, acquired in the GDR, had become worthless with the introduction of Western technologies. As a result, many felt that they had become worthless as well, because their *identities* were closely tied to their abilities to achieve and maintain employment. Also, many were well aware that the worth of a person is measured differently under capitalism than in socialism. Money is now the decisive factor. One administrative assistant described it as follows: "Well, life is totally different now. During GDR times, our lives were more peaceful in spite of all the shortages. We did not have this competitive way of thinking. We did not have to live with the fear of losing our incomes *and* dignity."

These women's perceptions of themselves were (still) deeply influenced by the norms and values they had grown up with in the GDR, which emphasized above all their productive labor. This stood in stark contrast to West Germany's values and norms, which emphasized women's unpaid work in the family and economic dependency, yet put a higher value on activities and economic power in the public sphere, increasing an already deep East-West divide.

Income from Paid Work and Other Sources

Unlike in the GDR, where East German women's income derived from paid work and labor performed in the informal economy, in reunified Germany income derives from gainful employment, but also from unemployment benefits, government-sponsored retraining programs, and social welfare programs. The incomes of the 52 women I interviewed were spread more widely over the income scale than was the case in the GDR.[8] The spread reflects women's new social status in reunified Germany, in that those who fall in the lower income categories are now on social welfare or receive unemployment benefits; whereas those who fall in the higher categories receive incomes from government retraining programs or from paid work. These categories make visible a widening gap of material well-being among this group of women, and thus clearer class distinctions.[9]

The remarks of this agricultural worker were typical of those whose incomes, and corresponding sense of control over their material well-being, had declined:

Our income [in terms of purchasing power] is less in reunified Germany than it was before. We did not have a lot of money to spend either in the GDR. But [it is more difficult now because] we have all these consumer goods and we can't afford to buy them. It is very difficult, especially for our children. It is very stressful. They ask, "Mommy, can we buy this? Can we buy that? Can we go here and can we go there? Can you give me DM 10, I need it for school." That is DM 10 here and DM 10 there. Where shall I take it from? It is very stressful. I can't give my children any money. I would like to, but I can't afford it. And they have difficulty understanding it, because [in the GDR] I could afford it.[10]

In contrast are the experiences of those who retained their income levels. They found it easier to catch up with a Western standard of living. Many had savings, and their purchasing power had increased because of the one-to-one exchange between the East German Mark and the West German "Deutsche Mark." This enabled them to buy previously unthinkable luxuries like Western-made cars, color televisions, and modern appliances.[11] This group of East German women was generally gratified with their situation in reunified Germany, as exemplified by this teacher:

My husband and I have the ideal situation. We both work. And from the point of view of running a household, . . . we can afford the new household technologies [that have become available since reunification]. Our family does not have to worry about, "Can we afford this [or] can we put food on the table?"

We can travel everywhere now, and buy what we need. I think that is wonderful. I am a great fruit lover. I have never eaten so much fruit as I eat now, because we could not get it in the GDR. And [it is] such a relief [and] help for women to have this [household] technology. It is great. When I think about [how it was in the GDR]! We used to wait five years for a [new] washing machine [to be delivered]. We still have one that does not spin the clothes. [But I also have a new washing machine], and I can leave the clothes in until they are ready to be put on the clothes line. It makes such a difference!

Women's material independence and ability to choose if, and to what extent, they wanted to participate in the new consumer society played a vital role in how they experienced and judged the outcome of German reunification. If they had access to, and control over, economic resources, they generally approved of the outcome. But if they struggled economically, they were keenly aware of the widening gap in terms of material inequality.

A capitalist society measures people's social status not only by how much they earn, but also by how much they spend, and what they spend it on. Thirty-seven women (71 percent) of the women in my sample said that they did not like the fact that access to money had become a predominant force in their lives, and that it had added to the stress they were already experiencing. The observations of this gardener were typical of many women: "Everything has become more corrupt [since reunification]. Everyone uses their elbows. Everything is about money. One is not concerned anymore about one's surroundings. It has become so much more difficult, significantly more difficult."

The concerns of one bookkeeper that the change from socialism to capitalism has encouraged people to focus on themselves rather than on the larger community were echoed by many other women as well:

Everyone is thinking of her/himself today because everyone has problems of some sort. No one is excluded. Those who have money want more money, and their problem is how to get their hands on it. And those who don't make any money have to find a way to make it, that is a big problem, too.

Similarly, the majority of women agreed with the comments of this health care worker: "Somehow we have lost our civility after socialism collapsed. Our way of thinking, our being available for each other, all that has gone. Now it's me, me, and again me. And money is the dominant word. There is no other vocabulary. I think it's horrible."

This stress was exacerbated because women felt structurally violated when competing with male workers for paid work and, therefore, access to money and other valued resources.

Sexual Stereotyping

The road to material well-being in reunified Germany entails additional and previously unknown pressures for East German women. One of these is to objectify and package their bodies to conform to sexual stereotypes. In reunified Germany, relationships—public and private—are built on the basis of socially defined sexual roles, less on rough equivalence between mature adults.[12] Social roles for women are now defined more clearly and in such a way that they create financial, emotional, and sexual dependence on spouses/partners. Many women in my sample said that, in the long run, such roles will make it difficult for them to enjoy satisfying relationships with men. They saw a danger in applying those standards to themselves and others because "How can it not lead to feelings of frustration and dissatisfaction?" These women resisted West German definitions and struggled to preserve and protect their *identities*. They objected especially to how women were portrayed in the media. In the words of a biologist: "In this society, women are sex symbols, symbols of [artificial] beauty. That is how they see women in this society. That was very different in the GDR."

Their conversations about women's portrayal in the media were accompanied by an array of feelings, particularly when they considered the power of institutions such as the media. They viewed the Western media as shaping women's images to become caricatures: The happy mother who can finally be at home with her child/ren; the uncaring mother who neglects her child/ren by insisting on working outside the home; the frustrated wife who has not figured out that her true calling is supporting her husband; the satisfied homemaker who has realized that her vocation is creating the perfect home for her family; the sex object who is available at any time, fulfilling her man's sexual fantasies; the calculating and/or ambitious career woman aspiring to be like a man; and the lesbian *Emanze* who is full of hatred toward all heterosexuals. Rarely were women portrayed the way they perceived themselves: as competent, professional women who can combine both professional and family life.

A manager echoed the sentiments of many: "I wish that women are not only seen as mothers [and wives] but more often as someone who is educated and competent in her profession, so that the relationship between these roles is more balanced."

Mostly the women in my sample objected to the media reducing women to sexual roles, as exemplified by a nurse who said that:

[In reunified Germany], equality between women and men is not like it was in the GDR. How can I say it? Women are presented more like a sex object, as playmates for the bed. That did not exist before. Now we have a house of prostitution [in Güstrow]. For me, that is degrading; it is generally shameful to have such an establishment.

Another health care worker, repulsed and feeling powerless to change how women are portrayed, commented:

And what makes me really angry . . . is all the dirt that is being swept over here [from the West]. It begins with the pornographic films and naked women in every newspaper and magazine. I have the feeling that *patriarchy* has become stronger, that men begin to believe that they are the strong ones. This is also suggested in films and magazines. Women are objects of lust, or [they are] mothers. They are there to keep the house clean. I really think that these are negative developments.

An educator described her experiences in a similar way:

I believe that women are in a much worse position than men, apart from being unemployed. For men there have not been the same dramatic changes. Women are affected so much more. Just take the devaluation of women through the media. I could not have envisioned [how women would be viewed] in newspapers, advertisements, and magazines. And all these sex papers, women are viewed as no more than sexual objects.

A bookkeeper was unable to categorize what was happening to her when she was approached on the street:

Prostitution is very much present nowadays. I myself have been approached. Someone pressed a card in my hand and said, "In case you need money, call that number." At first, I didn't grasp what was happening. I had to read it to realize that it was clearly prostitution. I showed it to a friend and he said, "My daughter gets these cards almost every day." And these [people] work at it without scruples and compromise.

Almost all women addressed the power of the media in redefining who and what they should be and the ambivalence they experienced when they were confronted, on a daily basis, with images of female bodies as objects to be packaged, bought, sold, violated, and devalued. Most felt that they were able to distance themselves from the influence of these images. But many were concerned about the impact of these images on their daughters and granddaughters. These women feared that girls (and boys) would grow up to regard media images of women as something girls should "naturally" aspire to, and that they would judge themselves and others by how closely their bodies and behaviors fit the images produced and communicated by a multibillion-dollar advertising industry.

Gendered Aspects of Becoming a Consumer

West Germany's capitalist system not only "encourages" women to objectify and package their bodies to conform to sexual stereotypes, it also "educates" women to become consumers. Material consumption, and not income-generating work roles, is to be the basis of how East German women define their *identity* and roles in reunified Germany. Because material consumption is essential for capitalism, it requires a set of corresponding values and behaviors and the construction of needs, wants, and preferences for nonessential goods. For consumption to become a "natural" part of East Germans' daily life, an *un*awareness has to be developed of the many powerful groups that continuously and purposefully influence desires and preferences for goods that can fulfill newly created unconscious yearnings (Bocock, 1993).[13]

The process of shifting a woman's *identity*, by "making" her a "natural" consumer, who packages her body in accordance with sexual and other stereotypes, and "persuading" her to embrace a life style that is defined by powerful commercial interests, met with resolute resistance by many East German women. It clearly exposes the tension between capitalistic and socialist practices, as exemplified by the words of this division director:

In reunified Germany, one has to document to the outside world who one is. West Germans carry their education and their travel on their sleeves so everyone will know what they know and where they have been, [to] the Louvre in Paris, the pyramids [in Egypt], to many spectacular places. At least that is how I perceive it. Everything is tuned to appearance. I think it is important to tread quietly, so one can hear the other voices as well. But that is not how West German society is. It is this trying to be noticed, this "look who we are, and what we have achieved" kind of attitude, that I find unbearable, but somehow it is so important nowadays to meet certain kind of criteria. It gives you a totally distorted picture of who the person is. But this is what is expected, it is the norm, and it is so untruthful.[14]

Many women were ambivalent about what it meant to be a consumer, and the prerequisites of consumption were considered with caution and skepticism, as did this gardener, who said that:

West Germans can handle debts. They don't have any problems with it. I am told that I have to learn to deal with debt as an object, to regard it as something normal. West Germans can live with that. I just can't handle it. I keep my expenses as low as I can. I would rather reduce them. West Germans lead a different life from us.

A secretary explained:

In the beginning, I could not handle the West German Mark. It took a while until we got used to it. It changed over night. One day we had the East Mark, and the next day we had the *Deutsche Mark*. And somehow we were supposed to act differently, too. We were expected to spend our money. I still can't spend my money the way they do in West Germany.[15]

Shifting women's social role and identity from an income-generating to a consumer role was not easily accomplished. Those who had lost their incomes through unemployment were simply "priced out" of the consumer market. For them, even providing food for the family was often more stressful than in the GDR. A shortage of commodities was replaced by a shortage of cash in reunified Germany. This was a dramatic *reversal* of the situation during state socialism, when people had considerable private savings but nothing to spend them on (Einhorn, 1993, p. 173).

For those who had sufficient money and tried to master the art of consumption, "going shopping" in the Western sense had to be learned. In the

GDR, women did not buy for the sake of buying. Shopping was a chore to be done. It meant standing in long lines, and more often than not, it meant being told, once one arrived at the front of the line, that the desired item was sold out and that another one was not readily available.

Many East German women were initially blinded and bewildered by the immediate availability, choice, and elaborate packaging of Western goods. That was quickly followed by a sense of feeling confused and overwhelmed by a host of unfamiliar brand names and varying qualities of goods that looked deceptively similar. A bookkeeper describes her experience: "I remember standing in front of a vegetable and fruit stand. Behind me people began to pile up. I did not know how to categorize what I saw."[16] And a midwife recalled: "Oh my God, the amounts of consumer goods they had [in the West]! I remember when we went [to the West] for the first time in December 1989, we walked and looked for hours and we did not know how to actually choose something."

Eventually, women began to question the inconsistencies they experienced. A manager's response was typical in this regard:

So much is complete nonsense. I am bombarded by the press and advertisers who tell me what I have to have and what I can't live without. I don't need all those things. We are totally saturated. It is crazy; now I have to learn again about what I really need, *who* I am, what I want. And the media continue to bombard me. How free does that make me?

Others learned, to their amazement, that being a consumer is very time- and energy-consuming. In the GDR, women had spent time and energy standing in line and running after goods. In reunified Germany, they spent time and energy comparing prices and making choices among a host of similar goods at shopping centers located farther away from their homes that could not be reached easily by bike or foot.

Many women also expressed concern about the effect of consumption on the environment and questioned whether things had really changed, as expressed by this teacher: "In the former GDR, we neglected the environment. Well, we destroyed it. But today [the market economy] educates us to become a throwaway society. There is often triple packaging! What is that all about?"

A nurse put it this way:

It is a throwaway society that we live in.[17] In the GDR, we had nothing and preserved everything. If we could not use it ourselves, we gave it to someone who could. Doing it that way was at least of some value to society. We always thought, "Is this of use to anyone?," before we discarded anything. We did not throw things away senselessly like we do now. We would not have to produce so much, especially the packaging. I am very afraid of the garbage we produce as a result of material prosperity and what that means for nature and for the entire environment!

Generally, women felt uncomfortable with the new pressures to continuously buy new things to replace older ones, and to strive for standards of beauty that were unattainable, unrealistic, and undesirable. The pressure to conform politically in the GDR was replaced with the pressure to conform to economic and cultural norms in reunified Germany. And like in the GDR, nonconformity prompted sanctions that were of a similar kind: being shunned, condemned to outsider status, restricted opportunities with regard to employment, promotion, and potential job loss or demotion.

PRIVATE PROPERTY

Private property, the very foundation of capitalism, was for most East Germans too abstract a concept to comprehend during the rapid transition from socialism to capitalism. The connection to their personal lives was often understood too late. For many, it took a huge leap to grasp that "Property [is key] to other wealth and economic advantage, for example, . . . as collateral for loans" (Seager, 1997, pp. 76–77). East German women were affected directly and immediately, both in positive and negative ways, when state-owned property was transformed into private property. Because more women than men were without income, their opportunities to obtain mortgages and loans for buying land and/or real estate were more limited, bringing to the fore clear class and gender distinctions.[18]

With state controls abolished, large portions of state-owned housing were sold off to private investors and/or reverted back to the previous owners in East and West Germany. Those who could afford and/or were able to obtain mortgages bought homes. For many, the quality of housing improved because government-funded programs encouraged people to purchase and renovate existing, and/or build new housing. For the unemployed, the housing conditions remained the same or worsened.

Twenty women (39 percent) in my sample said that their housing conditions had improved as a result of the conversion from state-owned to private property. Eighteen women (35 percent) said their housing conditions had remained the same, and nine (17 percent) said that their housing had deteriorated. (Five women did not address the subject.)

Those who felt that the quality of housing had improved had assumed ownership of the houses they lived in. They had gained more living space, made substantial renovations—often installed spacious bathrooms, central heating systems, warm water, and telephone lines, and acquired amenities such as fully automated washing machines and dishwashers. All this improved the quality of their daily lives and gave them a sense of security and control during times of great fluctuation.

A child-care worker explained: "We do not have to worry about [increasing] rent now. We own this house. We do not have to pay a mortgage on it either. The constant increase in rent puzzles me. Well, we do have to do work on our house. But now we can get all the materials we need [and we can afford them]."

Those who had rented apartments that were refurbished by the new owners were mostly satisfied with their housing conditions in spite of substantial rent increases. However, those who were paying significantly higher rents but had not benefited from any improvements in the conditions of their apartments and the buildings they lived in felt that their housing conditions had deteriorated and with it their quality of life.

A church worker saw the irony of two fundamentally different housing policies, neither of which—socialist or capitalist—had served the interests of many people:

Now we are faced with a real dilemma. We had created pictures of a perfect socialist world. We had this incredibly cheap rent, and we avoided looking at the situation closer, because somehow we did not want to know that it costs money to keep up a house. And now we experience the high costs [of renovating a house or an apartment]. Many say [the sad conditions of our housing stock] are due to reunification. But the houses are not in bad condition because of reunification. They are in bad condition because we have not done anything for years. And many houses have not been touched since the [end of World] War II.

The women who did not benefit from any improvements in the conditions of their housing were keenly aware that decision-makers in the GDR had mismanaged housing, and that tenants paid the price for that in reunified Germany. These women had to accept the current housing conditions because it was their only option. They did not qualify for loans and/or were unable to afford to move to better apartments. Many felt that they had as little control over their housing situation under capitalism as under socialism. Moreover, they often felt taken advantage of by what they defined as a profit-driven market system. A cook experienced it this way: "Today, all the landlords want is money. They don't do anything. Our landlord is new. Before [reunification], these apartments belonged to the community. [After reunification,] the [current] landlord bought the building. He has done nothing to improve it, but our rent has tripled."

An agricultural worker who had lost her job and was facing an uncertain future in every respect described her situation in a similar way:

To be honest, I have to say that I felt better before [reunification], much better. Especially with the costs in rent. It increases [all the time]. We do not have any say in it. It is simply being decided. The rent increases, everything increases all the time. And the income gets less. . . . My life is much more unsettled now and it is all so uncertain, especially with the [high] rent for [this apartment]. And now we can be asked to leave this place [should the owner want it for his use or should we not be able to pay]. That makes me so nervous. It destroys me.

A gardener who attended a job retraining program and tried to cope with a reduced family income concurred:

Our income is DM 3,000 per month. That is what we have to live on. From that, I have to pay DM 1,300 for rent. And this apartment is in terrible condition. But it is so difficult to get apartments here. I personally have great difficulty accepting that I am so taken advantage of by the owners.

The feeling of being taken advantage of was exacerbated by the return of housing to previous East and West German owners, who, by fulfilling certain conditions, were able to claim it back. This often prompted bitter feelings, particularly toward West German owners who claimed the space for their own use and asked tenants to vacate apartments or houses, as described by this agricultural worker: "We live in an old manor house. We have a large apartment in it, which costs DM 400 without any utilities. But the manor house now belongs to someone in West Germany, so we have to move out, of course."

Converting state-owned property into private property proved to be a double-edged sword. Those who were able to buy the property they lived in felt better off, but those who were not able to buy it had to absorb substantial increases in rent, or vacate the place and find something else, which was no easy task, given the available housing and high rents. In any case, those who had to bear higher housing rents also had less spending money and, thus, were less able to participate in the new consumer society. With a substantially higher proportion of women being unemployed, it follows that a higher proportion of employed men qualify for mortgages and loans, creating new gendered class lines between those who have access to property ownership and those who do not.

"MAKING DO" IN THE MIDST OF PLENTY

The steep increase in housing costs was part of the increase in overall costs of living. Like in the GDR, in reunified Germany, women usually assumed the responsibility for making ends meet with the resources available to them. But unlike in the GDR, in reunified Germany there were no opportunities to generate extra income by participating in an informal economy. The networks where goods and services were bartered had disintegrated because everything had become easily available for those who could afford it. The material situation many women found themselves in after reunification, with costs increasing and resources dwindling, often caused frustration and resentment. One textile worker expressed her feelings this way:

The prices for bread and meat have not changed a lot, but look at the pay we get in East Germany. The rent and insurance we have to pay is as expensive as in West Germany, but we only get paid 60 percent of what West Germans get paid. *As far as I am concerned, they can put the Wall back up again and build it 10 meters higher than it was before.* I cannot afford to live in reunified Germany. We have not had a vacation since reunification. We cannot afford it. Now they say you can travel wherever you want to, but what good does that do if I can't afford it? I can't even travel to the North Sea! It is too expensive. *I liked it better in the GDR.*

A sales assistant who had retained her job, but whose purchasing power had dwindled, observed: "When our son needed a pair of pants, I could afford to go out and buy them [in the GDR]. But today, I think about it many times, 'Do I go out and buy one or don't I?' A pair of baby shoes, those little ones they wear when they start walking, used to cost 9 Marks. Now they cost 69 Marks!"

And a gardener who was struggling to make ends meet said:

In the GDR, we did have things [to buy]. Alright, it is true, we could not get bananas every day, or oranges, or grapes. But, personally, I felt much better. I have to be honest. And I am very lucky because my husband is a civil servant [and his job future is secure]. But [I know] of many who have three and four children and both [parents] are unemployed. Just look at the rent we pay. We live in an old country estate. It is going to be sold to a *Wessi* (West German). Our apartment is 92 square meters. We pay 400 Marks rent [a month] without any utilities. And we need 2,000 Marks worth of coal [per year for heating the place], and that money has to come from somewhere. And we only have one income.

The collapse of the informal economy particularly affected women in the agriculture sector who had derived a significant part, and sometimes all, of their income from that sector. More important, for these women an entire way of life had disappeared, their skills became obsolete, and their social connections severed. A majority of the women (60 percent) in my sample felt that the quality of their lives had diminished because the type of social relations they had built through their daily interaction at work do not exist anymore. As a result, 58 percent said that interpersonal relationships are not as good as they used to be, and 62 percent said that they felt, generally, more isolated.

CONCLUSION

The transformation of state socialism to capitalism introduced capitalism's essential pillars into the everyday life of East German women: private property and consumption, and clearly defined gender roles and class distinctions—all reinforcing Germany's patriarchal structures. This impacted widely on women's material conditions and often, though not always, limited their opportunities.

The conversion of state-owned property to private property proved to be a mixed blessing for East Germans. On the one hand, private property improved living conditions; on the other hand, it made them worse. In any case, private property made class visible by drawing a clearly defined line between the *haves* and the *have-nots*, and imposed this unaccustomed social categorization on East Germans.[19] Privatization introduced and defined competitiveness, not cooperation, as a desirable trait, and defined social roles and corresponding behaviors in more gendered terms. It influenced how East German women were able—or unable—to provide for their own and their families' material well-being.

Consumption prompted ambivalent reactions. On the one hand, it was embraced because goods that had been difficult to obtain became instantly available for those who could afford them. On the other hand, it was met with caution, as consumption required a new set of behaviors that were perceived as "unnatural" by many East German women. Being a consumer included a female *identity* that violated the norms and values that many women in my sample had internalized under state socialism. Consumption provoked negative reactions because it entailed competitive and isolating elements and reduced women and men to their gendered roles.

Generally, the women I interviewed did not relate well to clearly defined gender roles either. They viewed women and men as occupying more mature adult roles with regard to producing the material well-being for themselves and their families. With material conditions profoundly changed, the women I interviewed were reluctant to adapt to those conditions, revealing that the difference between East and West Germany's competing gender ideologies is not easily closed.

In the next chapter, I summarize the study's main findings and discuss their implications for further research and social policy in reunified Germany in particular, and Eastern Europe in general.

NOTES

1. Marxists predicted, correctly, that an economic annexation would force state companies into bankruptcy and that half of the people would be unemployed. Social democrats voiced concern that unchecked competition would especially harm those groups that were already at a disadvantage like the elderly, women, and the young and the disabled. Grass-roots movements argued that a Western colonization would increase Eastern feelings of helplessness and inferiority. Few listened to these voices, because the neoliberal arguments about the effectiveness of the market justified the risks of a rapid reunification, and they won out (Jarausch, 1995, p. 240).

2. For a comprehensive analysis of structural change and its effect on occupational and income mobility, plus of individual strategies for responding to the changing social conditions, see Diewald and Mayer (1996).

3. See chapter 3 for details on this topic.

4. In this regard, see Bachmann and Wurst (1996), who show an increasing polarization among those who feel "integrated" into reunified Germany and those who feel "disconnected."

5. In this regard, Jutta Voigt, an editor at the newspaper *Wochenpost* in Berlin, relates her experience as a participant in a West German training workshop for managers:

We were asked [by a West German trainer] to create a list of all our acquaintances and friends. After each name we were asked to note if we give to that person or if we receive from that person. Then we were instructed to cross out the names to whom we only give. That is the new "Spiel" [in reunified Germany]. According to those instructions, I would have had to cross out many of my friends. They have not given me anything except the opportunity to be who I am.

Voigt wonders what kind of person she would have become had she grown up in capitalist Germany. She speculates that she would have been more successful, have little or no humor, and be more productive, without children, and more calculating. In reunified Germany, she does not talk as freely as she did in the GDR because someone else can now take her ideas and claim them as their own intellectual property. It never occurred to her in the GDR to consider an idea as property that can be sold for more than a penny or a smile (Voigt, 1992, p. 6).

6. The position of *Gleichstellungsbeauftragte* ("equality officer") was created to institutionalize gender equality at all levels of reunified society. *Gleichstellungsstellen*, also called "Women's Bureaus" or "Bureaus for Gender

Equality," were established in communities across the country. On the state and federal levels, ministries for women were established as well as programs instituted to promote women. The main functions of these offices are to check the law, to coordinate and make proposals for implementing political measures that promote gender equality, to advise and provide information for women as well as to keep the public informed about the state of gender relations (Seidenspinner, 1994, p. 7).

7. Dienel's (1996) research findings show that in West Germany's market economy, women find it difficult to have both family and professional careers. Dienel studied women in leadership positions in the private and public sectors in West Germany and found that 85.7 percent of the women in her sample had no children; 13.3 percent had one or two children; 57.1 percent were married or lived with a partner; and 42.9 percent were divorced or had never married.

8. See endnote 2 in chapter 6.

9.

Monthly Income of East German Women in My Sample After Reunification

Deutsche Mark (DM)	Number of Women*	Percent
less than 400	2	3.9
400–899	9	17.7
900–1,299	7	13.7
1,300–1,599	6	11.7
1,600–1,999	6	11.7
2,000–2,999	9	17.7
3,000–3,999	11	21.6
4,000–4,999	1	2.0
Total	51	100.0

*One interviewee did not repond to this question, decreasing the sample size by one.

10. Müller, Hauser, Frick, and Wagner (1995) studied income and income distribution and the standard of living in East and West Germany. They found that the income distribution in East Germany has become more unequal since reunification, but it has not reached the level of inequality in West Germany. Still, East Germans are far less satisfied with their incomes than are West Germans.

11.

Consumer Goods per 100 Households in Former GDR

Consumer Goods	1991	1996
Telephones	18	91
Washing Machines	73	97
Microwave Ovens	5	47

VCRs	40	78
Home Computers	15	40
Video Cameras	3	31
CD Players	2	22

Source: German Federal Statistics Office, cited in Drozdiak, 1998, April 25, p. A11.

12. With regard to gender relations, Wagner (1996, pp. 146–147) compared the relationships between female and male students at an East and a West German university. He found that the climate between female and male students at the *Freie Universität* in [West] Berlin was one of mistrust, accusations, and great distance, while, at the same time, being erotically charged. In contrast, the climate between female and male students at the University of Erfurt in East Germany was one of camaraderie. Couples could be recognized only because they appeared more often together. Demonstrative couple behavior was the exception. East German students did not appear to perceive each other as sexual beings in the way West German students did. Other tasks took priority. They appeared to have different criteria for mutual recognition and judgment, suggesting a different development in gender relations.

13. It is difficult to imagine Western culture, and in particular American culture, without shopping. For many Americans who feel bored, the first thought that comes to mind is to go to a shopping mall. The film *Affluenza*, a PBS special, co-produced by a public television station in Seattle and Oregon Public Broadcasting, shows that "on average [Americans], shop six hours a week and spend only 40 minutes playing with [their] children. . . . [I]n 1990, more Americans declared personal bankruptcy than graduated from college. [And] since 1950, Americans alone have used more resources than *everyone* who ever lived before them [emphasis added] (Thompson, December 20, 1998, p. 12).

14. Bettina Wegner, one of East Germany's well-known song writers, said that the *Zeitgeist* in reunified Germany forbids one from showing honest emotions. One is expected to be cool:

In the GDR, if someone was sad or cried, someone would actually see it and go and put an arm around that person and ask, "What is the matter?" Now, no one asks anymore, "Why do you cry?" And, after all, crying is healthy. So why are we forbidden to behave in a healthy, human manner? Because that is not the *Zeitgeist!* Everyone smiles. People also smile when they feel depressed. They smile in a desperate sort of way when they should really be very angry. But this is the smiling society. (Cited in Menge, March 12, 1998, p. 22)

15. The statistics for East German women and men show a somewhat different consumer behavior from the women I interviewed. The inexperience in handling consumer loans, combined with high unemployment in an overall uncertain economic environment, has resulted in personal bankruptcy for many East Germans. Personal bankruptcies increased by 72 percent between 1994 and 1997; the average debt of those who declared bankruptcy was DM 32,000 (*Tageszeitung*, January 14, 1999, p. 16).

16. This is an example of Kuhn's (1970) seminal work on *paradigms*: "different paradigms, different realities!"

17. In *Future Shock*, Toffler (1972, chapter 4) addresses the issue of the "throwaway society."

18. According to the United Nations, women own about 1 percent of the world's land. In the United States, for example, only 6 percent of agricultural land is owned by women (Seager, 1997, pp. 76–77).

19. Bachmann and Wurst (1996), for example, interviewed members of a community in the East German state of Saxony to explore how the newly established political and economic frameworks have affected this community and how its citizens have reacted. Attempting to assess the legitimacy of the transformation in East Germany, the authors examined the perceptions of women and men with regard to employment, social changes in women's lives, their material well-being, changes in neighborhood and regional relations, "emigration" of children to other parts of Germany, and how the community's *identity* has been affected. The researchers discovered an increasing polarization between those who are integrated in the new system because their life chances have remained the same or have improved and those who are increasingly alienated from the system because their life chances have considerably diminished with regard to employment, material well-being, and opportunities to consume. Those who are integrated conferred legitimacy upon the new system, albeit not without criticism. Those who feel alienated, on the other hand, present a potential for undermining the new system if they were to dissociate publicly from it and create an alternative system that would meet their needs and improve their opportunities.

8

Conclusion: Implications for Further Research, Theory, and Practice

INTRODUCTION

In this study, I examined the experiences of East German women under state socialism and capitalism, exploring their social space and status under socialism and how that space and status changed as a result of German reunification. In this regard, I pursued four central goals:

1. to listen to the voices and to recognize as valid the experiences of the 52 East German women I interviewed.
2. to create a record of East German women's knowledge and actions, and thereby direct the focus of German reunification away from changes at the institutional levels to women's daily lives.
3. to emphasize the crucial importance of the daily visible *and* invisible work women perform to mend the social fabric so that social stability is maintained during times of social upheaval. And
4. to explore why East German women resisted shifting their *identities* and *roles* to adapt to the new social structures of reunified Germany, by examining how the changes in the larger social structure related to changes in individual lives.

GENERAL FINDINGS

Both systems—East Germany's state socialism and West Germany's capitalism—grew from deeply rooted patriarchal structures sustained by male elites. These structures have remained unyielding in the face of profound political, economic, social, and cultural change. They constituted the common ground for the elites of both Germanies to implement the reunification of Germany. The patriarchal structures of state socialism can be described as flexible and "progressive" only to the extent to which they served the advantages of the male elites. In that sense, the socialist structures responded more comprehensively than the capitalist structures to the needs of women with regard to combining family and paid work responsibilities. This can be explained, in part, by socialist ideology, and in part, by the socialist system that depended for its very existence on women's productive and reproductive labor.

The Western perception that the German Democratic Republic (GDR) was an archetype of the Leninist, totalitarian state in which everyday life was strictly regimented and controlled, was not entirely supported by my study. Daily life was *complex*. The experiences of the women in my sample suggest that while everyday life followed a routine, it was not as rigid, subordinate, or linear as it is often portrayed by the Western perspective. For most women, daily life was full of improvisation and contradictions. Many East German women astutely bent the Communist Party's rules or evaded them altogether if they complicated their lives. This was particularly true during the last decade of the GDR's existence. Despite the Party's goal to control public and private space, it tolerated deviations to guarantee its own survival. Private space in the GDR was allowed to be "a free zone," where reflections on the present and hope for a better future could be pondered (Borneman, 1991, p. 17).

After West Germany's capitalist system was established in East Germany and powers were consolidated at all levels of society—political, economic, social, and cultural—East German women's social space for independence and self-realization was reduced. The age-old patriarchal structures forcefully asserted a fundamental value: control over women's lives and bodies. Although "public space [in reunified Germany is] the zone of officially endorsed 'freedom' and self-realization," many East German women feel squeezed out, and "private space [is now] consistently invaded by devices of publicity, advertising, and need-creation" (p. 17).

The predominantly male elites of reunified Germany have drawn a clear and more hierarchical division of public and private labor. They defined, once again, East German women's role as being *primarily* responsible for home and family. This is in contrast to the socialist elites, who had defined East German women's social roles as being primarily members of the paid labor force.

A consequence of redefining women's primary role has been that many East German women do not perceive West Germany's capitalist system as egalitarian and liberating as many Westerners assume it to be. For example, many women in my sample felt that reunified Germany limits their individual opportunities, choices, and actions in everyday life to a larger degree than socialist East Germany had done. Even those whose material circumstances had improved perceived the capitalist system as less just because it has largely failed to offer a majority of East German women better choices. A cosmetologist poignantly expressed the sentiments of many:

This is not what we went into the streets for, not for a capitalist society. No one took to the streets for that. We wanted more justice, more equality. We wanted an economic system that functioned reasonably well. We knew the socialist order was not working. We had not succeeded in realizing socialism [the way it was envisioned]. Well, and the capitalist state has not solved [any of our economic problems, either].

The shift to an emphasis on women's social role, which has been aided by severe cuts in social supports such as child care and diminished economic opportunities, has created a field of tension where the larger societal structures relentlessly impact on individual lives. These conditions illustrate the reverberation of the larger social environments—political, economic, and cultural—on women's individual and collective interests, abilities, needs, and efforts.

SPECIFIC FINDINGS

Occupational Opportunities and Choices under Socialism

Socialist society demanded women's full domestic and nondomestic participation in three closely related areas of everyday life—occupational, family, and material. East German women skillfully balanced multiple roles to meet daily workplace and family demands, tampering with but not permanently changing the patriarchal organization of socialist society.

Even though the socialist state had implemented laws and policies that guaranteed women formal rights, promoted equal educational and professional opportunities, and integrated the majority of women of working age into the work force, real gender equality was not achieved. Nevertheless, a comprehensive child-care system enabled women, albeit imperfectly to combine work and family life. These measures permitted them to be economically independent of their spouses/partners and to make independent choices and decisions, as exemplified by the words of this educator: "[In the GDR] when our marriages entered a crisis stage, we meant it when we said, 'Tomorrow I am going to leave you.' Because it was possible without being thrown into a deep financial crisis and without making any financial demands on men."

But women's economic independence was mandated from the top. The state declared, as early as 1975, that women's equality was *"realized* not only in the legal sense, but to a large degree in everyday life" (emphasis added). Gender equality was confined to the level of state ideology. It became a tool for denying any discrimination against women (Rai, Pilkington, and Phizacklea, 1992, p. 6). The state did not permit the questioning of gendered roles. As a result, a gendered division of labor persisted in the public *and* private spheres. Indeed, the division was reinforced by a complex and contrary belief system that prevailed in the GDR: Given equal rights and opportunities, women and men were *not* different; but given their biological distinctions, women and men were *essentially* different. Whereas the former was officially articulated and dominant, the latter remained unspoken and continued to exist beneath the surface. A health care worker noted:

I don't think we were emancipated in the GDR, but there was a sort of equality with regard to work and income. Women generally earned good money. But at a subconscious level, it was assumed that men were better than women. As I said, we gave the impression of being emancipated, but underneath, it was not quite like that.

Nevertheless, shifts in gender relations took place and the majority of women developed a new self-understanding as a result of being fully integrated in the work force. The socialist elites of the GDR may not have succeeded in translating the theoretical claims of gender equality to everyday life, but they succeeded in redefining women's *primary* social role from that of being responsible for home and family to that of being a fully integrated member of the paid labor force.

The East German women in my sample had internalized the redefinition that reflects the gender ideology of state socialism, in that they linked gender equality with their employment status, many saying: "Equality for us meant to be employed." They had learned to take for granted the right, but also the duty, to be gainfully employed, and because women's nondomestic work was publicly recognized, the women conveyed a sense of pride, strength, and practicality about their work. Most did not concern themselves with the gendered aspects of their situation at work. The political aspects, such as refusing to join the Party, were thought to be more often the reason for being overlooked for a promotion or a pay increase than the gendered aspects.

Combining full-time work and family responsibilities was not as easily accomplished as the state had planned, however. Women's daily lives involved improvising and deviating from the state's rigid rules. As a consequence, the state did not control women's private and public lives to the extent it had envisioned. Although the majority of East German women combined an uninterrupted work life with family responsibilities, a sizeable number reduced their work hours or dropped out of the work force altogether, at least for a while. This enabled them to respond to a myriad of personal and family needs that could not be routinized and subordinated to state demands.

Bending the rules, improvising, and changing schedules to fit individual needs, gave many East German women in my sample the feeling that they had choices. This, coupled with a vast array of social rights, led East German women to experience and perceive their lives under state socialism in a way that corresponds to claims made by *liberal feminism*: Social rights lead to women's equality, and a lack of social rights results in gender discrimination. If women are granted equal opportunities for education and professional advancement, equality between women and men can be achieved.

Family Life under State Socialism

Family life under socialism was not as uniform, monotonous, or controlled by the state as the Western perspective commonly assumes. Families related differently to the socialist system and acted in accordance with their needs, wants, values, and expectations. They adopted different strategies to deal with the daily demands of family life, and many were closely connected in the so-called *niches*: the carefully guarded spaces from which the state was kept out. Each family charted its own path toward creating a family life that was both supportive and satisfying.

Still, the choices for creating a happy family life were limited, shaped by the opportunities and constraints of the larger social environment in which families lived. Although at the very core of familial relations, a traditional gender-based division of labor persisted, gender relations were flexible, and changes were prompted by the demands of daily life that all families in my sample had to contend with: long work hours, household and family responsibilities, shortages of all sorts of consumer goods, and additional work in the informal economy and *niches*. To different degrees, all women in my sample dealt with the tension that resulted from their *real* struggle to combine family and paid work life in accordance with the socialist *ideal*. The *ideal* was based on male experience and male standards of work and family life. The *real* was the lived female experience. This led to contradictions that remained unresolved.

Material Conditions under State Socialism

By controlling the economy, abolishing private property, and developing an income structure that reduced income differences among the majority of East German citizens in general—and among women and men in particular—the Socialist Unity Party (SED) had created the perception that a socialist society was, materially speaking, more equitable than a capitalist society.

In reality, however, the Party did not succeed in distributing its material wealth equally. Old class structures in the form of Party hierarchy continued to exist. Party loyalty and active work on behalf of the Socialist Unity Party were rewarded with material privileges at the expense of those who did not join or who opposed the Party. A gender gap in earnings continued to persist as well. However, it can be argued that because paid work was a duty and, therefore, guaranteed, and because the earning differential between men and women was of a lesser degree, the difference in material wealth was, generally, less in the GDR than in reunified Germany.

This perception of the GDR being a more equitable society in which women had equal, or nearly equal, opportunities was reinforced further when the shortcomings of the planned economy led to a loosening of state controls over East Germans' lives and to the opening up of social spaces for individual action. In those spaces, women (and men) violated many socialist norms and values without incurring sanctions. The improvement of material well-being through private initiative was tolerated because it served the GDR elites and guaranteed their survival, at least for a while.

Many East German women seized these opportunities, mostly out of necessity, and as a result their daily lives were not as strictly controlled by the state. The women in my sample experienced themselves as able improvisers and as capable as the men they lived and worked with. It was "normal" for them to provide for their own, as well as their family's material well-being inside as well as outside the planned economy.

Summary

Paid work, family life, and material conditions under state socialism were closely intertwined in overlapping public and private spheres. Combining family and work responsibilities and creating a comfortable material base required the cooperation of female and male family members, friends, and colleagues. It was achieved *with* each other, never *against* each other. This is one reason why many women I interviewed regarded socialist society not as a perfect society, but as more equal than a capitalist society.

SPECIFIC FINDINGS

Occupational Opportunities and Choices in Reunified Germany

The close link that had existed under socialism between paid work, family life, and material conditions was severed under capitalism, resulting in sharply diverging private and public spheres and a more clearly defined gendered division of labor.

Paradoxically, it is at a time of accelerated modernization and the establishment of democratic institutions and processes in former East Germany that women's rights and opportunities have been curtailed. Specifically, deeply gendered employment patterns have openly emerged and are arrogantly pursued. The majority of women in my sample have struggled to survive materially, psychologically, and emotionally in a new and utterly unfamiliar social system. To survive has exacted a toll not least because, in a climate of increasing unemployment, many have lost their jobs and faced decreased occupational opportunities, discriminatory barriers, and increased social insecurity and stress. The women who have been fortunate enough to remain employed have experienced pressure to perform and conform in accordance with West German norms and rules, work longer hours, and deal with discriminatory salary structures, increasing mistrust among co-workers, and a more pronounced hierarchy at their workplaces.

Most of the women evaluated cautiously and critically the norms and values that the West German system has imposed on them. They recognized that they face *structural* as well as individual discrimination, and that it is likely to persist unless East German women succeed in changing the existing power disparity and secure equal "access to scarce and valued societal resources—material and nonmaterial" (i.e., income-generating roles, incumbency in elite roles, and time for leisure and personal growth) (Chafetz, 1990, pp. 83, 188–192).

Most of the women were facing this challenge head on: They were reluctant to adapt to West German conditions, making visible the tensions between East and West Germany's competing gender ideologies and images of a preferable society.

Family Life in Reunified Germany

The greatest, often *in*visible, task and accomplishment of East German women during the transition from state socialism to democracy has been the absorption and integration into daily family life—and by implication into the larger society—of the structural and institutional changes that have taken place on all levels of society.

For example, unemployment had far-reaching consequences, affecting, directly or indirectly, all families in my sample. In its wake social problems, such as alcoholism and violence within families, surfaced and had to be dealt with. Children, responding to the uncertainties and insecurities of the larger environment, had again become the sole responsibility of individual families, or more precisely, of mothers, while at the same time, East German women's style of mothering came under criticism by West German women and men.

In contrast to the GDR, in reunified Germany women are expected to be the primary caretakers of the family's physical and emotional well-being, while men are expected to be the primary caretakers of the family's economic well-being. These shifts make visible the emergence of a more distinct gender division of labor and, therefore, more unequal rank and power relations within families and consequently the larger society. Capitalist structures have not opened up more choices for women, as many had expected, but, instead, have foreclosed them.

The Material Conditions in Reunified Germany

Capitalism introduced its essential pillars into the everyday lives of East German women: consumption and private property, and clearly defined gender roles and class distinctions. This impacted widely on women's material conditions and often, though not always, limited their opportunities.

The conversion of state-owned property to private property proved to be a mixed blessing for East Germans in terms of material well-being. For those who could afford it, private property improved living conditions, but for those who could not afford it, living conditions worsened. In any case, private property made class visible by drawing a clearly defined line between the *haves* and the *have-nots*. Privatization introduced and defined (zero-sum) competitiveness, not (positive-sum) cooperation, as a desirable trait, and defined social roles and corresponding behaviors in more gendered terms. It influenced how East German women were able—or unable—to provide for their own and their families' material well-being.

Consumption prompted ambivalent reactions. On the one hand, it was embraced because goods that had been difficult to obtain became instantly available to those who could afford them. On the other hand, it was met with caution as consumption required a new set of behaviors that were perceived as "unnatural" by East German women. Being a consumer included a female *identity* that violated the norms and values that many women in my sample had internalized in the GDR: It provoked negative reactions because it entailed competitive and isolating elements, and often reduced women to their sexual roles.

Generally, the women I interviewed did not relate well to clearly defined gender roles because in the GDR gender roles were built on a rough equivalence between mature adults. And although most women were aware that income-generating work roles were not sufficient to achieve gender equality, they viewed it as an important step in the right direction: "In the GDR we were more emancipated because we participated in the work force. [In reunified Germany] we don't do that anymore." The majority of East German women have been "expelled" from an important social space and, thus, from participating in decision making and power sharing.

The critical stance of many East German women toward the West German system did not imply that they wanted the old system back. Many emphatically said that they were relieved that the pervasive influence of the Socialist Unity Party was gone. Few felt nostalgic about the "way it was." They welcomed change like this child-care worker, who said: "I don't want to have the old system back because I like to think for myself." They had been critical of the GDR system and had been well aware of its shortcomings. In the *niches*, many had learned to sharpen their critical skills, and once West Germany's capitalist system was installed, they evaluated it in a critical way, too, causing confusion for West Germans, who have little doubts about the superiority of their system.

East Germans' expectations in unified Germany have been high. Contrary to the beliefs of many Westerners, none of the East German women I spoke with had expected to catch up materially with the West overnight. They were ready and prepared to work for it, because they had worked hard all their lives. Indeed, most felt that they had succeeded in carving out a comfortable life in the GDR, even though they perceived room for improvement. Most had naively expected that a capitalist society was a more just society, in which goods and other resources were more fairly distributed. They had expected these principles to manifest themselves in their daily lives. Instead, for many, it had not turned out that way and they felt that, in *practice*, capitalism had pushed them from the center to the margins of society.

Summary

East German women's social status and roles have been redefined under capitalism. Their rights and opportunities have been curtailed, and a more sharply defined gendered division of labor and clearly diverging private and public spheres have emerged. This stands in contrast to accelerated modernization and the establishment of democratic institutions and processes in East Germany. Women have pointed to the paradox of their situation and resolved to resist the imposition of traditional gender roles by struggling for and asserting their needs and identities.

SIGNIFICANCE OF FINDINGS

Joan Kelly-Gadol (1977, p. 139), who studied the emancipation of women during the Renaissance,[1] found that "Women's historical experience often differ[ed] substantially from that of men's." While the Renaissance liberated men "from natural, social, and ideological constraints," it had different, even opposite, effects on women. The Renaissance, known for unlocking unimagined "possibilities for . . . social and cultural expression," restricted social and personal choices for women of *all* classes.[2]

Kelly-Gadol's findings about women's social status during times of profound social transformation hundreds of years ago are still relevant today, highlighting the *persistence of underlying patriarchal structures*. As my findings have demonstrated, the transition from state socialism to capitalism revealed itself as a gendered process in which the social status of women is being redefined by the new, mostly male, elites to ensure the continuity of their own power positions and social stability during times of great uncertainty. West German institutions—notably the *gender-based* division of labor—have defined East German women's position in the new Germany, supporting an important capitalist imperative for women: to regard domestic work and their roles as wives and mothers as *primary* and nondomestic work and corresponding roles as *secondary*.

The efforts of Germany's elites to redefine women's social roles coincided with efforts to incorporate the necessary changes to meet the demands of a global, information-based society of the twenty-first century.[3] Decision-makers seemed to perceive no inconsistency between pursuing, on the one hand, progressive goals while, on the other, striving to "turn back the clock," reinforcing a traditional division of labor that grants women less of the material resources, social status, power, and opportunities for self-actualization than men who share the same social position. Thus, a sharper line can be observed between the private sphere where women belong and the public sphere that men occupy.

For most women in my sample, family and work lives were closely intertwined in the GDR. They did not experience the private-public divide in the way it presents itself in reunified Germany. East German women lived in the overlapping area of these spheres and perceived each sphere as *complementing*—not competing against—the other. They value both equally. They did not have to choose one over the other, or glorify one at the expense of the other. This had implications for their roles as mothers, wives, and workers. Being embedded in both spheres, feeling recognized in public as well as in private for their contributions, resulted in social experiences that did not differ substantially from those of men. This created a distinct perception of social reality. And although women were less privileged than men under socialism, they did not perceive the gap as insurmountable. Power relations between women and men existed, but were perceived to be of a lesser degree than they are in reunified Germany.

This perception is also grounded, in part, in fundamentally different property relations. In the GDR, ownership of property did not exist; hence, women perceived themselves as equal to men in this regard. In accordance with the dominant ideology, everything was owned by the state and, thus, everything belonged to the people. When state-owned property was converted to private property in reunified Germany, the gendered aspects of access to material resources and, thus, the gendered aspects of social roles, were intensified. With their income potential drastically reduced, ownership of anything has become a distant dream for the majority of East German women.

Women's contributions, economic and otherwise, to GDR society were enormous. Yet, these contributions have been rendered largely invisible in reunified Germany. Knowledge about them is not deemed important, even though such knowledge would demonstrate the vast potential that is being wasted by efforts to relegate the majority of women once again exclusively to the home.

IMPLICATIONS FOR FURTHER RESEARCH, THEORY, AND PRACTICE

Women's changing social positions in the transformation from state socialism to capitalism offer a unique opportunity—a "real-life laboratory"—to study further the impact of institutional structures on subjective experiences, and the importance of subjective experiences in the establishment and maintenance of, and change in, institutional structures. Institutional structures cannot be known separately from everyday-life worlds, and everyday-life worlds are being shaped by institutional structures, which themselves are influenced by historical events and economic demands (Smith, 1987, 1990a, 1990b).

Because in the everyday-life worlds, the individual and societal institutions are inseparably linked, women's experiences in *transitional* societies make it possible to chart how, over time, changes in the structures of economy, polity, and ideology influence domesticity, subjectivity, and the intimate, private act of human reproduction, and vice versa (Smith, 1987, 1990a, 1990b).

Examining women's changing social circumstances in the transformation from state socialism to capitalism also directs attention to the limitations of the binary public-private model of social structure: It obscures the depth, breadth, and importance of East German women's daily interactions in the GDR, the majority of which took place in *overlapping* areas of the public and private spheres. In this regard, Hansen (1997, p. 273) points out that "the *dichotomous* language of public and private directs attention *either* to the state and the market, or to family and intimate relations, eclipsing community life" (emphasis added).

Community life played an important part in the GDR. According to Deess (1998), the state had "incorporat[ed women and men] throughout the society into small groups, or collectives, of 5–30 members, [and thus it had] structured dense social networks." Many activities in these networks were not divided into private and public. They involved productive work, socializing, discussions about family, helping each other, and debates about what worked and what did not work under state socialism. As such, these small groups "were [also] a mechanism for the collective articulation of dissent" (Deess, 1998, p. 2).

Accordingly, further research could include the exploration of spaces where private and public spheres *overlap*. Questions to be posed include: What are the implications for gender equality if social activities are not carried out in the public *or* private sphere, but in the *overlapping* space of both? How does that influence the perception of gender difference? How does that impact the definition of gender roles? How does that impact gender ideology?

By directing the focus to the *overlapping* area of the public and private spheres, further research could explore if a capitalist system can permit or even promote such a space, or if it has to insist on a clear either/or divide and, therefore, uphold gender inequality for the system's own survival. Answers to these questions may be arrived at by examining the same sample of East German women's perceptions and experiences five to 10 years later. (The research reported here was conducted in the winter and spring of

1996.) This would also illuminate the extent, and in which way, West Germany's institutional structures have continued to shape East German women's social space, status, and activities.

Conversely, further research should examine whether East German women's everyday-life experiences under state socialism have impacted, in any way, the institutional structures of reunified Germany. Possible questions include: Is there evidence that East German women have succeeded in asserting at home, the workplace, and/or in their communities principles and values that served them well under state socialism? Do the majority of East German women still define employment as essential for realizing gender equality? Does their sense of *identity* still derive from being integrated into the collective process of paid work? Do they still believe that women's participation in the work force is not only a right, but a necessity, because the material and other needs of a family cannot be met by any one person? Does paid work—and not the social status of men they are living with—still define their social status and their place in the wider society? Do they still hold on to the notion that family and paid work can be combined, and that the caring for children and the elderly should be the equal responsibility of both the individual family and the larger society?

Alternatively, has the lapse of time lessened East German women's perseverance and encouraged their compliance with the demands made by West Germany's economy, polity, and ideology, and thus made "inhabiting" *separate* spheres appear more "natural"? Has the resolve of the women to be economically independent of their spouses lessened since I conducted my interviews in the winter and spring of 1996? And if so, why? Has the exclusion of women's participation in the paid labor force limited their social horizons to family and circles of self-selected friends?

Betty Friedan (1995) once remarked that women's social position signals to democracy what the canary (or "budgy") signals to the miners. When elites of any country find it necessary to define women's social status and roles in such a way that they are confined to a space where they cannot breathe freely, and cannot participate fully, it does not bode well for democracy. East German women (and for that matter, women in other East European countries as well) will be reluctant to embrace the *spirit* of democracy and capitalism if their *needs*—for *identity*, *recognition*, and *security*: wants, and values are disregarded (Burton, 1997). Such a reluctance or rejection would also call into question the Western claim for the universality of its institutions (Offe, 1997).

Consequently, I propose further research on women's status in "transitioning" societies to generate *early warning* indicators for deficiencies and failures, as well as successes, of capitalist institutions; and to generate recommendations for *early action*. The elites of these newly established democracies must recognize that if the new social order is to have a viable future, issues concerning women's social conditions and status of equality cannot be ignored. Such research would have implications for feminist theory *and* practice: The design of the preferred society that transcends what *either* East *or* West Germany (or any other society) had to offer women *or* men.

In the meantime, one implication for social policy in reunified Germany has been glaringly revealed by the findings of this study: the direct relationship between the birthrate of the nation and women's social status. When East German women's economic opportunities were reduced or eliminated, they decided against bearing any (more) children. Securing their own survival as well as that of their families took priority. Reducing women's economic opportunities as well as the infrastructure (i.e., child care, after-school care facilities) that allowed women to combine family and paid work will keep the birthrate low. This will create a dependence on foreign labor for the state to survive. As this dependence increases, so might right-wing extremism and xenophobia: two major problems for Western European democracies. The implications are clear: Social peace cannot be achieved unless women participate *fully*—politically, economically, socially, and culturally—and live under social conditions that permit them to choose to have *both* paid work *and* a family.

NOTES

1. The Renaissance was the period of great revival in art, literature, and learning in Europe during the fourteenth, fifteenth, and sixteenth centuries. It began in Italy and spread gradually to other countries, marking the transition from the medieval to the modern world (*Webster's New Twentieth Century Dictionary*, 1975).

2. Courtly love, for example, had been the domain of "powerful feudal women who made it responsive to their sexual and emotional needs." During the Renaissance, it became the domain of "male princes and their courtiers, who had an interest in creating a dependency in women" (Kelly-Gadol, 1977, p. 137).

3. For more details, see Offe (1997) and Perrucci and Wysong (1999).

Appendix 1: Methods

TYPE OF STUDY: ITS SETTING

Professor Paul Shoup of the Woodrow Wilson Department of Government and Foreign Affairs at the University of Virginia (UVA) introduced me to Angelika Schmiegelow-Powell (who was, until her retirement in June 1997, bibliographer for Slavic/German Social Sciences in the Alderman Library at the University of Virginia [UVA]). He had recommended her as an indispensable resource person for my dissertation research. Moreover, Angelika had just returned from Güstrow (the place of her childhood) in the northern part of East Germany, where she had spent two years, at the invitation of the County Board of Supervisors of Güstrow to reorganize the *Volkshochschule* (School of Continuing Education). She had completed her task successfully and had earned the trust and respect of a great many people there. When we met, she took me under her wings and built a bridge for me to the women of Güstrow who eventually made up my *convenience* sample (Frankfort-Nachmias and Nachmias, 1996, pp. 184–185).

I went to Güstrow in the spring of 1996 to conduct field research to generate primary data for examining what changes East German women had experienced in their daily work and family lives as a result of reunification. I interviewed 52 East German women of different ages and from different socioeconomic backgrounds. All of them live in the town of Güstrow and surrounding areas in the state of Mecklenburg-Vorpommern. Because the women constitute a convenience sample, gathered in accordance with the "snowball" sampling method, and because the participants are located in a specific historical, temporal, and cultural context, I did not strive for generalization of findings to universal patterns, regularities, or laws (Jorgensen, 1989, p. 115). The goal of every interpretation in this study has been to increase understanding and not to claim that it is absolute, complete, or reflective of *external validity* (Frankfort-Nachmias and Nachmias, 1996, pp. 118–119). My aim has been only to clarify and enlighten, leaving room for further study.

METHOD OF DATA GATHERING AND TYPE OF INTERVIEW QUESTIONS

It was of enormous help to know Angelika Schmiegelow-Powell, who could open doors to women who were otherwise somewhat skeptical of people coming from the West to examine their lives.[1] To ensure that I communicated my respect for, and interest in, the women as individuals, and to make them feel comfortable with the interviewing process, I sent a letter in advance to those who had agreed to be interviewed in which I introduced myself and my study.[2]

My choice of a *qualitative* data-gathering method was, to a certain extent, influenced by "the *Verstehen* tradition" (Frankfort-Nachmias and Nachmias, 1996, p. 280). At the center of this process lies "empathic understanding" of events and the recognition of "both the historical dimension of human behavior and the *subjective* aspects of the human experience" (emphasis added) (p. 280).

My data-gathering technique was informed further—and primarily—by *Feminist Methods in Social Research* (Reinharz, 1992) and *The Focused Interview* (Merton, Fiske, and Kendall, 1990).[3] The focused interview is conducted with respondents who are "known to have been involved in a particular experience" and focuses on that experience (Frankfort-Nachmias and Nachmias, 1996, p. 234). I developed an interview guide (see Appendix 2) with semistructured questions so I could guide the inquiry, but, through an open-ended format, gave the respondents freedom to reply (Merton, Fiske, and Kendall, 1990, p. 16). This approach allowed me to record the women's ideas, reflections, and recollections as they perceived them (Reinharz, 1992, p. 19). It permitted me to involve them in the production of data about their everyday lives, and to ask them for clarification (Graham, 1984, cited in Reinharz, 1992, p. 18). Moreover, I could step in and draw out the interviewees, encouraging them to define the nuances of their perceptions and get as close as possible to a real understanding of the changes in East German women's daily work and family lives, how they experienced the changes that had occurred since German reunification and how they perceived related issues (Merton, 1990, pp. 70–79).

THE INTERVIEW

I began each interview with the question: "Looking back on life in the German Democratic Republic (GDR), can you tell me what a typical day looked like for you?" From there I continued gently at a pace set by the women to questions pertaining to changes (as a result of reunification) in their daily work and family life, in their relationships with people who were important to them, in their self-image, and in decision making; the relevance of their GDR education in the reunified Germany; the moral dilemmas they encountered; and opportunities and obstacles to their growth in reunified Germany.

I conducted the interviews during March and April 1996 in Güstrow and surrounding areas. Each interview took between 75 minutes and three and a half hours, the average time being about two hours.

In addition to interviewing the women, I asked them to provide, on a brief questionnaire, their demographic data, including employment status, income, age, education, and marital status.

DATA PROCESSING AND ANALYSIS

All interviews were conducted, recorded, and transcribed *in German*. At the center of my analysis are the experiences, perceptions, and beliefs of these women. Because I adopted Strauss' (1987) approach to *grounded theory*, I began my analysis while conducting and recording the interviews and continued while transcribing the tapes. In the process, I made notes of important themes, formulated hypotheses, discarded some, refined others, and formulated new ones (Frankfort-Nachmias and Nachmias, 1996, p. 292).

The analysis of each interview text included more systematic steps that involved continuous "questions as to fit, relevance, and workability about the emerging categories and relationships between them." The data steered the analysis, and the analysis was continuously adjusted to fit the data. The following questions are an example of systematic steps in the analysis of each interview text (Glaser, 1978, p. 39; Strauss, 1987, pp. 27–36):

1. What conditions does the interviewee describe?
2. What does the interviewee say is the basic reason/problem for this condition?
3. What accounts for the reason/problem?

4. What category does this incident indicate?

The answers to these questions led to the development of numerous themes, categories, and hypotheses. As respondents described the conditions of their daily work and family lives before and after German reunification, the themes, categories, and hypotheses were sorted according to whether they referred to "before German reunification" or "after German reunification."

I then compared and combined categories (separately for each of the above headings) into three dimensions or core categories:

1. *occupational* situation
2. *family* situation
3. *material* situation

Once organized under the three dimensions, the categories were analyzed further (for each "before" and "after" reunification) by posing the question: Does the respondent indicate (with regard to a specific category, e.g., employment in reunified Germany) that she is:

1. better off?
2. worse off?
3. the same?
4. no opinion?

Once answers to the above questions were obtained from each respondent, I coded them. I also coded the demographic data and entered all into the SPSS statistical program (see Frankfort-Nachmias and Nachmias, 1996, pp. 161–162) to generate summaries of answers to the various categories, or *nominal* variables.[4]

NOTES

1. The help of Uschi Reichel, my first East German friend, was also invaluable. She recruited the first group of women who volunteered to be interviewed. Then, in accordance with the snowball technique, they convinced more women to participate. Uschi put together the initial list of interviewees, including information on their backgrounds. She also arranged, on my behalf, with the Lutheran and Catholic church communities, to make available one of their cozy meeting rooms and kitchen facilities where many women came for a social gathering. It gave me the opportunity to introduce myself and get to know the majority of the women. I

took this opportunity to ask those who came to add their names to my schedule for interviews at times that were convenient for them. This meeting established a good rapport between us and set the stage for my interviews during the coming weeks. This was especially appreciated, as the area experienced one of the coldest winters and springs in decades during my stay.

Uschi and her family also generously provided me with an apartment that they had built for visiting friends on the upper floor of their house. It contained everything I needed to feel at home and to pursue my work.

2. In early 1996, not every woman in East Germany had a telephone. Hence, reaching them involved time and effort.

3. Belenky et al. (1986), Kreher (1995), and Stanley (1990) also guided me in my approach to this study.

4. For a more complete description of the methods employed, see Sandole-Staroste (2000).

Appendix 2: Interview Guide

INTRODUCTION

I am generally interested in how East German women view their situation today, five and a half years after reunification. I would like to find out how women assess, and have adapted to, the changes that have occurred.

Our conversation will be strictly confidential. Your name will not appear anywhere. With your permission, I would like to tape record it. This will allow me to concentrate on our conversation rather than on taking notes.

There are some specific questions I would like to ask you. At the end of our conversation, I would like to ask you to fill out a short questionnaire to gather background information. Please feel free to add anything you like.

THE QUESTIONS

1. I would like to begin by asking you about your work outside the home. Can you tell me about your job and your work place?

   a. When you think back to the GDR, can you describe what your work life was like?
   b. When you think about reunified Germany, what has work life been like since 1990?
   c. Do you think that the changes you have experienced have been a good or bad thing?

2. Now I would like to ask you about your situation at home. Can you tell me about your family life?

   a. When you think back to the GDR, can you describe to me what an average day at home looked like?
   b. What does your average day at home look like since reunification?
   c. Do you think that the changes you have experienced have been a good or bad thing?

3. Now I would like to ask you about changes in leadership and how you have experienced them.

   a. When you think back to the GDR, how did people in leadership or authority positions influence your work and family life?
   b. How would you compare people in leadership or authority positions in the GDR with people in such positions in reunified Germany?

4. When you think of all that has happened since 1990:

   a. Would you say that people in different occupations experienced reunification in different ways?
   b. Do you think that German reunification has impacted on women and men in the same way?
   c. How do you feel about yourself since reunification?

5. My last questions are about philosophical ideas. When you hear the following concepts, what do they mean to you?

   a. Gender equality?
   b. Women's emancipation?

Thank you for your time and cooperation. I appreciate it very much.

Appendix 3: Respondents' Occupational Status under Socialism (GDR) and Capitalism (FRG)

Respondent	Occupation in the GDR	Occupation in the FRG
1	technician (grain cultivation)	job retraining program
2	cook	job retraining program
3	zoo technician (mink breeding)	job retraining program
4	textile worker	job retraining program
5	gardener	job retraining program
6	teacher for the hearing impaired	teacher for the hearing impaired
7	child-care worker	unemployed
8	nurse	workshop director for disabled people
9	agricultural worker (cattle breeding)	job retraining program
10	cook	job retraining program
11	agricultural worker (cattle breeding)	job retraining program
12	church volunteer	retired
13	textile worker	job retraining program
14	bookkeeper	unemployed
15	teacher	unemployed
16	dairy technician	job retraining program

Respondent	Occupation in the GDR	Occupation in the FRG
17	post office worker	post office worker
18	midwife	chairperson of work council
19	agricultural worker (cattle breeding)	job retraining program
20*	technician (grain cultivation)	job retraining program
21	nurse/counselor	social service administrator
22	administrative assistant	administrative assistant
23	dairy technician	job retraining program
24	shepherd	job retraining program
25	self-employed cosmetician	self-employed cosmetician
26	nurse	unemployed
27	child-care worker	kindergarten teacher
28	retail (buyer)	unemployed
29	agricultural worker (vegetable production)	cafeteria manager
30	art historian	self-employed artist
31	salesclerk	job retraining program
32	salesclerk	unemployed
33	white-collar worker (trading division)	white-collar worker
34	health care worker	social worker
35	waitress/kitchen help	waitress/kitchen help
36	secretary	white-collar worker
37	gardener (orcharding)	unemployed
38**	book dealer	retired
39	school inspector	deputy director of school of continuing education
40	bookkeeper	retired
41	director (material distribution division)	bank manager
42	drug store manager	drug store manager
43	optician	optician
44	administrative assistant	administrative assistant
45	biologist	unemployed
46	professor/researcher	self-employed journalist/author

Respondents' Occupational Status

Respondent	Occupation in the GDR	Occupation in the FRG
47	salesclerk	salesclerk
48	teacher	teacher (short-term contract)
49	deputy school director	teacher
50	white-collar employee	early retirement
51	computer programmer	family counselor
52	director of child-care center	director of child-care center

*Finished school in 1989, the year state socialism collapsed.
**Retired in 1988.

Bibliography

Anderson, Harry, and Fred Coleman. 1989. "Gorbamania in Germany." *Newsweek*. 26 June, p. 31.

Apple, Rima D., and Janet Golden. 1997. *Mothers and Motherhood: Readings in American History*. Columbus: Ohio State University Press.

Assmann, G. and Frank Adler. (Eds.). 1983. *Wörterbuch der marxistisch-leninistischen Soziologie*. Berlin: Dietz.

Associated Press. 1995. "Germany Passes Compromise Law On 'Abortion.'" *Washington Post*. 15 July, p. A18.

Atkinson, Rick. 1995. "German Unification Lays Heavy Burden on Eastern Working Women." *Washington Post*. 29 March, pp. A25, A30.

Baca Zinn, Maxine, and D. Stanley Eitzen. 1996. *Diversity in Families* (4th Edition). New York: HarperCollins.

Bachmann, Ronald, and Claudia Wurst (Eds.). 1996. *Ostdeutsche Lebensverhältnisse unter Wandlungsdruck: Eine Gemeindestudie zu sozialen Seiten der Deutsch-Deutschen Vereinigung*. Frankfurt/Main: Peter Lang GmbH.

Ballauf, Helga. 1998. "Ein Problem wird Zerredet: Den Mangel an Lehrstellen kann nur ein wirksames Bündnis für Ausbildung beseitigen." *Die Zeit*. No. 38, September, p. 79.

Baureithel, Ulrike. 1994. "Vom Schwierigen Umgang der Deutsch-Deutschen Frauenbewegung Miteinander." In Katrin Rohnstock (Ed.), *Stiefschwestern: Was Ost und West-Frauen voneinander denken*. Frankfurt am Main: Fischer Taschenbuch Verlag.

Bebel, August. 1910. *Woman in Socialism*. New York: Socialist Literature.

Beck, Ulrich. 1986. *Risikogesellschaft: Auf dem Weg in eine andere Moderne*. Frankfurt: Suhrkamp.

Beck, Ulrich. 1994. "Vom Verschwinden der Solidarität: Individualisierung der Gesellschaft heißt Verschärfung sozialer Ungleichheit." In Warnfried Dettling (Ed.), *Perspektiven für Deutschland*. München: Droemische Verlagsanstalt Th. Knaur.

Begenau, Jutta. 1995. "Der andere Lebensalltag, die anderen Entscheidungs- und Handlungsspielräume von Frauen aus der DDR und die Schwierigkeiten des Beschreibens ostwestdeutschen Vergleichens." In Zentrum für Interdisziplinäre Frauenforschung der Humboldt-Universität Berlin, (Hg). *Unter Hammer und Zirkel: Frauenbiographien vor dem Hintergrund ostdeutscher Sozialisationserfahrungen*. Dokumentation der Tagung "OSTFEM II—Bestandsaufnahme, Forschungen zu Frauenbiographien," 25–27 November 1993, in Berlin. Pfaffenweiler: Centaurus Verlagsgesellschaft.

Belenky, Mary, Clinchy Blythe, Nancy Goldberger, and Jill Tarule. 1986. *Women's Ways of Knowing: The Development of Self, Voice, and Mind*. New York: Basic Books.

Beratung und Information für Frauen in Mecklenburg-Vorpommern. 1995/96. In M/V, Rostocker Str. 43–49, 17166 Teterow. "Rundbrief 7." Winter.

Berghahn, Sabine, and Andrea Fritzsche. 1991. *Frauenrecht in Ost und West Deutschland: Bilanz, Ausblick*. Berlin: Basisdruck Verlag.

Berghahn, Sabine. 1992. "Frauenrechte im Vereinigungsprozeß." In Christel Faber and Traute Meyer (Eds.), *Unterm Neuen Kleid der Freiheit: Das Korsett der Einheit*. Berlin: Sigma Rainer Bohn Verlag.

Bertram, Barbara. 1996. "Keine Wende zum Heimchen am Herd." Deutsches Jugendinstitut (DJI), Heft 42, November 1997, p. 6.

Blum, Linda M. 1997. "Tough Times for Feminism." *Contemporary Sociology: A Journal of Reviews*. Vol. 26, No. 3, May. Washington, DC: American Sociological Association, pp. 321–323.

Blumberg, Rae Lesser. 1995. "Introduction: Engendering Wealth and Well-Being in an Era of Economic Transformation." In Rae Lesser Blumberg, Cathy A. Rakowski, Irene Tinker, and Michael Monteón (Eds.), *Engendering Wealth and Well-Being: Empowerment for Global Change*. Boulder, CO: Westview Press.

Bocock, Robert. 1993. *Key Ideas of Consumption*. London: Routledge.

Böhm, Tatjana. 1992. "Wo stehen wir Frauen nach 40 Jahren getrennter Geschichte in Deutschland West und Ost?" *Feministische Studien*. 10. Jahrgang, Nr. 2, November, pp. 28–34.

Böhmer, Maria. 1994. *Gesetze zur Gleichberechtigung von Männern und Frauen in Bund und Ländern: Eine Vergleichende Dokumentation*. Konrad Adenauer Stiftung. Bornheim: Pfaffenholz.

Borneman, John. 1991. *After the Wall: East Meets West in New Berlin*. New York: Basic Books, A Division of HarperCollins Publishers.

Brähler, Elmar, and Horst-Eberhard Richter. 1995. "Deutsche Befindlichkeiten im Ost-West Vergleich." *Psychosozial*. 18.Jg. Heft 1, Nr. 59, pp. 7–20.

Braun, Anneliese, Gerda Jaspers, and Ursula Schröter. 1995. "Rolling Back the Gender Status of East German Women." In *German Unification: The Destruction of an Economy*. London: Pluto Press.

Bullfrog Films. 1995. *Who's Counting? Marilyn Waring on Sex, Lies & Global Economics*. P.O. Box 149, Oley, PA. 19547. E-mail: <bullfrog@igc. apc.org>, fax (610)370–1978, phone (610)779–8226. National Film Board of Canada, Studio B, Terre Nash (Director), Kent Martin (Producer).

Bundesministerium für Arbeit und Sozial Ordnung. 1995. "Soziale Sicherheit: Solidarität als Fundament." Bonn: Bundesministerium für Arbeit und Sozial Ordnung.

Bundesministerium für Familie, Senioren, Frauen und Jugend. 1994a. "Materialien zur Familienpolitik der Bundesregierung." Bonn: Bundesministerium für Familie, Senioren, Frauen und Jugend.

Bundesministerium für Familie, Senioren, Frauen und Jugend. 1994b. "Erziehungsgeld, Erziehungsurlaub." Bonn: Bundesministerium für Familie, Senioren, Frauen und Jugend.

Bundesministerium für Frauen und Jugend. 1992. "Frauen in der Bundesrepublik Deutschland." Köln: Kölnische Verlagsdruckerei GmbH.

Bundesministerium für Frauen und Jugend. 1994. "Männer und Frauen sind Gleichberechtigt." Gräfenhainichen: Druckhaus Thamhayn GmbH.

Burton, John. 1997. *Violence Explained: The Sources of Conflict, Violence and Crime and Their Prevention*. Manchester, England: Manchester University Press.

Bütow, Birgit, and Heidi Stecker. (Eds.). 1994. *Eigenartige Ostfrauen: Frauenemanzipation in der DDR und den neuen Bundesländern*. Bielefeld, FRG: Kleine Verlag.

Chafetz, Janet Saltzman. 1990. *Gender Equity: An Integrated Theory of Stability and Change*. Newbury Park, CA: Sage Publications.

Cherlin, Andrew J. 1996. *Public and Private Families: An Introduction*. New York: McGraw-Hill.

Clinton, Hillary Rodham. 1996. *It Takes a Village: And Other Lessons Children Teach Us*. New York: Simon and Schuster.

Collins, Randall, and Scott Coltrane. 1995. *Sociology of Marriage and the Family: Gender, Love, and Property*. Chicago, IL: Nelson-Hall Publishers.

Coltrane, Scott A. 1997. *Gender and Families*. Thousand Oaks, CA: Sage Publications.

Coole, Diana H. 1988. *Women in Political Theory: From Ancient Misogyny to Contemporary Feminism*. Boulder, CO: Lynne Rienner Publishers.

Costas, Ilse. 1994. "Das Geschlechterverhältnis in hochqualifizierten Berufen in den ehemals sozialistischen Ländern: Forschungsfragen und einige Erklärungsversuche." In Ruth Heidi Stein and Angelika Wetterer (Eds.), *Studierende und Studierte Frauen: Ein Ost-West Deutscher Vergleich*. Kassel: Verlag Jenior und Pressler.

Dahn, Daniela. 1990. "Ohne Frauen ist kein Staat zu machen." Presentation at The American Institute for Contemporary German Studies, Washington, DC, April 16.

Daniels, Arne. 1998. "Heute fällst Du Unten Durch. Was passiert in einer Stadt, in der jeder vierte arbeitslos ist? Das Beispiel Dessau." *Die Zeit*. No. 7, 5 February, p. 21.

de Beauvoir, Simone. 1952. *The Second Sex*. New York: Knopf.

Deess, Pierre. 1998. "Social Change in the German Democratic Republic: The Role of Institutional Pre-mobilization Practices (IPPs)." Paper presented at the 1998 Annual Meeting of the American Sociological Association, San Francisco, August 21–24.

Defense Diplomacy. Special Report. 1989. "German Democratic Republic." Vol. 7, No. 5, May, pp. 33–36.

Derbyshire, Ian. 1991. *Politics in Germany: From Division to Unification* (2nd Edition). Edinburgh (Scotland): W. & R. Chambers, Ltd.

Dienel, Christiane. 1996. *Frauen in Führungspositionen in Europa*. München: Verlag Deutsches Jugendinstitut.

Diewald, Martin, and Karl Ulrich Mayer. (Eds.). 1996. *Zwischenbilanz der Wiedervereinigung*. Opladen: Leske und Budrich.

Dölling, Irene. 1990. "Frauen- und Männerbilder. Eine Analyse von Fotos in DDR Zeitschriften." *Feministische Studien*. 8. Jahrgang, Nr. 1, Mai, pp. 35–49.

Dölling, Irene. 1992. "Between Hope and Hopelessness: Women in the GDR after the 'Turning Point.'" In Paul G. Lewis (Ed.), *Democracy and Civil Society in Eastern Europe*. New York: St. Martin's Press.

Dölling, Irene. 1995. "Zum Verhältnis von Modernen und Traditionalen Aspekten im Lebenszusammenhang von Frauen in der DDR." In Zentrum für Interdisziplinäre Frauenforschung der Humboldt-Universität Berlin (Hg). *Unter Hammer und Zirkel: Frauenbiographien vor dem Hintergrund ostdeutscher Sozialisationserfahrungen*. Dokumentation der Tagung "OSTFEM II—Bestandsaufnahme, Forschungen zu Frauenbiographien," 25–27 November 1993, in Berlin. Pfaffenweiler: Centaurus Verlagsgesellschaft.

Drozdiak, William. 1997. "Unlearning Marxism: East Germans Find New Education Both Liberating, Jarring." *Washington Post*. 11 February, p. A15.

Drozdiak, William. 1998. "Dreams Unfulfilled Leave Eastern Germans Dismayed: Chronic Economic Woes May Hurt Kohl's Chances in Key Regional Vote." *Washington Post*. 25 April, pp. A10–11.

The Economist. 1999. "One Society, Stretched and Divided." In "The Berlin Republic: A Survey of Germany." 6 February, p. 13.

Ehrenreich, Barbara. 1990. *Fear of Falling: The Inner Life of the Middle Class*. New York: Harper Perennial.

Ehrenreich, Barbara. 1996. "Zipped Lips: So You Think You're Guaranteed Free Speech on the Job? Try Telling That to Your Boss." *Time*. February 5, p. 80.

Eichler, Margrit. 1997. *Family Shifts: Families, Policies, and Gender Equality.* New York and Toronto: Oxford University Press.

Einhorn, Barbara. 1993. *Cinderella Goes to Market: Citizenship, Gender and Women's Movement in East Central Europe.* London and New York: Verso.

Eisenstein, Zillah. 1993. "Eastern European Male Democracies: A Problem of Unequal Equality." In Nanette Funk and Magda Mueller (Eds.), *Gender Politics and Post-Communism: Reflections from Eastern Europe and the Former Soviet Union.* New York: Routlege.

Eisenstein, Zillah. (Ed.). 1979. *Capitalist Patriarchy and the Case for Socialist Feminism.* New York: Monthly Review Press.

Eisler, Riane. 1988. *The Chalice and the Blade: Our History, Our Future.* San Francisco: Harper and Row.

Elsner, Gisela. 1982. "Clara Zetkin, 1857–1933." In Hans Jürgen Schultz (Ed.), *Frauen—Porträts aus Zwei Jahrhunderten* (pp. 158–171). Stuttgart: Kreuz Verlag.

Emundts, Corinna, and Adalbert Zehnder. 1998. "Das Weinen der Schmetterlinge." *Süddeutsche Zeitung.* No. 217. September 21, p. 3.

Engels, Friedrich. 1962. "The Origin of the Family, Private Property and the State." In *Karl Marx and Fredrick Engels*, Vol. II. Moscow: Foreign Language Publishing House.

Eshleman, J. Ross. 1997. *The Family* (8th Edition). Needham Heights, MA: Allyn and Bacon.

Falk, Gabriele, and Margit Hohmann. 1993. *Situationsbericht 1992 der Stadt Güstrow.* Güstrow: Town Council.

Festinger, Leon. 1957. *A Theory of Cognitive Dissonance.* Evanston, IL: Row Peterson.

Fisher, Marc. 1992. "Court Blocks German Law on Abortion." *Washington Post.* 5 August, p. A25.

Fisher, Marc. 1995. *After the Wall: Germany, The Germans and the Burdens of History.* New York: Simon and Schuster.

Flax, Jane. 1990. *Thinking Fragments: Psychoanalysis, Feminism, and Postmodernism in the Contemporary West.* Berkeley: University of California Press.

Footnotes. 1997. "Major ASA Awards Recipients Honored in Toronto." September, October, p. 4.

Forrester, Viviane. 1997. *Der Terror der Ökonomie.* (The terror of the economy.) Vienna, Austria: Zsolnay Verlag.

Fox Keller, Evelyn. 1985. *Reflections on Gender and Science.* New Haven, CT: Yale University Press.

Frankfort-Nachmias, Chava, and David Nachmias. 1996. *Research Methods in the Social Sciences* (5th Edition). New York: St. Martin's Press.

French, Marilyn. 1985. *Beyond Power: On Women, Men, and Morals.* New York: Summit Books.

Friedan, Betty. 1976. *The Feminine Mystique*. Harmondsworth, England: Penguin Books.

Friedan, Betty. 1995. *A New Paradigm in American Politics*. Lecture conducted together with Seymour Martin Lipset in the Harris Theater at George Mason University, March 7.

Friedrich Ebert Stiftung. 1987. *Organisationen und Verbände der DDR*. Bonn: Friedrich Ebert Stiftung.

Fröhling, Jörg, Reinhild Meinel, and Karl Riha. (Eds.). 1996. *Wende-Literatur: Bibliographie und Materialen zur Literatur der Deutschen Einheit*. Frankfurt/Main: Europäischer Verlag der Wissenschaften.

Funk, Nanette. 1993. "Abortion and German Unification." In Nanette Funk and Magda Mueller (Eds.), *Gender Politics and Post-Communism: Reflections from Eastern Europe and the Former Soviet Union*. New York: Routledge.

Gaschke, Susanne. 1998. "Im Auftrag von Frau Meier." *Die Zeit*. No. 8, 12 February, pp. 11–12.

Gerhard, Ute. 1990. *Gleichheit Ohne Angleichung*. München: Beck'sche Verlagsbuchhandlung.

Gerson, Kathleen. 1997. "Dismantling the 'Gendered Family': Breadwinning, Gender, and the Family Values Debate." *Contemporary Sociology*. Vol. 27, No. 3, pp. 228–230.

Giffin, Frederick C. (Ed.). 1973. *Woman as Revolutionary*. New York: Signet Classics.

Gillis, John R. 1997. *A World of Their Own Making: Myth, Ritual, and the Quest for Family Values*. Cambridge, MA: Harvard University Press.

Glaser, Barney G. 1978. *Theoretical Sensitivity*. Mill Valley, CA: Sociology Press.

Glazer, Nona Y. 1993. *Women's Paid and Unpaid Labor: The Work Transfer in Health Care and Retailing*. Philadelphia: Temple University Press.

Grosser, Dieter. 1998. *Das Wagnis der Währungs-, Wirtshafts-und Sozialunion*. Stuttgart: Verlags-Anstalt.

Gysi, Jutta, and Dagmar Meyer. 1993. "Leitbild: Berufstätige Mutter—DDR Frauen in Familie, Partnerschaft und Ehe." In Gisela Helwig and Hildegard Maria Nickel (Eds.), *Frauen in Deutschland 1945–1992*. Berlin: Akademie Verlag.

Häder, Michael, and Sabine Häder. 1995. *Turbulenzen im Transformationsprozess: Die Individuelle Bewältigung des Sozialen Wandels in Ostdeutschland 1990–1992*. Opladen: Westdeutscher Verlag.

Hagemann-White, Carol. 1997. "Current Debates in German Social Science." *Contemporary Sociology: A Journal of Reviews*. Vol. 26, No. 5, September, pp. 556–559. Washington, DC: American Sociological Association.

Hahn, Toni, and Gerhard Schön. 1995. "Besonderheiten ostdeutscher Langzeitarbeitslosigkeit." In Hans Jürgen Andreß (Ed.), *Fünf Jahre Danach: Zur Entwicklung von Arbeitsmarkt und Sozialstruktur im vereinten Deutschland*. Berlin: Walter de Gruyter.

Haller, Michael. 1992. *Bezahlen die Frauen die Wiedervereinigung?* München: Piper Verlag.

Hansen, Karen V. 1997. "Rediscovering the Social: Visiting Practices in Antebellum New England and the Limits of the Public/Private Dichotomy." In Jeff Weintraub and Krishan Kumar (Eds.), *Public and Private in Thought and Practice: Perspectives on the Grand Dichotomy*. Chicago and London: The University of Chicago Press.

Harding, Sandra, and Merill B. Hintikka. (Eds.). 1983. *Discovering Reality: Feminist Perspectives on Epistemology, Metaphysics, Methodology and Philosophy of Science*. Boston: D. Reidel.

Hartmann, Heidi. 1981. *Women and Revolution: A Discussion of the Unhappy Marriage of Marxism and Feminism*. Montreal, Quebec: Black Rose Books.

Hartsock, Nancy C.M. 1983. *Money, Sex and Power*. New York: Longman.

Hays, Sharon. 1996. *The Cultural Contradictions of Motherhood*. New Haven, CT: Yale University Press.

Heins, Martin. 1994. *Transformationsprozesse in Ostdeutschland: Norm-, Anomie-, und Innovationstheoretische Aspekte*. Wiesbaden: Deutscher Universitäts Verlag.

Heintz, Jim. 1999. "Swedish Scandal Has Modest Proportions: Top Official Used Contacts to Acquire Small Apartment in Tight Housing Market." *Washington Post*. 20 March, p. K8.

Helwerth, Ulrike. 1991. "Wenn Mutti Früh zur Arbeit geht. . . ." In *TAZ-DDR Journal Zur November Revolution*, April, pp. 138–140.

Hill Collins, Patricia. 1991. *Black Feminist Thought: Knowledge, Consciousness, and the Politics of Empowerment*. London: HarperCollins Publishers.

Hoffmann, A. 1992. *Facts about Germany*. Frankfurt/Main: Societätsdruck.

Holst, Elke, and Jürgen Schupp. 1995. "Erwerbsbeteiligung von Frauen in West- und Ostdeutschland. In Wolfgang Glatzer and Heinz-Nobert Noll (Eds.), *Getrennt Vereint: Lebensverhältnisse in Deutschland seit der Wiedervereinigung*. Frankfurt: Campus Verlag.

Horn, Erdmute. 1992. "Überlegungen zur staatlichen Gleichberechtigungspolitik in der Bundesrepublik Deutschland und in der Deutschen Demokratischen Republik." In Christel Faber and Traute Meyer (Eds.), *Unterm Neuen Kleid der Freiheit: Das Korsett der Einheit*. Berlin: Sigma Rainer Bohn Verlag.

Icks, Annette. 1995. *Der Transformationsprozeß in der ehemaligen DDR 1989–1991: Politische, soziologische und wirtschaftliche Aspekte*. Hamburg: Verlag Dr. Kovac.

Institut für Angewandte Sozialwissenschaft. 1990. *Frauen in den Neuen Bundesländern*. Bad Godesberg: INFAS, Kompetenz in Forschung und Anwendung.

Institut für Demoskopie Allensbach. (Ed.). 1993. *Frauen in Deutschland: Lebensverhältnisse, Lebenstile und Zukunftserwartungen.* Köln: Bundverlag

International Herald Tribune. 1996. "Women in Work Force." 12 February, p. 5.

Jaggar, Alison M. 1983. *Feminist Politics and Human Nature.* Totowa, NJ: Rowman & Allanheld.

Jaggar, Alison M., and Paula S. Rothenberg Struhl. (Eds.). 1984. *Feminist Frameworks.* New York: McGraw-Hill.

Janert, Josefina. 1998. "Die Meckerecken der DDR." *Die Zeit.* No. 47. 12 November, p. 85.

Jansen, Rolf. 1995. "Arbeitsbedingungen und Arbeitsbelastungen." In Wolfgang Glatzer and Heinz-Nobert Noll (Eds.), *Getrennt Vereint: Lebensverhältnisse in Deutschland seit der Wiedervereinigung.* Frankfurt: Campus Verlag.

Jarausch, Konrad H. 1995. *Die Unverhoffte Einheit 1989–1990.* Frankfurt Main: Suhrkamp.

Johnson, Allan G. 1997. *The Gender Knot: Unraveling Our Patriarchal Legacy.* Philadelphia: Temple University Press.

Johnson, Miriam M. 1997. "Review?" *Contemporary Sociology: A Journal of Reviews.* Vol. 26, No. 3. Washington, DC: American Sociological Association, pp. 395–399.

Jorgensen, Danny L. 1989. *Participant Observation: A Methodology for Human Studies.* Applied Social Research Methods Series, Vol. 15. Newbury Park, CA: Sage Publications.

Kaplan, Abraham. 1964. *The Conduct of Inquiry: Methodology for Behavioral Science.* Scranton, PA: Chandler Publishing Company.

Kaufmann, Eva, Ursula Schröter, and Renate Ullrich. 1997. *"Als Ganzer Mensch Leben": Lebensansprüche Ostdeutscher Frauen.* Berlin: Trafo Verlag.

Kaufmann, Franz-Xaver. 1995. *Zukunft der Familie im Vereinten Deutschland: Gesellschaftliche und Politische Bedingungen.* München: C.H. Beck'sche Verlagsbuchhandlung.

Kelly-Gadol, Joan. 1977. "Did Women Have a Renaissance?" In Renate Bridenthal and Claudia Koonz (Eds.), *Becoming Visible: Women in European History.* Boston: Houghton Mifflin.

Kreher, Simone. 1995. "Einige Bemerkungen über den Standort von Biogaphieforschung in der Soziologie." In Zentrum für Interdisziplinäre Frauenforschung der Humboldt-Universität Berlin (Hg.). *Unter Hammer und Zirkel: Frauenbiographien vor dem Hintergrund ostdeutscher Sozialisationserfahrungen.* Dokumentation der Tagung "OSTFEM II—Bestandsaufnahme, Forschungen zu Frauenbiographien." 25–27 November 1993, in Berlin. Pfaffenweiler: Centaurus Verlagsgesellschaft.

Kreisky, Eva. (Ed.). 1996. "Vom Patriarchalen Staatssozialismus zur Patriarchalen Demokratie: Der Politische Systemwechsel in Osteuropa aus der Gender-Perspektive." In Eva Kreisky (Ed.), *Vom Patriarchalen Staatsozialismus zur Patriarchalen Demokratie.* Wien, Austria: Verlag für Gesellschaftskritik.

Kuhn, Thomas S. 1970. *The Structure of Scientific Revolutions* (2nd Edition). Chicago: The University of Chicago Press.

Kumar, Krishan. 1992. "The Revolutions of 1989: Socialism, Capitalism, and Democracy." In *Theory and Society.* Vol. 31, No. 3, pp. 309–356.

Kurz-Adam, Maria. 1994. "Spaziergang durch den Feminismus? Versuch einer Standortbestimmung der Frauenforschung zwischen modernen Weltbildern und postmoderner Vielfalt." In Gerlinde Seidenspinner (Ed.), *Frau sein in Deutschland: Aktuelle Themen, Perspektiven und Ziele Feministischer Sozialforschung.* München: Verlag Deutsches Jugendinstitut.

Lengermann, Patricia Madoo, and Jill Niebrugge-Brantley. 1992. "Contemporary Feminist Theory." In George Ritzer (Ed.), *Contemporary Sociological Theory.* New York: McGraw-Hill.

Lenin, Vladimir Illich. 1951. "Woman and Society." In *The Woman Question: Selections from the Writings of Marx, Engels, Lenin and Stalin.* New York: International Publishers.

Lessing, Doris. 1997. *Schritte im Schatten.* Hamburg: Hoffmann und Campe Verlag.

MacKinnon, Catharine A. 1989. *Toward a Feminist Theory of the State.* Cambridge, MA: Harvard University Press.

Marks, Elaine, and Isabelle de Courtivron. 1981. *New French Feminisms.* New York: Schocken Books.

Marx, Karl, and Friedrick Engels. 1964. *The Communist Manifesto.* New York: Washington Square Press.

Mathews, Jay. 1995. "Poll Finds Women Favor Dual Roles. Most in Survey Proud of Ability to Blend Work, Home Responsibilities." *Washington Post.* 11 May, p. B13.

Menge, Marlies. 1998. "Ick bin der Antizeitgeist." *Die Zeit.* No. 12. March, p. 22.

Merton, Robert K., Marjorie Fiske, and Patricia L. Kendall. 1990. *The Focused Interview: A Manual of Problems and Procedures.* New York: The Free Press.

Michaelis, Rolf. 1998. "Glut in der Asche: Irmtraud Morgners Nachlaß 'Das heroische Testament.'" *Die Zeit.* No. 48, 19 November, p. 63.

Misselwitz, Hans J. 1996. *Nicht länger mit dem Gesicht nach Westen.* Bonn: Verlag J.H.W. Dietz.

Misselwitz, I. 1991. "Zur Identität der DDR Bürger—Eine erste Gedankensammlung." *Psychosozial.* Heft I, Nr. 45, pp. 30–33.

Mitchener, Brandon. 1995. "A Warning in East Germany's Dependent Status." *International Herald Tribune.* 30 June, p. 5.

Morgener, Irmtraud. 1998. *Das heroische Testament: Ein Roman in Fragmenten.* München: Luchterhand Literaturverlag.

Müller, Klaus, Richard Hauser, Joachim Frick, and Gert Wagner. 1995. "Zur Entwicklung der Einkommensverteilung und der Einkommenszufriedenheit in den neuen und alten Bundesländern 1990 bis 1993." In Wolfgang Glatzer and Heinz-Nobert Noll (Eds.), *Getrennt Vereint: Lebensverhältnisse in Deutschland seit der Wiedervereinigung.* Frankfurt: Campus Verlag.

Münkler, Herfried. 1998. "Zielloses Dahintreiben: Richard Sennett analysiert die Folgen des flexiblen Kapitalismus für die Lebensführung der Menschen." *Die Zeit.* No. 14, 26 March, p. 26.

Nickel, Hildegard Maria. 1993. "Mitgestalterin des Sozialismus: Frauenarbeit in der DDR." *Frauen in Deutschland 1945–1992.* Berlin: Akademie Verlag.

Nickel, Hildegard Maria. 1995. "DDR-Sozialisationserfahrungen: Chance oder Risiko für weibliche Erwerbsbiographien?" In Zentrum für interdisziplinäre Frauenforschung der Humboldt- Universität Berlin (Hg.), *Unter Hammer und Zirkel: Frauenbiographien vor dem Hintergrund ostdeutscher Sozialisationserfahrungen.* Dokumentation der Tagung "OSTFEM II—Bestandsaufnahme, Forschungen zu Frauenbiographien." 25–27 November 1993, in Berlin. Pfaffenweiler: Centaurus Verlagsgesellschaft.

Offe, Claus. 1997. *Varieties of Transition: The East European and East German Experience.* Cambridge, MA: MIT Press.

Ortner, Sherry B., and Harriet Whitehead. (Eds.). 1981. *Sexual Meanings: The Cultural Construction of Gender and Sexuality.* New York: Cambridge University Press.

Ostner, Ilona. 1995. "Arm ohne Ehemann? Sozialpolitische Regulierung von Lebenschancen für Frauen im Internationalen Vergleich." In *Aus Politik und Zeitgeschichte.* Supplement to Weekly Paper of *Das Parlament.* B36–37, p. 10.

Parmentier, Klaus. 1995. "Die Arbeitsmarktentwicklung in der Bundesrepublik Deutschland unter besonderer Berücksichtigung der Situation in den neuen Bundesländern." In Wolfgang Glatzner and Heinz-Nobert Noll (Eds.), *Getrennt Vereint: Lebensverhältnisse in Deutschland seit der Wiedervereinigung.* Frankfurt: Campus Verlag.

Peltak, Jennifer. 1998. "Challenges of Having It All in the 90s." *The Community Newspaper.* 19 March, p. A7.

Penrose, Virginia. 1990. "Vierzig Jahre SED-Frauenpolitik: Ziele, Strategien, und Ergebnisse." In *Frauenforschung: Informationsdienst des Forschungsinstituts Frau und Gesellschaft.* Hannover, 8. Jahrgang, Heft 4, pp. 60–78.

Perrucci, Roberts and Earl Wysong. 1999. *The New Class Society.* Boulder, CO: Rowman and Littlefield Publishers.

Pinzler, Petra. 1996. "Der alltägliche Skandal." *Die Zeit.* No. 32, 2 August, p. 22.

Pollack, Detlef. 1990. "Das Ende einer Organisationsgesellschaft. Systemtheoretische Überlegungen zum gesellschaftlichen Umbruch in der DDR." *Zeitschrift für Soziologie.* No. 19, pp. 292–307.

Pond, Elizabeth. 1993. *Beyond the Wall: Germany's Road to Unification*. New York: The Twentieth Century Fund, Inc.

Potuchek, Jean. 1997. *Who Supports the Family? Gender and Breadwinning in Dual-Earner Marriages*. Stanford, CA: Stanford University Press.

Prantl, Heribert. 1998. "Hilflos vor rechter Gewalt." *Süddeutsche Zeitung*. No. 217. September, p. 2.

Press and Information Office of the Federal Government. 1991. *The Unification of Germany in 1990*. Bonn: Press and Information Office of the Federal Government.

Presser, Harriet B. 1994. "Employment Schedules Among Dual-Earner Spouses and the Division of Household Labor by Gender." *American Sociological Review*. Vol. 59, No. 3, June, pp. 348–364.

Rabe, Christine. 1998. "Wenig Zeit für Feminismus." *Die Zeit*. No. 8, 12 February, p. 14.

Rai, Shirin, Hilary Pilkington, and Annie Phizacklea. 1992. *Women in the Face of Change*. London and New York: Routledge.

Reicherzer, Judith. 1991. "Der letzte Schnitt: 250,000 Frauen verlieren ihren Job." *Die Zeit*. Nr. 48, 22 November, p. 23.

Reinharz, Shulamit. 1992. *Feminist Methods in Social Research*. New York: Oxford University Press.

Rhode, Deborah. 1997. *Speaking of Sex: The Denial of Gender Inequality*. Cambridge, MA: Harvard University Press.

Rocksloh-Papendieck, Barbara. 1995. *Verlust der Kollektiven Bindung: Frauenalltag in der Wende*. Pfaffenweiler: Centaurus Verlag-Gesellschaft.

Roemer, Annemarie. 1995. *Geboren 1949: Lebensläufe von Frauen in Ost und West*. Dresden: Referat Gleichstellung von Frau und Mann an der Technische Universität Dresden.

Root Aulette, Judy. 1994. *Changing Families*. Belmont, CA: Wadsworth Publishing.

Rosenberg, Dorothy. 1991. "Shock Therapy: GDR Women in Transition from a Socialist Welfare State to a Social Market Economy." *Signs*. Vol. 117, No. 1, Autumn, pp. 129–151.

Rudolph, Hedwig. 1990. "Brot und Rosen zu DM-Preisen? Frauenarbeit im wirtschaftlichen Umbruch." In *Frauenforschung. Informationsdienst des Forschungsinstituts Frau und Gesellschaft*. Hannover, 8. Jahrgang, Heft 4, pp. 1–13.

Rueschemeyer, Marilyn. 1994. "Women in the Politics of Eastern Germany: The Dilemmas of Unification." In Marilyn Rueschemeyer (Ed.) *Women in the Politics of Postcommunist Eastern Europe*. New York and London: M.E. Sharpe.

Sandole-Staroste, Ingrid. 2000. *East German Women's Struggle to Resist the Strengthening of Traditional Gender Roles in the Reunified Germany*.

Doctoral Dissertation. Charlottesville: University of Virginia, Department of Sociology, January.

Sauer, Birgit. 1996. "Transition zur Demokratie? Die Kategorie 'Geschlecht' als Prüfstein für die Zuverlässigkeit von sozialwissenschaftlichen Transformationstheorien." In Eva Kreisky (Ed.), *Vom Patriarchalen Staatssozialismus zur Patriarchalen Demokratie*. Wien, Austria: Verlag für Gesellschaftkritik.

Schmid, Klaus-Peter. 1998. "The fünfte Kolonne: Wie die PDS um den ostdeutschen Mittelstand wirbt." *Die Zeit*. Nr. 38, 10 September, p. 29.

Schmidt, Renate. 1994. "Jenseits des Patriarchats." In Warnfried Dettling (Ed.), *Perspektiven für Deutschland*. München: Droemersche Verlagsanstalt Th. Knaur Nachf.

Schmitz, Michael. 1995. *Wendestress: Die Psychosozialen Kosten der Deutschen Einheit*. Berlin: Rowohlt.

Schneider, Norbert F., Angelika Tölke, and Bernhard Nauck. 1995. "Familie im gesellschaftlichen Umbruch—Nachholende oder Divergierende Modernisierung?" In Bernhard Nauck, Norbert Schneider, and Angelika Tölke (Eds.), *Familie und Lebenslauf im Gesellschaftlichen Umbruch*. Stuttgart: Ferdinand Enke Verlag.

Scholz, Hannelore. 1994. "East-West Women's Culture in Transition: Are East German Women the Losers of Reunification?" *Journal of Women's History*. Vol. 5, No. 3, Winter, pp. 108–116.

Schröder, H. 1991. "Identität, Individualität, und Psychische Befindlichkeiten des DDR-Bürgers im Umbruch." *Zeitschrift für Sozialisationsforschung und Erziehungssoziologie*. I Supplement, pp. 163–176.

Schröter, Ursula. 1995. "Ostdeutsche Frauen zwischen Verlieren und Gewinnen." In *Sozialer und Demographischer Wandel in den Neuen Bundesländern*. Berlin: Akademie Verlag GmbH.

Schweriner Nachrichten. 1996. "Klassenkampf von gestern." 7 March, p. 2.

Schweriner Volkszeitung. 1996. "Arbeitslosigkeit vor Neuer Rekordmarke." 3 March, p. 5.

Schweriner Volkszeitung. 1996. "Begrüßungsgeld allein lockt keine Klapperstörche an." 5 March, p. 4.

Schweriner Volkszeitung. 1996. "Arbeitslosigkeit klettert von Rekord zu Rekord." 6 March, p. 1.

Schweriner Volkszeitung. 1996. "Frauen sind die Lösung, nicht das Problem." 8 March, p. 3.

Schweriner Volkszeitung. 1996. "Dienstmädchen ist die Lösung." 8 March, p. 7.

Schweriner Volkszeitung. 1996. "Frauen wehren sich gegen die Rolle als Heimchen am Herd." 9 March, p. 19.

Schweriner Volkszeitung. 1996. "Winziges Cafe in Wittenburg." 20 March.

Schweriner Volkszeitung. 1996. "Mehrheit der Bürger einig: Land muß Vulkanfirmen retten." 21 March, p. 5.

Seager, Joni. 1997. *The State of Women in the World*. London: Penguin Group.

Seidenspinner, Gerlinde. 1994. "Frauen forschen für Frauen." In Gerlinde Seidenspinner (Ed.), *Frau sein in Deutschland: Aktuelle Themen, Perspektiven und Ziele Feministischer Sozialforschung*. München: Verlag Deutsches Jugendinstitut, pp. 7–14.

Sennett, Richard. 1998a. *Der flexible Mensch: Die Kultur des neuen Kapitalismus*. Berlin: Berlin Verlag.

Sennett, Richard. 1998b. *The Personal Consequences of Work in the New Capitalism*. New York: W.W. Norton & Company.

Sennett, Richard. 1998c. "Why Good Workers Make Bad People." In *New Statesman*. 9 October, pp. 25–27.

Shaffer, Harry G. 1981. *Women in the Two Germanies: A Comparative Study of a Socialist and a Non-Socialist Society*. New York: Pergamon Press.

Sherif, Muzafer. 1967. *Group Conflict and Cooperation: Their Social Psychology*. London: Routledge and Kegan Paul.

Sichtermann, Barbara. 1998. "Ein Weg der aus Gewalt und Armut hinausführen sollte." In *Die Zeit*. Nr. 14, 26 March, p. 17.

Simon, Annette. 1995. *Versuch Mir und Anderen die Ostdeutsche Moral zu Erklären*. Gießen: Psychosozial Verlag.

SIPRI (Stockholm International Peace Research Institute). 1976. *World Armaments and Disarmament*. Cambridge, MA: The MIT Press.

SIPRI (Stockholm International Peace Research Institute). 1991. *World Armaments and Disarmament*. Oxford: Oxford University Press.

Skolnick, Arlene S. 1996. *The Intimate Environment: Exploring Marriage and the Family* (6th Edition). New York: HarperCollins.

Smith, Dorothy E. 1987. *The Everyday World as Problematic: A Feminist Sociology*. Boston: Northeastern University Press.

Smith, Dorothy E. 1990a. *The Conceptual Practices of Power: A Feminist Sociology of Knowledge*. Boston: Northeastern University Press.

Smith, Dorothy E. 1990b. *Texts, Facts and Femininity: Exploring the Relations of Ruling*. London: Routledge and Kegan Paul.

Spiegel. 1995. "Ostdeutsche wußten eben, 'wie man in einem fixierten System überlebt.'" No. 29. http://hamburg.bda.de:800/bda/int/spiegel/article/sp29050.html>. Accessed July 18, 1998.

Staatliche Zentralverwaltung für Statistik. 1988. *Die Frau in der DDR: Fakten und Zahlen*. Berlin: Staatsverlag der Deutschen Demokratischen Republik.

Stanley, Liz. (Ed). 1990. *Feminist Praxis: Research, Theory, and Epistemology in Feminist Sociology*. London and New York: Routledge.

Staud, Toralf. 1998. "Reise zu den Brandstiftern. Mecklenburg: Die NPD auf dem Vormarsch." *Die Zeit*. Nr. 38, 10 September, p. 3.

Stein, Ruth Heidi, and Angelika Wetterer. (Eds.). 1994. *Studierende und Studierte Frauen: Ein Ost-West Deutscher Vergleich*. Kassel: Verlag Jenior and Pressler.

Strauss, Anselm L. 1987. *Qualitative Analysis for Social Scientists*. Cambridge: Cambridge University Press.

Szepansky, Gerda. 1995. *Die Stille Emanzipation: Women in der DDR*. Frankfurt: Fischer Taschenbuch Verlag.

Tageszeitung. 1999. "In der Schuldenfalle: 2,6 Millionen Haushalte werden von Zinsen und Tilgung erdrückt." 14 January, p. 16.

The Week in Germany. 1995. "Government, Industry and Unions Join Forces in Effort to Put the Long-term Unemployed Back to Work." 27 January, p. 1.

The Week in Germany. 1995. "Youth Report '94: For Young Eastern Germans, Greatest Concern is Employment." 27 January, p. 6.

The Week in Germany. 1995. "German Unions Lost Over a Half-Million Members in 1994." 2 June, p. 5.

The Week in Germany. 1995a. "Promoting Upward Mobility for Women in the Corporate World: A Matter of Language." 22 September, p. 5.

The Week in Germany. 1995b. "Berlin's Youth Facing Increasing Poverty, Report Says." 22 September, p. 5.

The Week in Germany. 1998. "Earlier Than Usual Seasonal Increase in Unemployment." 11 December, p. 4.

Thompson, Bob. 1998. "Consumed." *The Washington Post Magazine*. 20 December, pp. 10–15, 25–30.

Thompson, J.D., and D.R. Van Houten. 1970. *The Behavioral Sciences: An Interpretation*. Reading, MA and London: Addison-Wesley.

Toffler, Alvin. 1972. *Future Shock*. New York: Bantam Books, Inc.

Tong, Rosemarie. 1989. *Feminist Thought: A Comprehensive Introduction*. Boulder, CO: Westview Press.

Trappe, Heike. 1995a. "Handlungsstrategien von Frauen unterschiedlicher Generationen zur Verbindung von Familie und Beruf und deren Beinflussung durch sozialpolitische Rahmenbedingungen." In Zentrum für Interdisziplinäre Frauenforschung der Humboldt-Universität Berlin (Hg.), *Unter Hammer und Zirkel: Frauenbiographien vor dem Hintergrund ostdeutscher Sozialisationserfahrungen*. Dokumentation der Tagung "OSTFEM II—Bestandsaufnahme, Forschungen zu Frauenbiographien." 25–27 November 1993, in Berlin. Pfaffenweiler: Centaurus Verlagsgesellschaft.

Trappe, Heike. 1995b. *Emanzipation oder Zwang? Frauen in der DDR zwischen Beruf, Familie und Sozialpolitik*. Berlin: Akademie Verlag.

Trebilcot, Joyce. (Ed.). 1984. *Mothering: Essays in Feminist Theory*. Totowa, NJ: Rowman & Allanheld.

Unabhängiger Frauenverband (Independent Women's Union). 1990. Berlin: Haus der Demokratie.

Vereinte Nationen Informationsdienst. 1996. Internationales Zentrum Wien, May.

Vertrag über die Schaffung einer Währungs-, Wirtschafts- und Sozialunion zwischen der Bundesrepublik Deutschland und der Deutschen Demokratischen Republik. 1990. Nr. 63/S. 517, 18 May. Bonn: Presse und Informationsamt der Bundesregierung.

Voigt, Jutta. 1992. "Der Kühle Charme der Konkurrenz." *Zeitmagazin.* Nr. 14, 27 March, p. 6.

Wagner, Wolf. 1996. *Kulturschock Deutschland* (Germany's cultural shock). Hamburg: Rotbuch Verlag.

Waldrop, M. Mitchell. 1992. *Complexity: The Emerging Science at the Edge of Order and Chaos.* New York and London: Simon and Schuster.

Waring, Marilyn. 1999. *Counting for Nothing: What Men Value and What Women Are Worth.* Toronto: University of Toronto Press.

Washington Post Health. 1998. "Kitchen Patrol." Vol. 14, No. 42, 20 October, p. 5.

Watson, Peggy. 1997. "(Anti)feminism after Communism." In Ann Oakley and Juliet Mitchell (Eds.), *Who Is Afraid of Feminism?* New York: The New York University Press.

Webster, Noah. 1975. *Webster's New Twentieth Century Dictionary* (2nd Edition). New York: William Collins & World Publishing Co.

Weslus, Elisabeth. 1994. "Wo wir doch jetzt die Freiheit haben." In Katrin Rohnstock (Ed.), *Stiefschwestern: Was Ost-Frauen und West-Frauen voneinander denken.* Frankfurt-Main: Fischer Taschenbuch Verlag.

Winkler, Gunnar. 1990. *Frauenreport '90.* Berlin: Verlag die Wirtschaft.

Zimmer, Dieter E. 1996. "Amtlich betrogen: Wie die Bundesrepublik mit deutschen Wissenschaftlern verfährt." *Die Zeit.* No. 32, 2 August, p. 35.

Author Index

Subject Index

ABOUT THE AUTHOR

INGRID SANDOLE-STAROSTE is adjunct professor in the Department of Sociology and the Women's Studies Program at George Mason University.